NEUROPSYCHOLOGICAL EFFECTS OF THE PSYCHIATRIC DISORDERS

Simon F. Crowe

La Trobe University,
Bundoora, Australia

harwood academic publishers
Australia • Canada • China • France • Germany • India • Japan • Luxembourg
Malaysia • The Netherlands • Russia • Singapore • Switzerland

Amsteldijk 166
1st Floor
1079 LH Amsterdam
The Netherlands

British Library Cataloguing in Publication Data

A catalogue record for this book is available from the British Library.

ISBN 90-5702-377-6

COVER   Albrecht Dürer 1471-1528 German
Melancolia I 1514
engraving
23.9 × 18.7 cm
Felton Bequest, 1956
National Gallery of Victoria, Melbourne.

CONTENTS

Preface   ix

Chapter 1   The Association between Psychiatric Illness and
             Neuropsychological Disorder   1
Chapter 2   The Schizophrenias   19
Chapter 3   Mood Disorders   39
Chapter 4   Anxiety Disorders   63
Chapter 5   Somatoform, Factitious and Dissociative Disorders   81
Chapter 6   Disorders of Sleeping and Eating   93
Chapter 7   Physical Treatments of the Psychiatric Disorders   107
Chapter 8   Pharmacological Treatment of the Psychiatric Disorders   123
Chapter 9   Conclusion   137

References   143
Index   171

PREFACE

The aim of neuropsychology is to attempt to correlate behavioural dysfunction with brain dysfunction. The success of this attempt since the Second World War has been little less than astounding, beginning with a trickle of papers in the fifties and sixties and growing to a raging river in the latter parts of this century. Neuropsychological investigation has become a cornerstone in the behavioural assessment and treatment programming in the neurosurgical and neurological spheres and increasingly the models proposed by neuropsychology have found a sympathetic ear in the understanding of the degenerative disorders. This book aims to present the current state of this enterprise and the implications of its numerous findings to the understanding of psychiatric conditions.

The title 'Neuropsychological Effects of the Psychiatric Disorders' grows out of a movement originating in the US but now more popular in the UK, which views psychiatric symptomatology as a manifestation of the disordered brain processes associated with the respective psychiatric conditions. Whilst the evidence surrounding this hypothesis has largely centred on the issue of schizophrenia, it is the contention of this discussion that all psychiatric illness can be analysed as neuropsychological disorders, and that the most productive advances in the understanding, categorisation and treatment of psychiatric disorders will arise from this synthesis. Time and again the literature has indicated that the effects of brain lesions are capable of influencing neurological function, neuropsychological functioning and psychiatric symptomatology. Much of the disorder observed in psychiatric patients is attributable to disruptions in the integrity of the cerebral systems and their consequent effects on cognition, affect, emotion and reality orientation.

The chapters in the book closely follow the categorisation of disorders set up by the Diagnostic and Statistical Manual of Mental Disorders (DSM-IV), with the focus only on those disorders generally considered to be psychiatric as opposed to degenerative (e.g. Dementia of the Alzheimer Type) or dispositional disorders (such as the personality disorders).

The book takes a clinical or hypothesis testing approach to the individual clinical cases as this allows for the apprehension of the nature of the individual's problems within the confines of their biological, psychological and social milieu. Each of these components is complex of itself but when they are taken in association, this interaction of factors makes for a quantum leap in the levels of complexity. Thus, while the book attempts to present the characteristic features of the various conditions described, each of these is supplemented with a worked clinical case example to allow the reader to develop a sense of the clinical aspects of the presentation, against which the previous experience and the 'clinical eye' of the reader act to humanise and deepen the experience of each condition and to educate the eye to interesting and unusual behavioural changes in subsequent clinical work.

The enterprise of the neuropsychological examination of psychiatric disorders is very much in its infancy, as you will soon note in reading the issues raised in this book. Nonetheless, I hope that this introduction to the topic acts as a stepping off point to further speculation, hypothesis generation and eventually data collection on this fascinating application of neuropsychology.

Obviously no one can finally produce a book such as this without help, support and a sympathetic ear. I would like to thank my wife Jan for putting up with every gruelling minute and also my students (particularly James Danckert, Mathew Summers, Marc Seal, Kirsten Hoogenraad and Phillip Dingjan) for their fascination with this topic which proved so infectious and sustaining.

Entry, Kentry, Cutry, Corn,

Apple seed and apple thorn

Wire, Brier, Limber, Lock,

Three geese in a flock,

One flew East, One flew West,

One flew over the cuckoos nest,

O-U-T, spells out

Nursery rhyme, Traditional

CHAPTER 1

THE ASSOCIATION BETWEEN PSYCHIATRIC ILLNESS AND NEUROPSYCHOLOGICAL DISORDER

It seems unlikely that the person who suffers from schizophrenia actually experiences the hallucinations, delusions, and disordering of thought which characterises this disorder in a direct physical way. Although it is possible, it seems improbable that the consultant psychiatrist is able to read his/her thoughts or that the FBI has inserted a radio transmitter into his/her tooth. Clearly, if the individual believes that a radio transmitter has been inserted into his/her tooth, then this must probably be at some metaphorical level.

If we are as yet unprepared to accept that there is some external force covertly inserting radio transmitters, then we still must explain how it is that this person believes that such a device has somehow been put there. The task of this book is to present an explanation of these phenomena which allows for a respectful interpretation of the reality of the sufferer, whilst not disabusing you of your view that your amalgam is a threat for reasons other than its putative connection to Alzheimer's disease.

In some sense the individual who has the hallucination or delusional percept is also correctly interpreting his/her reality, and the numerous times that clinicians throughout the years have talked themselves blue in the face trying to convince these individuals that they are not, must be viewed as an elaborate and fruitless waste of time. How then can both of us be right?

It is the contention of this book that individuals who suffer from psychiatric disorders, whilst participating in the same workaday world as you and I, are somehow reading it wrong. They are misinterpreting the information coming in through their sensory systems, and as a consequence of this error are responding to the aberrant reality as if it were real. And why not? After all, they are using the same sensory apparatus as you and I. How then could reality be so misinterpreted?

1

At some level the processing of this information must have gone awry. Somewhere between sensation, perception and behavioural output the message has become unstuck; its reading frame has slipped and its significance has been magnified or minimised. It has not been processed as a 'sane' thought. This deficit in information processing may be different for each of the psychiatric disorders, with the massive distortions of reality associated with schizophrenia the most compelling.

The elaboration of this argument will take place in a number of steps. In this chapter an overview of how we might look at these disorders most effectively, particularly from a neuropsychological point of view, will be made. A discussion of the respective psychiatric disorders will be presented in the following chapters, each in terms of their defining characteristics and then in the context of the literature regarding their neuropsychological effects. The discussion will then move to an examination of the treatments used in psychiatric disorder including physical and pharmacological approaches and discuss the effects of the treatments themselves on cognitive functioning. In the final chapter, an attempt will be made to pull the various threads of the discussion together in an examination of the implication of the neuropsychological interpretation of psychiatric disorder to the understanding of these disorders.

NEUROPSYCHOLOGICAL MODEL

For the most part the approach taken to the reporting of the various deficits in each of the psychiatric conditions will attempt to be 'atheoretical' in terms of the neuropsychological approach adopted. Whilst the model of neuropsychology I have been trained in and that I teach is the 'hypothesis testing' or 'process' approach (Lezak, 1995; Walsh, 1994), the material presented in this book is atheoretical in that we know so little about these conditions from a neuropsychological perspective that anyone who has anything useful to say about these disorders, irrespective of which approach to the study of these disorders that they come from, is welcomed with open arms. I hope this book will bring to your attention just how little we know about the connection between psychiatric dysfunction and neuropsychological dysfunction, and that it might encourage you to demand, or even better collect, more data.

In the case report included at the end of each chapter I use the process approach, not just because it is where I have come from, but because I believe that this approach provides a useful way to evaluate each case. The use of the process approach should not be construed as an endorsement of 'clinical' over 'statistical' clinical decision making. No one can argue with Meehl's (1986) observation that whilst in psychology very few things are consistently established to be true, one thing that is, is that statistical methods are vastly superior to clinical ones. This model is employed because it is both flexible enough to be able to cope with the massive variability in performance which characterises patients with a psychiatric disorder, and it allows for the apprehension of the nature of the individual's problems within the confines of their biological, psychological and social milieu.

One of the great benefits of a neuropsychological view of a particular clinical syndrome is that it allows the examination of the various behavioural and information processing modules of the working brain to be examined and compared simultaneously within the one individual. Inferences about the impairment of a particular individual are thus based on a number of tests of the cognitive functions that constitute the complete system. In this context it is precarious to interpret the results of a group study in terms of the individual impairment of a particular information processing module, as these changes may be masked by the inherent noise in the system.

This problem is indicated, for example, by the experiment in which drug treatment X is compared to placebo. Subjects 1, 3, 5 and 9 improve, while subjects 2, 4, 6, 7, 8 and 10 remain the same. On a statistical comparison of the means there was found to be no significant difference between the treatment and the control group. As a consequence, agent X is consigned to the pharmacological scrap heap as yet another inert compound.

However, what we are missing in our interpretation of this study is that this averaging procedure is disguising a genuine and welcome response in four of our individuals and demonstrating a complete lack of efficiency in the others (David, 1993). This approach, referred to as the black swan approach, is perhaps the most telling way to determine if a given drug or even a theoretical position on brain function is viable or not. The approach was named as such because in Europe (where all the swans are white) it is possible to put forward the particularly geocentric view that 'All swans are white'. Such a view would be resoundingly dismissed if we came across a single instance of a black swan. Clearly, if one back swan exists not all swans are white. A single disconfirmatory case thus allows the falsification of the position in a single blow. Coming from Australia I am unsure why this approach is called the black swan approach, because as all Australians know, *all* swans are black. Nonetheless, I will assume that there was a proofreading error in the original description of this point of view.

Neuropsychology has a massively rich tradition of the single-case methodology, with cases such as Phineas Gage and HM acting as the cornerstone of the edifice of the neuropsychological study of the frontal lobes, in the case of Gage, and of memory research, in the case of HM. This is not to suggest that the single case exists in isolation. Data from single cases cannot be interpreted without the understanding and explanation provided by the group norms for particular tests.

Another problem with the single-case methodology is that single-case methods are unreliable for the purpose of localisation. The individual diversity associated with localisation within the human cerebrum can best be highlighted by the description of the distributions of the calcarine and parieto-occipital arteries. These arteries supply blood to the primary and secondary visual cortices in the occipital lobe and are characterised by their variability within the population. The work of Marinkovic and his colleagues (1987) clearly indicates the massive spread of distribution of the area of the brain supplied by these arteries, with some individuals featuring large wedge shaped areas supplied by the artery in question, while others feature only a sliver. Obviously, a haemorrhage in an individual with a large area subserved by the artery will show more marked levels of impairment as a result of the infarction than would an individual with a lesser distribution. The brain as an organ has the least consistent pattern of perfusion of any organ in the body, so the likelihood that your parieto-occipital stroke will produce the same cognitive sequelae as mine is at least equally as variable.

The interest for the neuropsychologist applying the single-case methodology is to determine whether function X is impaired while functions P, Q and R are not. As Benton (1981) has argued, symptoms must be viewed as expressions of disturbance in a system not as a direct expressions of focal loss of neuronal tissue.

In the history of psychiatry the lack of any obvious neuropathological manifestation of these disorders has resulted in years of delay and imprecise interpretations of these disorders, which has its clearest manifestation in the use of the term 'functional' disorder. A 'functional' disorder is one for which there is overtly no 'organic' cause. So for example epilepsy, Parkinson's disease or an astrocytoma might be considered to be suitable organic causes for a neuropsychological impairment. On the other hand, schizophrenia, depression or obsessive–compulsive disorder might be considered to be non-organic or functional causes of a disorder. Whilst psychiatrists defend this distinction (e.g. Lishman, 1987), it seems that the attempt to delineate the contribution of 'organic' causes of mental dysfunction from 'functional' or psychiatric ones has not proven to be a particular fruitful way of looking at psychiatric disorders.

Time and again the literature has indicated that the effects of brain lesions are capable of influencing neurological function, neuropsychological functioning and psychiatric symptomatology. Much of the disorder observed in psychiatric patients is then attributable to disruptions in the integrity of the cerebral systems and their consequent effects on cognition, affect, emotion and reality orientation. The right question to ask then is: What is the effect of this patient's psychiatric disorder on their cognitive functioning? Hopefully by the time you get to the end of this book the answer to this question will be clearer.

LOCALISATION OF FUNCTION IN THE BRAIN

The notion of where particular brain functions are localised stretches back, at least, to the ancient Egyptians. They believed that the Ba spirit (the soul) was located in the intestines. At some time or another in history every organ of the body has been elevated to the status of the seat of the soul, spanning from the liver through to the heart, to Plato's rather curious position that because the senses exist only to mislead, the seat of the soul must be in that place which represents the most suitable vessel for the spirit. To classical Greek mathematicians the sphere was considered to be the most perfect shape. As the only organ of the body that is vaguely spherical, they believed the head must contain the seat of the soul.

Ancient Greece, in an unhappy marriage with the early fathers of the church, went on to produce yet another aberration for the understanding of the function of the brain in the form of the cell doctrine of brain function. In essence they contended that the ventricles of the brain are filled with a vital spirit distilled in a number of steps, with nutriment from the intestines and air from the nose which act to animate the muscles of the body. The doctrine, originally developed in the 4th century, was maintained for the ensuing eleven centuries as the orthodoxy of brain function. It was not until the Renaissance that the back of this idea was broken, and reason and observation were allowed to colour church orthodoxy.

There are some wonderful drawings arising from this era by Leonardo da Vinci, who in early sketches of the brain clearly details the series of circular connected ventricles of the classical doctrine. Some fifteen years later however, da Vinci presented what were clearly his own dissections of the brain—sketches which lack the censorious eye of faith and are much more consistent with the anatomical realities of the brain *in situ*.

The next step in our historical journey is the work of Gall, the father of phrenology. Gall noted, early in his experience, that a colleague who had large bulging eyes also had a good memory. As a consequence of this observation he concluded that all individuals with bulging eyes have good memories. From this observation he developed a model which covered some one hundred and fifty personality attributes. Gall maintained that particular brain regions, because of their larger area and greater activity, caused the skull overlying them to buckle out. Thus the character of the individual could be determined by feeling the bumps on their head. Interestingly it was not until 1963 that the Phrenological Society in Britain finally closed its doors, indicating the long-term significance of a good bump on the head.

The problem with Gall's view and any narrow localisation of the functions of the brain generally is to determine exactly how many cognitive domains there are. Within the history of brain localisation we are a shuttlecock batted back and forth from the narrow localisation of Gall and Spurzheim to the absence of localisation proposed by Karl Lashley. Lashley in his work with rats noted that the ability of rats to run a maze is conditional upon the amount of tissue that they lose, not upon where that tissue comes from. As such he contended that the brain is equipotential: all parts of the brain subserve similar functions so that if one part is removed another can take up the role.

The deadlock between the narrow localisationists and the equipotentialists was finally broken by Luria. The model presented by Luria (1973) proposes that there are three slave systems within the working brain, each of which is hierarchically organised. These systems are: (1) the system for maintaining cortical tone and arousal, (2) the system for gathering and retrieving information, and (3) the system for motor planning and output.

To Luria the fundamental task of neuropsychology is to 'ascertain by careful analysis which group of concertedly working zones of the brain are responsible for the performance of complex mental activity; what contribution is made by each of these zones to the complex functional system; and how the relationship between these concertedly working parts of the brain in the performance of complex mental activity changes in the various stages of development' (p. 34). I believe that Luria's mission for his fledgling discipline of neuropsychology is as fresh today as it was when he first formulated the view.

The implication of this principle is that the symptom of itself does not tell us a lot about the neuroanatomical site of the damage which causes its behavioural manifestation. For example, in the case of apraxia, or the impairment of the skilled execution of motor sequences, the lesion causing the disturbance may impinge on a number of levels of the behavioural loop, between the apprehension of the outside world, through the decision to effect an action, culminating in the directive to the musculature to effect, for example, brushing the hair. Voluntary movement constitutes a complex functional system incorporating a number of conditions or factors dependent upon the concerted working of a group of cortical zones and subcortical structures, each of which makes its own contribution to the performance of the movement and supplies its own factor in the structure.

Such speculations about the localisation of behavioural programs in the brain give rise to a 'syndrome analysis' of change in behaviour, as a consequence of a brain lesion. Thus, a number of lesions may result in disruption of a function such as

memory or executive functions, and the location of these lesions may be in a number of different sites distributed throughout the brain. The neuropsychological sign only indicates that the distributed network subserving the particular function has been disrupted, and by itself the symptom tells us little about any specific localisation of the focus causing its appearance. Each neuropsychological function is effected by a complex functional system incorporating a number of conditions or factors dependent upon the concerted working of a group of cortical zones and subcortical structures, each of which makes its own contribution to the performance of the function and supplies its own factor in the structure (Luria, 1973). The disruption of the function would occur irrespective of the site of the damage to the distributed system. The specific site of the lesion would, however, add a characteristic flavour to the disruption of function based on the area affected.

As noted above, Luria maintains that there are three principal functional units of the brain: (1) a unit for regulating tone or waking, located in the brain stem; (2) a unit for obtaining, processing and storing information, located behind the central sulcus; and (3) a unit for programming, regulating and verifying mental activity located in the frontal lobes. Each of these basic units is hierarchical in structure and consists of at least three cortical zones built one over the other: the primary (projection) area which receives impulses from or sends impulses to the periphery, the secondary (projection-association) areas where incoming information is processed and programs are prepared and the tertiary zones or the zones of overlapping, the latest system to develop and responsible in man for the most complex forms of mental activity requiring the concerted participation of many cortical areas.

Three basic laws govern the working of the individual cortical regions composing the second and third functional systems (Luria, 1973). These are: the law of hierarchical structure of the cortical zones, the law of diminishing specificity of the hierarchically arranged cortical zones composing it, and the law of the progressive lateralisation of functions.

The law of hierarchical structure of the cortical zones contends that the relationship between the primary, secondary and tertiary zones does not remain constant throughout development. In the child the formation of properly working secondary zones cannot take place without the integrity of the primary zones which constitute their informational basis. The proper working of the tertiary zones would be impossible without adequate development of the secondary cortical zones which supply the necessary material for the creation of the major cognitive syntheses such as the development of language, which requires sensory, motor and planning components for its successful execution. A disturbance of the lower zones in the course of infancy would thus inevitably lead to incomplete development of the higher cortical zones, which run from the bottom up. In an adult person who has fully assumed higher psychological functions, the higher cortical zones have assumed the dominant role. As such the highest zones control the working of the secondary zones which are subordinate to them. Thus the level of disruption caused by a lesion of the subordinate zones is not as devastating as it would be during development as the superstructure overlying the deficit is capable of compensating for and papering over the deficit in the subordinate zone.

The law of diminishing specificity of the hierarchically arranged cortical zones composing it contends that those zones which are in most direct contact with the outside world, the primary sensory reception areas or the primary motor effector area in the frontal lobe, maintain the most modal specificity. The secondary zones possess modal specificity to a much lower degree, and in the tertiary areas modal specificity is all but gone. In a sense, the function of the tertiary areas could be considered supramodal in character. It is also interesting to note on this issue that it is rarely the primary sensory or motor areas which are disrupted by degenerative conditions. In Alzheimer's disease for example, rarely is it the case that the individual features deficits in primary sensory or motor function. The disorders are invariably associated with the secondary and tertiary association areas.

The law of the progressive lateralisation of functions states that the cognitive functions are progressively transferred from the primary, to the secondary, and ultimately to the tertiary areas. The principle of lateralisation of higher functions in the cerebral cortex begins to operate only with the transition from the primary zones to the secondary zones, and in particular with the transfer from the secondary to the tertiary zones which are principally concerned with coding of information reaching the cortex, most specifically with the aid of speech. It is for this reason that the functions of the secondary and tertiary zones of the left hemisphere begin to differ radically from the functions of those on the right (Luria, 1973).

A more recent approach to the localisation and explanation of the function of the various regions of the brain has been proposed by Marcel Mesulam (1985). The 'topologic approach' to brain function expands on the theories proposed by Luria amongst others and presents them in what I believe to be the most satisfying model of the brain's function to date. Mesulam's topological model proposes five functional areas of the brain which can be classified from those areas with closest connection to the internal environment to those areas which are responsible for the apprehension of stimuli in the extra-personal space. The five areas are:

1. Limbic areas including the septum, the substantia innominata, the amygdala complex, the hippocampal formation and the piriform complex. These areas

are in closest association with the centres in the brain stem and hypothalamus which control homeostasis or maintenance of the internal state of the body.

2. Paralimbic areas including the temporal pole, the orbitofrontal cortex, the insula, the parahippocampal gyrus and the cingulum. These areas are responsible for the modulation of drive and control of the homeostatic urges as they impinge on the environmental demands, including emotion and memory.

3. Unimodal (modality specific) association areas. These areas surround the primary reception and transduction areas and are responsible for attachment of meaning to the patterns of sensory activation, e.g. perception as opposed to sensation.

4. Heteromodal (higher order) association areas. These areas are equivalent to Luria's zones of overlapping and are responsible for the integration of material from each of the sensory systems, as well as developing motor programs for responding to the implications of the sensory input.

5. Idiotypic or primary sensory and motor areas: the primary sensory areas for vision, touch, hearing and the other sensory and motor systems. These areas are in closest contact with the outside (extrapersonal)world.

Each of these systems has connections to the others either horizontally or vertically, although their connection is strongest with the immediately adjacent zone. The limbic areas are unique in so far as they have direct connection to the hypothalamus, the head ganglion of the internal milieu. This unique role has led some investigators (e.g. Cytowic, 1996) to speculate that the urges of the limbic areas (i.e. feeding, feeling, fighting, fornicating) may be the motor that drives all behaviour, and that the remainder of the brain is involved in carrying out the directions of the limbic system in the most effective and appropriate way.

HOW MANY COGNITIVE FUNCTIONS ARE THERE?

Before we launch into further discussion about the clinical syndromes or issues associated with methodology or theory, we must attempt to determine the answer to a question that has vexed neuropsychology from its very beginning: How many cognitive functions are there? One answer to this question might be that the number of cognitive functions is equivalent to the number of instruments which have been proposed to test them. Clearly then if we examine neuropsychological test compendiums, the number of neuropsychological functions is massive. How can we pare this massive number down to a more manageable set?

One system, which I believe has some features of interest, is to break the functions into more discernible cognitive domains, as illustrated in the cognitive pyramid presented in Figure 1.

The use of the pyramid is not merely because of my fascination with things Egyptological, but because there is a hierarchy to these cognitive functions, in that if there is a breakdown at the lower levels of function it has significant implications for the performance at the higher levels. This is not to suggest there is a direct one-to-one association between the breakdown at one level of the hierarchy to the breakdown at higher levels, but merely to indicate that the higher levels of the pyramid cannot be successfully negotiated if the lower ones are not intact. The pyramid also has the advantage of mirroring a number of the issues raised regarding the Lurian model, in so far as the base of the pyramid represents Luria's functional unit one (i.e. arousal and cortical tone), the sensation, perception, gnosis, praxis and memory represent unit two, and language, spatial cognition and executive function represent unit three.

For example recently there has been a debate in the literature concerning what it is that the Wisconsin Card Sorting Test (WCST: Grant & Berg, 1948) measures. The WCST is a task that requires the subject to sort a series of cards which have the shapes circle, cross, triangle and star in four colours, red, blue, green and yellow. The subject's task is to sort the cards into categories under four example cards, with the only available feedback being the correctness or incorrectness of the response. After the subject correctly sorts for a sequence of ten correct placements, the rules change in the order colour, form or number. The subject is not informed when the category changes.

Historically (Milner, 1963;1964), the WCST has been considered to be an excellent test of frontal lobe or executive dysfunction. Over the last few years, however, a number of studies have indicated that performance on the WCST may be equally compromised by posterior (Anderson, Damasio, Jones & Tranel, 1991; Grafman, Jones & Salazar 1990) or diffuse lesions (Robinson, Heaton, Lehman, & Stilson, 1980). These issues have culminated in Mountain and Snow's review (1993) which cautions against the use of the WCST to identify lesion sites or in the diagnosis of frontal dysfunction. If we return to our pyramid it allows some explanation of this problem.

Deficits at lower orders of performance can equally impair performance at the highest levels of the pyramid. For example, an individual with hemineglect may fail to attend to the left side of space producing aberrant responding on the task. Equally an individual with dementia of the Alzheimer type (DAT) has difficulty recalling the previously sorted card, the category and possibly, the name for triangles, all of which makes it difficult to perform the task.

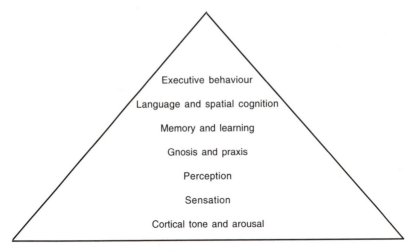

Executive behaviour

Language and spatial cognition

Memory and learning

Gnosis and praxis

Perception

Sensation

Cortical tone and arousal

Figure 1 Pyramid of cognitive skills

Cognitive tasks are multifactorial in nature (Brown, 1989) and even the most apparently simple task calls on many, if not all, of the levels of the cognitive hierarchy proposed in Figure 1. How then is it possible to say anything about neuropsychological deficit in a way that doesn't classify it all as generalised or global?

The great advantage of the hypothesis testing approach is that it is possible to examine performances at the lower level of the hierarchy and to rule them out as contributing to the observed neuropsychological deficit. Thus if our patient with the right sided stroke is assessed on a visual tracking task in our examination of gnosis or spatial cognition and is found to be impaired, then it is fair to say that the poor performance on the WCST is due to a lower order deficit and as a consequence the deficit cannot be considered to be one exclusively attributable to frontal/executive impairment. How can we conclude that a particular deficit is attributable to compromise in the frontal executive system? If we exclude deficits at all other levels of the hierarchy then it is likely that the problem is due to an executive problem.

NEUROPSYCHOLOGICAL INSTRUMENTS

As this book is intended for use by those who have some knowledge of neuropsychological techniques and theory, it seems unnecessary to detail all neuropsychological tests. Thus the focus is on only a few select instruments, in particular those used in the case reports presented at the end of each chapter. For more detail on neuropsychological techniques refer to the neuropsychological test compendia such as Lezak (1995) or Spreen and Strauss (1998) for more detail.

The tests we will consider are the Wechsler Adult Intelligence Scale-Revised (WAIS-R), the Wechsler Memory Scale-Revised (WMS-R), the Trail Making Test (TMT), the Austin Maze Test (AMT) and the Controlled Oral Word Association Test (COWAT).

The Wechsler Adult Intelligence Scale-Revised (WAIS-R)

The Wechsler Adult Intelligence Scale-Revised (WAIS-R) is a compendium of 11 subtests, six constituting the Verbal Scale (Information, Digit Span, Vocabulary, Arithmetic, Comprehension and Similarities) and five constituting the Performance Scale (Picture Completion, Picture Arrangement, Block Design, Object Assembly and Digit Symbol). The scales respectively measure well learned information in the case of a number of the Verbal subtests and problem solving and executive functions in the case of the Performance Scales. The factor analytic studies of the WAIS reveal that there are three constituent factors: (1) Verbal Comprehension which has its highest weighting on Information, Comprehension, Similarities and Vocabulary, (2) Perceptual Organisation which loads on Block Design, Object Assembly and to a lesser extent Picture Completion and Picture Arrangement, and (3) a Freedom from Distractability factor which weighs significantly on Arithmetic, Digit Span and to a lesser extent Digit Symbol. If we refer back to the pyramid in Figure 1, the Verbal Comprehension factor assesses language and comprehension functions, the Perceptual Organisation Factor assesses spatial cognition, and the Freedom from Distractability index measures working memory and other attentional functions.

The Wechsler Memory Scale-Revised (WMS-R)

The Wechsler Memory Scale-Revised (WMS-R) consists of 13 subtests which measure new learning, memory and recall of material after a delay. The subtests include: Information and Orientation, Mental Control (the ability of count backwards from twenty and recite the alphabet), Figural Memory (recall of shapes), Logical Memory 1 (recall of a prose passage), Visual Paired Associates 1 (recall of colour and shape pairs), Verbal Paired Associates 1 (recall of pairs of words), Visual Reproduction 1 (recall of line drawings) and Digit Span. The Scale also measures a number of these sub-tests after at least a 30 minute delay. These are Logical Memory 2, Visual Paired Associates 2, Verbal Paired Associates 2 and Visual Reproduction 2. The Scales divides the scores into five indices, Verbal Memory, Visual Memory, General Memory, Attention and Concentration and Delayed Recall. The WMS-R measures memory, working memory and learning.

Recently, both the WAIS-R and the WMS-R have been extensively revised and renormed in their respective third editions. As the older instruments are used in the case reports presented at the end of each chapter, the description of the new editions is best left to the technical and administration manuals of each instrument.

The Trail Making Test (TMT)

The Trail Making Test (TMT) was originally developed as part of the Army Individual Test Battery (1944) and is one of the most commonly used tests in neuropsychological practice due to its high sensitivity in diagnosing brain impairment (Armitage, 1946; Lewinsohn, 1973; Reitan, 1958; Spreen & Benton, 1965). The test requires the subject to perform a tracking task under two conditions. In the first part of the test (Trails A), the subject must trace a trail through a series of circles numbered from 1 through to 25 variously spread over an A4 page. In the second part of the test (Trails B) the subject must perform an alternation between circles containing numbers and letters. The sequence proceeds from the first number to the first letter alphabetically and then to the second number and the second letter. TMT(B) contains 13 circles numbered 1 to 13, alternating with 12 circles lettered A to L.

Whilst the task is an excellent index of the presence of brain impairment, poor performance on the task is relatively non-specific in so far as it does not indicate why the brain impaired individual is performing poorly and this may be attributable to motor slowing, poor coordination, visual scanning difficulties, poor motivation or conceptual confusion (Lezak, 1995) to name only a few possible causes. The performance on Trails B can be quite illuminating as it can indicate concreteness in idea generation and disinhibition, useful indicators of impairment of the executive functions.

The Austin Maze Test (AMT)

The Austin Maze Test (AMT) is a ten-by-ten press button maze which requires the subject to find a pathway through the maze contingent upon feedback. The task is an excellent test of visual memory and visuospatial problem solving involving executive functions, memory and visuoconstructive skills.

The Controlled Oral Word Association Test (COWAT)

The Controlled Oral Word Association Test (COWAT) assesses the ability of the subject to generate words governed by a number of rules. The technique has been found to be a sensitive indicator of brain dysfunction (Lezak, 1995). Frontal lesions, particularly those of the left side, cause depression of fluency (Miceli et al., 1981;

Milner, 1964; Perret, 1974). Benton (1968), for example, has found that patients with left-sided damage produced one third less words than did those with right-sided lesions, while those with bilateral involvement had even greater reductions in performance on the task. The COWAT is thus an excellent test of language functions as well as a useful index of executive functions including disorders of drive and disorders of control (Crowe, 1992, 1996a, 1996b).

* * *

In the context of the pyramid presented above, the assessment of cortical tone and arousal has not been addressed, nor has the areas of gnosis and praxis. Cortical tone is, I think, something that is best addressed by observation of the client at interview: Are they alert? Are they keeping track of what is going on around them? The issue of gnosis and praxis I address in an abbreviated neurobehavioural battery which is a subset of the Luria Battery of Tests (Christensen, 1975). This involves some basic language testing including confrontational naming, repetition, execution of a three-part command, reading, and a writing sample. I also do some basic tests of gnosis including the Poppelreuter Figures, finger gnosis and right/left orientation (see Christensen, 1975 for details), and some praxic tasks from the Boston Diagnostic Aphasia Examination. I include these tests to ensure that at a basic level the client is capable of comprehending, understanding and taking on the information that I present. A number of these brief examinations are available (e.g. Mini-Mental Status Examination which can be useful as a basic screening tool).

One final aspect of the function of the brain which is crucial in a discussion of psychiatric disorders but perhaps less so in a discussion of the effects of lesions of the brain is the issue of neurotransmission. Within the brain there are divisions not just on the basis of lobar divisions, and on the basis of the proximity to the external world. Within the brain their are specialised areas or tracts of fibres which can have an effect on the whole brain or on a particular cell type by the uses of chemical substances called neurotransmitters. A select few of these will now be reviewed.

THE NEUROTRANSMITTERS OF THE BRAIN

Over the last century nearly thirty biochemicals have been identified as neurotransmitters in the brain. A neurotransmitter can be defined as an endogenous chemical which is capable of producing rapid effects on cells of the central nervous system. This issue has become somewhat clouded over more recent decades by the fact that some of these agents actually may act more slowly than this and nowadays,

the hard and fast distinction between the rapidly acting neurotransmitters and the more slowly acting agents or neuromodulators has become blurred.

For the purposes of this discussion only three neurotransmitter systems will be considered in any detail as these are the three which have been the principal focus of modelling of the psychiatric disorders and which also stand as the basis of the principal pharmacological approaches to these disorders. The three neurotransmitters are: dopamine, serotonin and noradrenaline.

These transmitters are characterised by the fact that they have their origin in the brain stem, and from this location they project to the entire cortex of the brain. Each of these tracts will now be considered in more detail.

Dopamine

Dopamine is synthesised from the amino acid tyrosine which is freely available in a balanced diet, and is broken down in the body by the action of the monoamine oxidases (MOA which has A and B forms) and by Catechol O Methyl Transferase (COMT). There are three dopamine tracts in the brain: (1) the nigrostriatal pathway which runs from the pars compacta of the substantia nigra through to the corpus striatum, (2) the mesolimbic and mesocortical pathways which run from the ventral tegmental area to the limbic system and the neocortex, and (3) the tubero-infundibular pathway which runs from the hypothalamus to the pituitary.

Cell loss in the nigrostriatal pathway (which contains nearly three quarters of the dopamine in the brain) leads to the clinical state of Parkinson's disease. Interestingly, more than 90% of the pigmented cells in the zona compacta of the substantia nigra must be lost before the first clinical symptoms of the disorder emerge, indicating that considerable planned obsolescence of these cells was expected in the first place.

The treatments for Parkinson's disease aim to increase the level of effective dopamine at the neurotransmitter terminal. This can occur in a number of ways, firstly and most importantly by adding in a biochemical later in the synthesis of the transmitter by leaping over the missing biochemical step in the pathway for the synthesis of dopamine in the form of L-dopa. It would appear that the loss of these cells prevents the synthesis of dopamine from tyrosine. However, if L-dopa (a later step in the biosynthetic pathway) is administered the patient can synthesise dopamine from this precursor. A second approach is to prevent the breakdown of these agents once they have been released from the synapse by inhibiting the agents which cause the breakdown of the transmitter (i.e. monoamine oxidase inhibitors, MAOI).

The discovery in the 1950s of the basis of Parkinson's disease as a flaw in a specific biochemical pathway gave rise to massive speculation regarding the 'cure' of other degenerative disorders such as Alzheimer's disease. This initial promise, however, has not materialised. This is probably due to the fact that Parkinson's disease (85% of cases of which have no known cause) constitutes the loss of a biochemical step in the synthesis of an identifiable neurotransmitter, while Alzheimer's disease features compromise in at least four neurotransmitter pathways, as well as having massive intra- and extracellular deposits of a glycoprotein (i.e. plaques and tangles) in the tissue.

Up until the present time five types of dopamine receptors have been identified (Smith & Darlington, 1996), three of which we know little about. As we will discuss later on, the action of dopamine on the D_2 receptor is crucial in the discussion of schizophrenia.

Noradrenaline (norepinephrine)

Noradrenaline is a further step down the biochemical pathway in the synthesis of dopamine from tyrosine and both of these agents are referred to as catecholamines. The noradrenergic tract begins in the brain stem in the locus coeruleus which innervates the entire cortex.

There are two main types of adrenergic receptor: α and β. There are now seven classified subtypes of the α receptor and three of the β receptor. The noradrenergic system has its principal roles in the generation of arousal in the form of the fight/ flight response, has a significant effect upon mood and arousal and is important in the regulation of the cardiovascular system.

Levels of noradrenaline are increased by inhibition of the re-uptake of the trans- mitter into the synapse by agents such as the tricyclic antidepressants, or by the prevention of their breakdown once released from the synapse in the from of the monoamine oxidase inhibitors.

Serotonin

Serotonin is also known as 5-hydroxytryptamine or 5HT and is synthesised from the dietary amino acid tryptophan. The origins of the serotonergic tracts is similar to those for the noradrenergic tracts and it appears there may be considerable overlap both structurally and functionally between the two transmitter types. The origin of the tract is in the raphe nuclei in the brain stem, and the cortex, the limbic system, the hypothalamus and the cerebellum are each subserved by the median forebrain bundle.

To date there have been fourteen subtypes of serotonin receptor identified and thus it is not surprising to find that serotonergic innervation is involved in numerous functions. The list includes control of mood, aggression, sleep and pain transmission.

* * *

As we will later see, the role of alteration of the activity of the neurotransmitters of the brain has opened a whole new chapter in the discussion of the psychiatric disorders. One possible way to look at the role of the brain, and the neurotransmitters which activate and inhibit it, is to suggest that the brain is nothing more than a series of chemical reactions which we imbue with the mystical qualities of personality, individuality and spirituality. Let us now examine this issue in more detail.

REDUCTION AND EXPLANATION

It remains for us to determine in this introductory discussion what the relationship between psychiatric illnesses and neuropsychological disorders is. One possible association between them is that they reduce to each other.

Reductionism is founded on certain propositions. These include: (1) that the various sciences can be hierarchically ordered with physics the most fundamental science through chemistry, physiology, psychology and psychiatry through to sociology; (2) that the concepts and laws of one science can be translated into those of another adjacent science in the hierarchy; (3) that the derivability of one science from another proceeds only in one direction, such that the concepts and laws of the 'higher' science are reduced to those of the 'lower' science; and (4) it is assumed that the lower the level of the explanation used the more powerful the explanation.

At this point an example may throw some light on this matter. An engineer who designs a bridge must think at different levels of complexity as he works. His/her overall plan for the bridge is in terms of spans, piers, abutments and the like, however when he/she reaches the level of the design of a single span he/she must think in terms of lower order units such as the I beam. Such a conception is still quite a wide screen view for the engineer convinced as he /she is that the I beam itself is only constituted of protons and electrons. At a microscopic level of analysis, the bridge is nothing more than a collection of atoms and subatomic particles swirling around each other, and the I beam merely a convenient fiction created and maintained as a concession to the limitations of the human imagination. Yet at another level of analysis, the I beam is an elementary unit of the bridge, obviously real and not fictitious. At that point in time the engineer sets aside his purely theoretical conception of the I beam as atoms whirling, and gets on with the job of making the bridge work. Analogy obviously cannot be construed as proof, but the example does serve to illustrate that the appropriateness of any form of explanation will depend upon the questions that are posed and the context in which they are asked.

As behavioural engineers, this book asks you to suspend your conceptions of hallucination, delusion and thought disorder as the I beams of the psychiatric reality, and to entertain the possibility that the swirling components of our cognitive and emotional pyramid may be able to allow us to see these disorders in a new light.

The phenomena of psychiatric disorders do not occur as a consequence of altered experience on the part of those individuals affected with these disorders. It seems very unlikely that individuals who hallucinate have access to the devil and the Holy Ghost on a regular basis. Similarly individuals with an overemphasis on what will happen (anxiety disorders) or what has previously happened (depressive disorders) seem to have had not too dissimilar experiences to those of us who have not as yet suffered from a psychiatric illness. Therefore there must be something about the way in which they have processed that reality that distinguishes them from those of us who are so far unaffected. The thrust of this book is to attempt to examine this processing difference, with a view to a new synthesis of the ancient art of psychiatry with the relatively new discipline of clinical neuropsychology.

CHAPTER 2

THE SCHIZOPHRENIAS

Historically the study of psychiatric disorders and schizophrenia in particular has been viewed as the graveyard of almost any subdiscipline of the medical sciences which has attempted to study them. Few findings stand the test of time, and it seems at times that the categorisation of the various disorders is more for the sake of neatness than to characterise any actual clinical phenomena. Time and again researchers in the area of schizophrenia have maintained that the only consistent finding to be made is that of the marked variability in the clinical samples.

Within this discussion, schizophrenia (or better, the schizophrenias) will not be considered as a disease, but like epilepsy as a syndrome consisting of a collection of signs and symptoms, which has a diverse pathogenesis.

The term *dèmence prècoce* was originally introduced by the French psychiatrist Benedict-Augustin Morel in 1856, who used the term to describe a 14-year-old boy who had previously been an excellent student but had undergone a rapid deterioration in his intelligence and behaviour. In 1870 Hecker described a similar state with an onset at around the time of puberty and with a pervasive pattern of disorganisation of personality, as hebephrenia (Hebe was the Greek goddess of youth).

The distinction between dementia paranoides and catatonia was made by Kahlbaum in 1863. Kahlbaum noted that with dementia paranoides there was a clear pattern of prominent delusions in association with the gross disorganisation of behaviour, and paranoia, characterised by systematised delusions, whilst there was an overall preservation of intellect and behaviour. The notion of catatonia on the other hand was used to describe a pattern associated with the patient's tendency to remain mute and motionless.

In 1896 Emil Kraepelin noted the similarities between these various syndromes and applied the term dementia praecox to all three forms. He subsequently accepted the notion of a fourth form, dementia praecox simplex characterised by a gradual onset and a lack of initiative. For Kraepelin the defining features of his dementia was the onset early in life, and the irreversible progression of the state to a permanent dementia. The system of disorders under the umbrella of dementia praecox proposed by Kraepelin was well accepted and was preserved as a part of the official nomenclature of the disorder in the US until 1950.

The more recent term schizophrenia can be attributed to the Swiss psychiatrist Eugen Bleuler who proposed the term in his classic text *Dementia Praecox* (or the Group of Schizophrenias) in 1911. Bleuler differed from Kraepelin in that he did not believe that the irreversible decline in function observed in these states was an essential or even defining feature of the disorder. Bleuler maintained that the illness was characterised by a particular type of thinking and feeling in response to the outside world, rather than merely a degenerative pattern.

Such a split in the perceptions of the disorder between Bleuler and Kraepelin underlines an often visited issue regarding the nature of these disorders: do these conditions represent a degenerative state or a particular set of defining behavioural aberrations? As recently as the theories of Crow (1980) in dividing the disorder into positive (Bleulerian) and negative (Kraepelinian) syndromes, the issue cannot really be said to have been settled.

The term schizophrenia, which has generally been interpreted as a splitting of the mind, actually refers to the fragmentation of the psyche into its component parts. Thus there is a split within the individual between cognition and emotional responses or motor behaviours. Bleuler divided the symptoms of schizophrenia into those that were fundamental to the condition (i.e. present in every case of the disorder such as disorders of affect, attention and volition) and those that were accessory (i.e. those not considered to be permanent features such as hallucination and delusion).

In 1952 and 1953 a whole new chapter in the perception of these conditions was opened by the introduction of the agent chlorpromazine for the treatment of various psychiatric conditions. This was followed closely by the agent reserpine which had a similar application (Delay & Deniker, 1961). Simultaneously numerous clinical reports appeared in the literature describing the efficacy of these treatments in the schizophrenias. This new chapter also caused a further challenge to Kraepelin's concept of schizophrenia. The new agents had their exclusive effects on hallucination, delusion and thought disorder, whilst having virtually no effect on the disorders of affect, attention and volition. It thus seemed that there were at least two groups of symptoms within the spectrum of schizophrenia, those that responded to the new antipsychotic medications and those that did not.

Kurt Schneider (1959) having noted the effect of these agents on what were to become known as the positive symptoms of schizophrenia, began to categorise these symptoms. In contrast to the earlier work of Kraepelin, who contended that the negative symptoms were the defining nature of schizophrenia, Schneider maintained that a series of symptoms observed in schizophrenia and in no other condition, could be developed. The list of his ten first rank symptoms of schizophrenia included:

1. hearing one's own voice spoken aloud;
2. hallucinatory voice talking about the patient in the third person;
3. hallucinatory voices making a running commentary on the patient's actions;
4. somatic hallucinations that the patient blames on external agencies;
5. though withdrawal, the subject feels that the thoughts have been taken from his head, as if a person or some external force were removing them;
6. thought insertion, the subject believes that thoughts that are not his own are being put into his head;
7. thought broadcasting, the subject feels that his thoughts are being broadcast, so that other people know what he is thinking;
8. thought blocking, the stream of though becomes disordered and gaps or lapses in the continuity of the thought appear;
9. delusional perception;
10. all experiences of feeling, drive or volition which are judged to be made or influenced by others.

Schneider also proposed the existence of a series of second rank symptoms, which were not diagnostic of schizophrenia themselves but nonetheless contributed to the diagnosis. Whilst Schneider's first rank symptoms have been very influential in the formulation of the diagnostic criteria of schizophrenia, a number of investigators have criticised Schneider's approach in neglecting the core negative symptoms (e.g. Andreasen, 1983). It is also the case that there is significant variability regarding the prevalence of first rank symptoms in different cultures which may indicate that culture has a significant contribution to make to the emergence of these symptoms in these patients (Ndetei & Vadher, 1984).

On the basis of the differential effects noted with the antipsychotic medications, Tim Crow (1980) proposed that schizophrenia consisted of two semi-independent syndromes. He described these syndromes in a manner originally proposed by the father of English neurology, John Hughlings Jackson, as comprising positive symptoms (symptoms which were additional to those seen in the normal state) and negative symptoms (features which are present in the normal state but which are absent in the condition). The suggestion of two types of schizophrenia was also supported by the work of Nancy Andreasen, who provided a more comprehensive definition of the two syndromes, and a more reliable means of measuring them, in the form of the Scales for the Assessment of Positive and Negative Symptoms (SAPS and SANS) (Andreasen, 1983; 1984; Andreasen & Olsen, 1982). The positive symptoms included:

- Hallucination: Sensory experiences in the absence of any stimulation from the environment e.g. audible thoughts/voices arguing/voices commenting.
- Delusion: Holding a belief that the rest of society would generally disagree with or view as misinterpretations of reality.
- Bizarre behaviour: The practice of unusual or uncharacteristic behaviours or rituals such as aggressiveness, or saving body products.
- Thought disorder: Problem with the form of thought. Including such features as incoherence, neologism (generation of non-words), loosening of association, clang associations, poverty of speech, perseveration and thought blocking.

These symptoms are clearly quite consistent with the descriptions made by Schneider. The positive symptoms are relatively responsive to the actions of the antipsychotic agents (which it was later established had their principal mode of action by blocking dopamine receptors), and Crow suggested that these symptoms were thus attributable to dopamine uptake. In contrast, the negative symptoms which were not amenable to the actions of these agents must be attributable to some other cause.

The negative symptoms are much in line with Kraepelin's original formulation. These include:

- Flattening of affect: Virtually no stimulus can elicit an emotional response (blunting and apathy). These individuals may also show inappropriate affect where the response that they make is out of context with the usually accepted response.
- Alogia: Decrease in the flow and spontaneity of speech.
- Avolition: Decrease in the ability to motivate oneself or get things started.
- Anhedonia: Inability to be able to feel pleasure in any activity.
- Attention deficit: Inability to attend and track mental operations.

As the symptoms were considered to be chronic and irreversible, Crow proposed that they must be attributable to structural changes to the brain itself, in the form of ventricular dilatation.

The typology proposed by Crow has proven extremely fruitful and has resulted in numerous papers, conference presentations and books. It is fair to say that Crow's original speculations have led to a renaissance into the inquiry into the nature and causes of the schizophrenias. Recently, however the simple dichotomous approach to the classification of schizophrenia has been questioned due to its failure to comfortably fit with the data. This doubt or perhaps more appropriately, refinement, of Crow's original typology has come from factor analytic approaches to the domains of symptoms within the spectrum of the schizophrenias. While the original factor analytic approaches advocated by Andreasen (Andreasen & Olsen, 1982) appeared to support the notion of the positive and negative dichotomy, more recent work by Liddle and his colleagues (Liddle, 1987) indicated that the puzzle may be slightly more complex.

Using scales based upon the SAPS and SANS, Liddle's factor analysis revealed three syndromes. These were a psychomotor poverty syndrome much like Andreasen's negative symptoms, a disorganisation syndrome consisting of formal thought disorder, inappropriate affect and poverty of content of speech, and a reality distortion syndrome consisting of delusional and hallucinatory symptoms. A recent review of the clinical heterogeneity of schizophrenia (Buchanan & Carpenter, 1994) has noted that no less than fifteen studies have arrived at a three factor solution to the number of syndromes under the umbrella of schizophrenia using a range of different diagnostic scales.

Andreasen et al. (1995) does sound a cautionary note on the rush to yet another series of symptom profiles in schizophrenia. She observes that the three clusters must be recognised as a dimension of psychopathology determined by the artificial statistical technique of factor analysis, rather than as subtypes of the disorder. A subtype by its definition is a unitary individual phenomenon while a dimension of psychopathology can have magnitude which may overlap and which can be additive within the given individual. Thus the statistical existence of a particular syndrome cluster does not necessarily mean that the next individual who walks into your office will feature any such thing.

NOSOLOGY

DSM-IV (American Psychiatric Association, 1994) lists six criteria on which the diagnosis of schizophrenia can be made. The most salient of these are:

1.   The presence of two or more characteristic symptoms which must be present for a significant proportion of a one month period. These symptoms include delusions, hallucinations, disorganised speech, disorganised or

catatonic behaviour, and negative symptoms including flattening of affect, alogia or avolition.

2. Social or occupational dysfunction.
3. A continuous duration of the disturbance for a period or six months. (Consult DSM-IV for the full listing of the criteria.)

DSM-IV also lists four subtypes of schizophrenia. These are: (1) paranoid type characterised by delusion and frequent auditory hallucinations and a relative absence of negative symptoms; (2) disorganised type, characterised by disorganised speech, behaviour and affect; (3) catatonic type characterised by motor symptoms including immobility or hyperactivity in association with posturing; and (4) undifferentiated which includes the features listed in one above but which does not meet the criteria for the other subtypes and residual type, when the features are largely of the negative state.

THE BIOLOGICAL ORIGINS OF SCHIZOPHRENIA

Not all of the speculation regarding the schizophrenias has centred around the issues of nomenclature. A number of attempts to provide a biological basis for the disorder have been proposed with varying success. One of the interesting historical notes in the evolution of the story of schizophrenia are the observations regarding the Akerfeldt test. In 1956 Akerfeldt reported a simple test which gave a positive response when the serum of patients with schizophrenia was tested calorimetrically. It soon became clear, however, that the test was only proving positive for those patients who had been in hospital for quite a long time, not for those recently diagnosed. The results were also positive for some chronically hospitalised general hospital patients who did not have a diagnosis of schizophrenia. In the end a positive result on the Akerfeldt test proved to be attributable to a deficiency in vitamin C occurring as a consequence of institutionalisation rather than to the 'schizococcus' as originally hoped.

A similar phenomenon occurred following the proposal of Harley-Mason in 1952, who suggested that schizophrenia might arise from the faulty transmethylation of catecholamines. Based on considerable contemporary interest at the time in hallucinogenic agents including peyote, daytura and LSD, Harley-Mason proposed that schizophrenia may be occurring as a consequence of the natural synthesis of hallucinogens within the subject leading to the observed similar features. The substance that he proposed as the target metabolite was

3,4-dimethoxyphenylethylamine (DMPEA). Interestingly 10 years later this substance was identified as that which caused the urine of patients of schizophrenia to produce a pink spot on chromatography paper. Unfortunately the pink spot was also observed in patients who did not have schizophrenia and was also noted in subjects who were treated with chlorpromazine. The finding, although interesting, remains of unclear significance.

Soon after the introduction of the major tranquillisers in 1952/3 it was noted that they also seemed capable of producing Parkinsonian side effects. The discovery in the late 1950s that the neurotransmitter dopamine was significantly depleted in post-mortem examination of patients who suffered from Parkinson's disease lead to the speculation that the two conditions were related. In the early 1960s it was discovered that the principal mode of action of the neuroleptics was their ability to block dopamine receptors. Furthermore the ability of these drugs to block dopamine receptors correlated better than other biochemical effects with their efficacy in the control of psychotic symptoms. The suggestion was supported by the fact that agents which cause an increase in the level of dopamine in the central nervous system, such as amphetamine, methylphenidate and L-dopa, also exacerbated the symptoms of schizophrenia in patients who were in remission.

The dopamine hypothesis thus suggests that schizophrenia is the result of overactivity of dopamine neurotransmission in the central nervous system (CNS) and that neuroleptics act by reducing this. To date this theory remains the dominant explanatory theory of schizophrenia, particularly of the positive symptoms which are considered to be attributable to excess activity at the dopamine D_2 receptors.

Support for the dopamine hypothesis is by no means universal and some of the problems of the theory yet to be resolved include: (1) it takes about three weeks following the treatment with an antipsychotic agent before there is detectable symptom relief, a unlikely finding if the association between the drug and the target transmitter is a direct one; (2) the new generation of atypical antipsychotic agents such as clozapine seem to affect 5HT, dopamine D_1 and D_4, but not D_2 receptors; and (3) positron emission tomography (PET) studies have failed to show the up-regulation of D_2 receptors, indicating that the observation of this finding may have been due to prior antipsychotic drug treatment.

The contemporary shift to other single agent explanations of schizophrenia (e.g. the phencyclidine model: Kim et al., 1980; Ishimaru, Kurumaji & Toru, 1994; Lahti et al., 1995), seems to be slowing and the generally held view now seems to be a recognition that the neurochemical causes of schizophrenia are complex and interacting.

NEUROPATHOLOGY

Despite the fact that neuropathologists have investigated the brains of subjects with schizophrenia for many years, it is only recently that there has been a consistent pattern of deficits emerge. Several research groups have reported atrophy, aplasia or dysplasia of temporal lobe structures and the related fronto-limbic cortical areas. Previous studies have noted enlargements of the temporal horns (Brown et al., 1986), decreases in the cortical thickness of the parahippocamal gyrus (Brown et al., 1986) and in the volume of the hippocampus, and alterations in the number (Falkai & Bogerts, 1986), and orientation of pyramidal cells in the hippocampal formation (Altshuler et al., 1987; Kovelman & Scheibel, 1984). With respect to this latter finding a number of replication studies have failed to note similar findings to Scheibel's group (e.g. Arnold, 1994; Benes, Sorensen & Bird, 1991). Decreases have also been noted in the cell density of the anterior cingulate and prefrontal cortices (Benes, Davidson & Bird, 1986; Benes & Bird, 1987). An excellent review of this area has recently been completed by Chua and McKenna (1995).

STRUCTURAL AND FUNCTIONAL IMAGING DATA

Over 30 pneumoencephalography (PEG) and more than 40 computed tomography (CT) studies of schizophrenia have been conducted. In the latter, patients were shown to display abnormalities, mainly ventricular dilatation. It seems that despite the fact that the differences between schizophrenic and normal subjects is clear, the magnitude of this difference is at best minor (Chua & McKenna, 1995). There does not seem to be any clear association between the clinical profile or schizophrenia subtype and the level or type of ventricular dilatation.

Magnetic resonance imaging (MRI) studies seem to echo the findings noted with CT. There seems to be no consistent evidence for a consistent reduction in brain size and only a minority of studies point to focal frontal reduction in these subjects. Chua and McKenna (1995) have concluded that 'it is likely that any brain substance abnormality in schizophrenia will be found to be localised to the temporal lobe, where it will be predominantly subcortical and perhaps also predominantly left sided' (p. 569).

The exciting findings of Weinberger and his colleagues, which consistently demonstrated deficits in the Dorso-Lateral Pre Frontal Cortex (DLPFC) of schizophrenic subjects using regional cerebral blood flow studies whilst the subjects were performing the Wisconsin Card Sorting Test (WCST), proved to be a focus of much of the work that has transpired in the ensuing decade (Berman, Zec & Weinberger, 1986; Weinberger, Berman & Illowsky, 1988). Subsequent replications of this study have been less than unanimous, although support for the original observations has been found. Although the activation studies present possibly the most exciting avenue for further exploration in this area, the results so far could at best be considered to be inconclusive.

NEUROPSYCHOLOGICAL FEATURES

Impaired cognitive performance can be considered a characteristic feature of schizophrenia, and the growing body of neuropsychological research suggests that cognitive impairment may be of diagnostic significance in this disorder (Gold & Harvey, 1993). Recent attempts to establish if these cognitive deficits constitute a generalised or differential deficit continue to remain inconclusive (Blanchard & Neale, 1994). Inquiry into the structural changes of the brain associated with the schizophrenias have been plagued by the failure to apply clear methodological techniques in the interpretation of the cognitive deficits associated with the disorder.

Numerous psycho-anatomical models of the disease have been proposed implicating a subcortical dysfunction, a lateralised dysfunction, a right hemisphere deficit, a left hemisphere deficit, left hemisphere overactivation, impaired interhemispheric integration, and a frontal dysfunction (Levin, Yurgelun-Todd & Craft, 1989). In short, both sides of the brain or their relationship to each other, the cortex and the subcortex, the temporal, frontal and parietal lobes and either underactivation or overactivation or a combination of these have each been implicated in the pathogenesis of schizophrenia. Due to the relative imprecision of these findings, this review will attempt to present both the flavour of the research conducted in this area, as well as the consistently reported findings with this group.

Attention and working memory

At least as far back as the discussions of this disorder by thinkers such as Kraepelin, the notion that patients with schizophrenia have difficulties with attention have been axiomatic. The deficits in attention have been consistently postulated to be the single underlying deficit which characterises these disorders, and the faulty filter model of schizophrenia (i.e. the subject is incapable of screening the array for salient information only), has had some currency. Direct examination of this matter however has been considerably less satisfying. At the outset it should be noted that the faulty filter model (Broadbent, 1958, 1971) is postulated on a now largely discredited view of attentional performance (see van Zomeren & Brouwer, 1994). Nonetheless, attention deficits have been consistently identified in schizophrenic patients using a range of assessment techniques.

Studies examining attentional asymmetry in schizophrenia subjects indicate a pattern of right sided neglect (e.g. Fuller-Torrey, 1980). Subsequent studies by Posner et al. (1988) and Tomer (1990) have attributed attentional asymmetry in schizophrenia to hyper-orientation to the Left Visual Field (LVF) rather than neglect of the Right Visual Field (RVF). Tomer (1990) found that omission of targets on a cancellation task was associated with a preference in reporting targets from the opposite hemifield in a double simultaneous extinction task. This suggests that the observed attentional asymmetry arise from hyper-orienting to the LVF rather than by a failure to orient to the RVF.

Posner et al. (1988) in a study of covert visual attention in schizophrenia suggests a performance asymmetry in these patients' ability to shift visual attention. Schizophrenic patients' response times to targets presented in the right visual field (RVF) and left visual field (LVF) are equal if attention is first cued to the target location. However, if attention is initially cued to the visual field opposite to where the target will appear, the response times to RVF targets are consistently slower than to LVF targets. Posner et al. (1988) postulate that schizophrenic patients have difficulty in disengaging their attention from the LVF in order to shift it in a rightward direction consistent with the notion of hyper-orientation to the LVF. In addition Posner et al. (1988) describe a general slowing of reaction time in the schizophrenic group when compared to the controls, and that the findings were independent of medication status. Unlike controls, the schizophrenic patients demonstrated no advantage in Reaction Time (RT) for validly cued trials over invalidly cued trials in either the RVF or the LVF.

In their review of the literature, Levin, Yurgelun-Todd and Craft (1989) note that attention deficits are characteristically noted with schizophrenia, and these are consistent with the notion that there is frontal system involvement with the disease. They also note that there are different attentional abilities in the different clinical subgroups of schizophrenia. Non-paranoid and negative state schizophrenics demonstrate deficits consistent with reduced arousal and distractability, while paranoid and positive state schizophrenics may demonstrate performances better than normals. There is also evidence of lateralised deficits in the disengagement and redirection of visual attention in schizophrenia.

Gnosis and praxis

Rarely does schizophrenia impinge on the functions of the secondary association areas, and if these deficits are observed they are more than likely due to an inter-current process of some origin other than the psychiatric disorder.

Language and spatial cognition

A classic analysis of the speech and language functions of subjects with schizophrenia was conducted by Nancy Andreasen in 1979. In her study of psychotic patients she noted that 29% of her sample reflected impoverishment of speech production in the form of monosyllabic responding, 40% featured poverty of content, presenting empty speech with little informational content, 36% demonstrated tangentiality such that there was at best only a passing association between the topic in hand and the subjects' response, 56% presented derailment, or inability to connect their response with the flow of the discussion, 16% were incoherent, 27% were illogical, 44% featured a loss of the goal orientation of a particular utterance, 24% featured perseveration, and a further 13% displayed heightened self-reference in their speech. Perhaps the most distinctive feature of the speech of the subjects with schizophrenia is that associated with the tendency to produce neologism or non-words (LeVine & Conrad, 1979).

Examination of the available literature reveals little evidence for deficits in basic language functions in schizophrenia. The studies indicate impairments in semantic content, discourse and complex language, all of which may be secondary to the cognitive deficits, particularly attentional and executive functions.

The data on visuospatial impairment has been inconsistent. Stuss, Kaplan, Benson et al. (1983) noted that non-leucotomised schizophrenic subjects performed worse than both normal subjects and leucotomised subjects on tasks requiring integration of constructional components such as the Block Design and Object Assembly sub-tests of the WAIS. Kolb and Whishaw (1983) have noted that simple perceptual and constructional abilities were intact.

Overall, it seems likely that in tasks which load on frontal functions (e.g. block design) deficits are more likely to be observed with these subjects but at the basic level these skills seem largely unaffected by the disorder.

Learning and memory

There are diverging opinions as to the specificity and extent of memory deficits in schizophrenia (Calev, Edelist, Kugelmass et al., 1991). It has previously been argued that there was no evidence for a specific amnesic syndrome associated with schizophrenia (O'Carroll, 1992), nonetheless recent research indicates the presence of distinctive memory performance in schizophrenia (Gold & Harvey, 1993; Saykin et al., 1991).

Both visual and verbal recall deficits have been consistently observed in schizophrenia, suggesting extensive disruption of cortical networks (Corcoran & Frith, 1993). Chronic schizophrenic patients perform consistently worse on verbal memory tasks than either schizo-affective patients or normal controls, even when matched for age, IQ and education (Beatty et al., 1993; Landro, Orbeck & Rund, 1993).

There are contradictory findings with respect to the effect that length and severity of illness has upon memory performance. It has been claimed that mildly disturbed patients are more impaired in encoding and organisation of material, whereas patients with severe symptoms demonstrate retrograde amnesia (Levin, Yurgelun-Todd & Craft, 1989, p. 353). However, Hoff et al. (1992) conducted comprehensive comparisons of first-episode schizophreniform and chronic schizophrenic patients with respect to memory performance. Controlling for age and education, they found no differences between these groups with respect to verbal and visual memory performance, although both groups performed significantly worse than normal controls.

The memory processing deficit is not restricted to the processing of verbal information. Schizophrenic patients have also been distinguished from bipolar patients and normal control subjects with respect to performance on spatial memory tasks that do not require working memory (Park & Holtzman, 1992). Park & Holtzman claim that this further supports a failure in representational processing in schizophrenic patients, which is independent of modality. Schizophrenic patients were also less accurate than depressed patients and normal control subjects at recognising familiar faces, determining the appropriate emotion of a person from a photograph and recalling unfamiliar faces when presented with a variety of options (Archer, Hay & Young, 1992). Thus, schizophrenic patients appear to have demonstrated a generalised failure of recognition of visual items.

It has been proposed that the complex pattern of observed memory deficits in schizophrenia are the result of inefficient and faulty attentional systems, rather than a general memory deficit per se (Braff, 1993).

In a thorough examination of possible types of memory failure in schizophrenia, Gold et al. (1992) observed poor recognition, recall, and frequency estimation performance across both effortful and automatic tasks. They theorise that memory deficits are due to a disruption in the encoding of material, resulting in a lack of distinctiveness and specificity of verbal items.

Schizophrenic subjects benefit more from semantic priming in word recognition tasks than bipolar or normal control subjects (Capel et al., 1990). This finding suggests that there are anomalies in the way associated memories are activated and recalled in schizophrenia.

Accurate recall of verbal material in acutely psychotic patients has been shown to be related to the nature of thought-disorder in the patients (Speed et al., 1991). While normal control subjects find it easier to recall organised material than non organised material, thought disordered subjects (manic, schizoaffective and schizophrenic) were more successful at recalling non-organised material.

Selective logical and semantic memory impairments have been identified in unmedicated patients, consistent with the involvement of the temporal-hippocampal system (Saykin et al., 1991). Calev et al. (1991) found no evidence of a disparity between verbal and visuospatial memory in schizophrenia, which is inconsistent with claims of laterality of functioning (Corcoran & Frith, 1993). These findings have led to claims that memory deficits in schizophrenia may be the result of hypofrontal blood flow—failure of the frontal lobe to appropriately supervise decision processes in memory retrieval and recognition. Wood and Flowers (1990) examined cerebral blood flow (rCBF) in normal control, schizophrenic, bipolar and unipolar depressive subjects over trials of a verbal recognition memory task. They found that both the schizophrenic and bipolar groups could be distinguished from the other groups on the basis of their performance on narrative prose tasks. However, on the basis of their neurological findings, they claim that schizophrenia is 'uniquely associated' with a failure in activation of Broca's and Wernicke's areas during memory task performance (Wood & Flowers, 1990, p. 423). This difference was independent of age, sex, education, anxiety and prose recall ability. They did not find any support for decreased frontal activity in schizophrenic subjects during verbal recall tasks.

The literature on the memory functions in patients with a diagnosis of schizophrenia consistently reports deficits in basic verbal and visuospatial recall, particularly in severely disturbed schizophrenics, that are similar to the classic amnesic syndrome suggesting bilateral hippocampal involvement. In mildly disturbed patients and in subjects with bipolar affective disorders the deficits in memory are associated with poor organisation of material, which results in a disruption of encoding as a consequence of disruption of attentional and organisational functions.

Adaptive behaviour

Kolb and Whishaw (1983) assessed a number of schizophrenic patients using a battery of tests previously validated on a neurologically impaired population and noted that their performance was impaired on tests measuring right and left temporal and frontal functions, but not on tests measuring parietal functions. A similar finding was reported by Taylor and Abrams (1984). Both studies, however, failed to include a psychotic control group undermining the conclusion that such deficits were specific to schizophrenia.

Gruzelier, Seymour, Wilson et al. (1988) have noted that schizophrenics with a preponderance of positive schizophrenic features demonstrated relatively intact and, in some cases, superior performance on putative tests of left frontal lobe function while those with the defect state demonstrated the reverse pattern. Liddle and Morris (1991) using the WCST, the Stroop, the COWAT and the TMT examined a group of schizophrenic patients and found that on the whole they were impaired. The impairments were correlated with the severity of psychomotor poverty and disorganisation but not with the severity of reality distortion.

To date the vast majority of the research into the adaptive behaviour functions of patients with schizophrenia has used a single test, the WCST, as the principal data of interest (Corcoran & Frith, 1993). Weinberger and his colleagues have consistently demonstrated deficits in the Dorso-Lateral Pre Frontal Cortex (DLPFC) of schizophrenic subjects using regional cerebral blood flow studies whilst the subjects were performing the WCST (Berman, Zec & Weinberger, 1986; Weinberger, Berman & Illowsky, 1988, Weinberger, Berman, & Zec, 1986). On the basis of these findings, Weinberger has suggested that the DLPFC plays a major role in the pathophysiology of schizophrenia. Drewe (1974) working with the WCST has implied that the medial frontal areas rather than the DLPFC or Orbital PreFrontal Cortex (OPFC) may be crucially involved in failure to perform the task appropriately. The work of Sagawa, Kawakaisu and Shiboya (1990) however, has noted that the left inferior frontal region, some distance from the DLPFC, shows the metabolic changes observed by Weinberger. Perhaps all of these results can be explained by suggesting that the schizophrenic patient relies unduly on the frontal lobe to perform this test (David, 1992). Berman and Weinberger (1990) have suggested that inner speech is a crucial element in successfully carrying out this task, and this factor may well underlie the left hemisphere asymmetry in blood flow for both normals and schizophrenics on this task.

Caution should, however, be exercised in the interpretation of this result. As Miller (1983) has succinctly observed, failure on tests of cognitive functioning occurs as a consequence of a number of factors and the clinician must be constantly alert to the various causes of poor performance. In psychotic groups this caution is doubly appropriate due to the effects of medication, compliance, motivation and preoccupation. Summerfeldt et al. (1991) have observed that the compromise in performance of schizophrenic patients on the WCST can be ameliorated to some degree by including a financial inducement to sort correctly. They interpret this result as consistent with the observation that the observed poor performance of schizophrenic patients on this task is as a consequence of poor motivation. The observations of Summerfeldt et al. (1991) serve to underline the fact that this problem in the case of the schizophrenic patients may be overcome by increasing reward. These observations concern treatability, but do not undermine the fundamental observation of poor initiation of behavioral programs in this clinical groups in comparison to normal controls.

HEMISPHERIC CONTRIBUTIONS TO THE SCHIZOPHRENIAS

The original conception of Flor-Henry (1976, 1979) that schizophrenia is a left hemisphere disorder continues to remain largely unsettled. An equal and opposite push from Cutting (1991) continues to support the notion of a right hemisphere deficit in the disorder. Equally as well, numerous other authors have contended that it may well be both. Whilst the notion of a hemisphere being at fault in a particular disorder is very engaging in the early analysis and development of a hypotheses, as time progresses and the weight of evidence increases, these earlier hypotheses tend to give way to more sophisticated and productive ones. This is not to undermine the massive contribution of the earlier approximations of the neuropsychological bases of the disorder but merely to use the knowledge they have given us to develop more sophisticated models of the disorder.

HOW ARE THE DEFICITS PRODUCED?

The review of the deficits associated with the schizophrenias indicate defects in attention, memory and planning. A combination of each of these is characteristic of each of the disorders in the spectrum of the schizophrenias. It seems that in the positive symptom states of schizophrenia the prototypical deficits are the failure to recognise the internal mentations as belonging to the self. This might be thought of as an 'autopsychagnosia', or an inability to be able to recognise that the person who speaks to you inside your head as actually being you. This suggestion has received considerable attention from English neuropsychologists including Frith, David and Bentall (see Frith, 1992; David & Cutting, 1994), although empirical evidence to support what presents as a very intriguing notion remains scant (see Seal, Crowe & Cheung, 1997).

In the negative state of schizophrenia the deficits are most in keeping with the notion of a subcortical dementing process (Pantellis & Nelson, 1994). Here we see marked compromise in attention, concentration, memory, planning and activation. The pattern of executive functioning is not consistent with the disinhibited basal forebrain style of executive disorder and is more in keeping with erosion of the levels of drive and activation (Crowe, 1992, 1996a). This is consistent with a compromise in the DLPFC and its connections in the brain stem which results in an avolitional state characteristic of the subcortical dementias.

The young man examined in the following case report provides a graphic illustration of the issues raised with regard to the negative state pattern of schizophrenia just discussed.

CASE REPORT

BD was referred to me by his caseworker at a government employment office. She asked me to assess his strengths and weaknesses with a view to him returning to paid employment. She noted in her referral letter that BD was a diligent, verbally expressive, but naive and vocationally immature person who was living with his parents. He was 25 years of age and had a long-term schizophrenic condition, first diagnosed when he was 20.

BD had previously worked as a dishwasher and briefly as a builder's labourer, and had attempted voluntary clerical work. A number of training attempts have been made including a two-year part-time catering course at the local college, one semester of a drafting course and several weeks of a wool classing course. Whilst he had experience in a range of areas, and with family encouragement had made various attempts to develop work skills, it was apparent that he had major difficulty sustaining work, reporting his past jobs as monotonous and that learning in the classes he had attended had been problematic. These failures had badly damaged his self-confidence. In speaking with his Technical and Further Education teacher about his study performance, it was apparent that virtually one-to-one teaching in the module based self-paced program that BD was involved in was required. His cognitive problems finally resulted in him ceasing the course. These problems included substantial problems with concentration and memory, poor retention of a discrete piece of information once mastered, problems understanding the meanings of words and requiring a considerable amount of time having these words explained to him. BD was distracted by information other than that which he was supposed to learn and featured considerable loss of information over a brief period of time. He had difficulty unless the tasks were very clearly structured. He appeared generally naive but particularly so with regard to words, concepts and activities to the extent that he sought very detailed information to get himself up to speed. Even when these were explained, however, he did not appear to integrate them well into a bigger picture.

Background

BD attended primary at a private school and had gone from the preparatory year through to Year 12 at the same school. He completed two Year 12 subjects. His reason for only doing two subjects was that he felt 'stressed out' by the requirements of the school, and consequently felt that he could not return. He observed that he couldn't make himself go back to school. He attributed these problems to remembering all of the insecurities associated with his academic performance and was prone to critical evaluation of himself, although on a number of occasions he noted that many of his school mates had undertaken their senior year without difficulty and he couldn't see why he couldn't also.

Following leaving school BD took a Christmas job in a large department store as a toy wrapper and did this for about four weeks. He then attempted a catering course which he didn't complete due to a schizophrenic breakdown and hospitalisation. In the following year he studied civil engineering according to his report, and found that he couldn't do it because it was 'too precise'. BD got sick again with the schizophrenia and was admitted to the local public hospital for three months. In the Christmas of that year he left hospital and went to live in a group home for about 1–2 years. During this time he attended a supported employment program where he did woodwork. Of this he noted that he was not very good with his hands.

During this time BD had always thought of becoming a seaman but observed that he didn't think he would be very good at it. He then studied kitchen work and undertook employment orientation, but again this resulted in a poor outcome. Early in the next year that I saw him, he had started a course in wool classing but had great deal of difficulty due to his very bad memory problem and he noted that he had 'a mental block in his head' which had been there from the pressure of Year 12, some five years before.

BD had his first presentation for schizophrenia when he was 20 and the problems he had include poor concentration, constant worry and fear due to his disastrous, as reported, hallucinations. He was hearing voices nearly 24 hours a day and couldn't get rid of them. During this time he saw heaven and hell, and he was responding to 'the funny stories in his head made up by the hallucinations'.

Over the three months before I saw him there had been a marked improvement in BD's function due to the application of the agent Clozapine. The voices, according to BD's report, had now stopped for the greater part. Due to the massive improvement in performance as a consequence of Clozapine, the employment agency was trying to get him back to work.

Formal Assessment

I conducted a number of tests with BD to determine his level of function and to see if we could gain any insight into the nature of his information processing. Formal testing with the Wechsler Adult Intelligence Scale Revised indicated that BD had a Verbal Intelligent Quotient of 85, a Performance Intelligence Quotient of 87 and a Full Scale IQ of 84. This placed his intelligence in the low average range. He had his greatest difficulties with the Arithmetic and Digit Symbol Substitution Test which indicated that BD has a problem with attention, concentration and the rapid processing of information to be able to produce desired output.

Results from the tests of memory functions were extremely interesting. BD had a Verbal Memory Quotient of 106, Visual Memory Quotient of 91 and a General Memory Quotient of 102, but displayed marked difficulties with Delayed Recall demonstrating a Delayed Recall Index of 69. BD was capable of recalling information immediately after I had presented it to him. For example I read him two, 25 item passages of information and he was capable of recalling 14 items from the first passage and 17 items from the second. He demonstrated a good learning curve for both Visual Paired Associates and Verbal Paired Associates, and was capable of recalling the line drawn figures of the Visual Reproduction Test quite well. However, after as brief as a thirty minute delay he retained virtually no information from the two passages remembering only three items from the first and three from the second. He also indicated some losses in his recall of the Visual Paired Associates and marked losses of the Visual Reproduction items. This clearly indicated that there was a marked deterioration in memory functions after the briefest of delay in BD's case; this loss was not material specific and applied to both verbal and visuospatial information.

Tests of the frontal executive functions indicated that BD was capable of solving the Porteus Mazes Test to the adult level, but he did have some false starts. The most telling problem for him however was observed on the WCST. This is a test that requires the subject to sort cards into categories underneath an example card according to either their colour, their number or their shape. The pattern that BD demonstrated on this occasion was to sort originally for colour and irrespective of any of the instructions that I gave him, he could not shift from his original approach to the task, and proved unable to sort them in any other way for the remainder of the pack of 128 cards.

VERBAL TESTS (Age Scaled Scores)									
Information									7
Digit Span									8
Vocabulary									8
Arithmetic									7
Comprehension									8
Similarities									8
VIQ									85
PERFORMANCE TESTS									
Picture Completion									10
Picture Arrangement									8
Block Design									8
Object Assembly									8
Digit Symbol									6
PIQ									87
FSIQ									84
WECHSLER MEMORY SCALE-REVISED									
Verbal Memory Index									106
Visual Memory Index									91
General Memory Index									102
Attention/Concentration									83
Delayed Recall									69
PORTEUS MAZES									
Year	6	7	8	9	10	11	12	14	Adult
Number of Trials	1	1	1	1	1	1	2	3	1

WCST (C = colour)
CCCCCC/CCCCCCCCCCCCCCCCCCCCCCCCCCCCCCCCCCCCCCCCCCCCCCCC

Conclusion

The pattern of performances that BD demonstrated on this occasion indicates that he is premorbidly of low average intelligence with deficits in attention and concentration, marked losses in information after a very brief delay and concreteness and inability to be able to shift set on tests of the frontal executive functions. These patterns are very characteristic of the negative symptoms of schizophrenia, and I would not anticipate that despite the massive improvements in his behavioural responding as a consequence of the Clozapine that these would not resolve all that much in the future. The observations of the teachers at the TAFE college are consistent with the sorts of deficits often observed, with marked deficits in memory function, difficulty attending and concentrating, difficulty in generalising from the specific to the general, and 'stickiness' in terms of his over-concentration on word meaning and word importance. These features taken together indicate that BD will not be a successful candidate in any sort of advanced training that the employment agency may hope to propose for him and I think that another attempt at Year 12 for BD with his past history of failure is destined to be unsuccessful.

By way of suggestions for what might meet with the employment needs in this particular case, the provision of an employment situation which features structure, and in which BD is capable of referring back to the information available to him time and again to monitor his progress was essential. What I suggested was something akin to process work or gardening. Whilst I acknowledged BD's aspirations to advanced academic achievement, his level of premorbid function as well as his marked memory deficits must make this a very unlikely eventuality. I appraised BD of my concerns about his memory and attention and also advised him that I did not think that an advanced education was suitable to his particular personality style. I wrote this down for him also and prevailed upon the employment agency to reinforce the findings in their further dealings with BD.

SUMMARY

The schizophrenias remain a mystery in terms of how they are capable of producing distortions of reality, emotion and behaviour. Nonetheless it is possible for us to make some observations regarding their effects on the individual. Positive symptom schizophrenia may only be associated with the distortions of reality associated with hallucination, delusion and thought disorder and probably not too much else by way of disruption of higher level cognitive functions. The deficit can be thought of as an autopsychagnosia or an inability to recognise personal mental activity as belonging to one's self. The negative state on the other hand is associated with a massive disruption of attention, memory and executive functioning. This results in a marked avolitional state which is characterised by lack of effort and an overall diminution of drive and direction.

CHAPTER 3

MOOD DISORDERS

Mood disorders or affective disorders are defined as those conditions in which a disturbance of mood is the predominant clinical feature. This simple definition conceals a number of uncertainties and disagreements regarding these disorders that requires considerable elaboration. The disorders themselves only refer to the extremes of mood which manifest as poles on the continuum running from depression to elation and not directly to either of the other primary mood states, fear or anger. According to Beck (1967), describing these disorders as only disorders of affect is as misleading as referring to scarlet fever as only a disease of the skin. Clearly many other aspects of self-concept, activity level and vegetative (i.e. body maintenance) functions are altered in these disorders, as much if not more than the changes in mood.

The understanding of the affective disorders must take place at three levels of inquiry. These include: (1) the experience of the mood disorder, which refers to the conscious feeling of depressive affect or sadness at one end of the continuum or of the elation and euphoria at the other; (2) the outward expression of the affective disorder including changes in the level of activity and neurovegetative functioning; and (3) the cognitive components of these disorders characterised by the either unduly negative or unduly positive appraisal of internal or external events.

This chapter deals with both the unipolar and bipolar affective disorders. The focus will surround the effects of these conditions from the neuropsychological perspective and will present the various models of causation attributed to these conditions from a neurochemical and behavioural standpoint. The discussion will then move to detail the nature of the effects of the mood disorders on cognitive functioning.

HISTORICAL BACKGROUND

The notion of depression extends back in time at least as far the Greeks. In 1621, Burton in *Anatomy of Melancholy* wrote of Hippocrates, the father of medicine, observing Democritus dissecting animals with the hope of finding the black bile characteristic of depression.

It was Kraepelin who originally proposed the unitary notion of the mood disorders and included a number of the previously unconnected mood disorders including mania, depression, depression with mania, and elderly depression under a single diagnostic umbrella. This monolithic view of mood disorders was challenged through the 1950s by Sir Martin Roth and his group at Newcastle (Roth, 1955), who proposed that depression should be divided into a psychotic or endogenous form of depression versus a neurotic or reactive form of depression.

Reactive depression was thought to be caused by ambient life stressors and in form it was thought to be dominated by psychological-type factors. On the other hand, endogenous depression was thought to be biological as opposed to intrapsychic in origin and was characterised by loss of interest, loss of appetite and weight, deceased interest in sex, sleep disturbances, psychomotor retardation and agitation. It has now become clear that psychological traumas often act as the triggering events which in the end lead to endogenous depression in some individuals. Paykel has noted that only 15% of a clinically depressed sample evidenced a lack of precipitating events, and that the triggering event or events may have occurred two years or more before the onset of the problem (Paykel et al., 1969).

The distinction between unipolar and bipolar depression was proposed by Leonhard in the 1950s based upon his genetic studies. The distinction of the nature of the depression in each instance has been reviewed by Bowden (1993) and by Mitchell et al. (1992) who note that in the unipolar disorder, the depressive episode tends to be longer and more serious and is usually characterised by somatic symptoms, anxiety, psychomotor agitation, suicidal ideas, muddled thoughts, loss of weight and initial insomnia. In bipolar disorder the depression is usually characterised by hypersomnia and a seasonal pattern of occurrence with a tendency to increasing symptoms in the winter and the autumn. It has also been suggested that unipolar depressed subjects may be more likely to successfully attempt suicide (Lester, 1993).

Depression affects about 5% of the population of the United States at any given time. In addition, about 1–2% of the adult population of the US have acute bipolar illness. The lifetime incidence of depression is about 30% of the population. If left untreated, 25–30% of adult depressives will commit suicide

(Richelson, 1993). The risk of depression is two to three times higher amongst women than men (Young, Schefter, Fawcett, & Klerman, 1990). The incidence of affective illness in an individual raises the risk of a similar diagnosis in a first degree relative by two to three times (Young et al., 1990), but such findings are by no means straightforward and considerable dispute exists (McGuffin & Katz, 1989).

About 65–70% of patients respond to antidepressant drug therapy and will go on to complete recovery. Electroconvulsive therapy (ECT) works in a further 10–15% of patients, leaving about 20% of individuals relatively intractable to treatment (Richelson, 1993).

NOSOLOGY

The mood disorders are characterised by the presence of the loss of emotional perspective. The DSM-IV (American Psychiatric Association, 1994) divides these into two principal groups of disorders: (1) depressive disorders (major depressive disorder, dysthymic disorder, and depressive disorder not otherwise specified) and those due to aetiological factors (mood disorder due to a general medical condition and substance-induced mood disorder), and (2) bipolar disorders (bipolar I disorder, bipolar II disorder, cyclothymic disorder and bipolar disorder not otherwise specified). The defining distinction between the two groups of mood disorders is the presence or history of manic, mixed or hypomanic episodes accompanied by the presence or history of major depressive episodes.

The focus of the present discussion will largely centre on the distinction between unipolar depression, or depression without mania where the depression is continuous and unremitting and may come in episodes, and bipolar affective disorder, which is characterised by the alternation of mania and depression.

The major depressive episode is characterised by at least two weeks during which there is depression of mood, or loss of interest or pleasure in most activities (American Psychiatric Association, 1994) and, in association with this, a number of other features of both physical and emotional disturbance. These include a change in neurovegetative functioning, including a change in appetite, sleep and activity pattern, decreased energy, feelings of worthlessness or guilt, difficulty in thinking, concentrating and making decisions, or recurrent thoughts of death or suicidal ideas, planning or attempts. These behaviours must be new to the individual or have worsened from the pre-depressive state and must persist for much of the day nearly every day for the preceding two weeks. Major depressive disorder is characterised by one or more major depressive episodes without a history of manic episodes (American Psychiatric Association, 1994).

The manic episode is defined by the presence of a persistently abnormal elevated, expansive or irritable mood. This must go on for at least one week unless it leads to an earlier hospitalisation. The mood disturbance must be accompanied by at least three additional symptoms including inflated self-esteem or grandiosity, decreased need for sleep, pressure of speech, flight of ideas, distractability, increased interest in goal directed activities or psychomotor agitation, and excessive involvement in pleasurable activities with a high potential for painful consequences. The episode must be sufficiently severe to cause marked impairment of social or occupational functioning, and must not be caused by drug effects, toxin exposure or due to the physiological effects of a general medical condition (American Psychiatric Association, 1994).

It is also the case that there are recognised stages of mania which roughly correspond to the severity of the manic episode. Stage I mania manifests as hypomania with mild euphoria or irritability, expansive speech and increased energy and usually a reduced need for sleep. It is, as such, difficult to differentiate from the ideal normal state or mild intoxication. Stage II mania features grandiosity, euphoria, increased energy, impulsivity, increased sexuality, increased rate of speech and interpersonal interaction, frank insomnia, paranoia and irritability. Stage III mania features clear psychotic symptoms including hallucinations and delusion, confusion, incoherent speech, agitation or catatonia, in association with insomnia. It is thus very difficult to differentiate this latter state from the other psychotic conditions (Gerner, 1993). Interestingly, the vast majority of patients pass through these stages in sequence and recover in the reverse sequence (Gerner, 1993).

THE BIOLOGICAL ORIGINS OF THE AFFECTIVE DISORDERS

The fact that depression can be treated by serotonin-specific re-uptake inhibitors (SSRIs), tricyclic antidepressants (TCAs), and the monoamine oxidase inhibitors (MAOIs: see Chapter 8), all of which are monoamine agonists, suggests the monoamine hypothesis of depression, i.e. that depression is caused by insufficient activity of mono-aminergic neurones. Because the syndrome does not respond to dopamine agonists such as amphetamine and cocaine, most investigators have concentrated on NA and 5HT as the likely suspects.

It has been proposed that the 'lack of effort' observed in depressed patients, including their increased dependency and indecisiveness, is the result of a reduction in brain catecholamine levels. The locus coeruleus is a subcortical structure which is intimately involved in arousal. Cells of the locus coeruleus contain the neurotransmitter norepinephrine, and they innervate virtually the entire central nervous system (CNS) from the spinal cord to the cerebral cortex. Although the function of the locus ceruleus is not known with certainty, it is thought to have some sort of overall biasing effect on the CNS. This notion is consistent with the finding that the discharge rate of the locus ceruleus neurones increases as an animal's state of arousal increases, decreases with drowsiness, and is nearly absent during sleep (Nolte, 1994).

In major depressive illness, an elevated level of serum cortisol is also a common but variable finding at different phases of the illness. The most well-established finding is that depressed subjects feature an oversecretion of the hormone cortisol of a magnitude at times resembling the level seen in Cushings disease (Gold, Goodwin, & Chrousos, 1988). Normally the secretion of hydrocortisone (cortisol) fluctuates, peaking at about 8:00 a.m. and virtually ceasing in the evening. In contrast, about 50% of depressed subjects secrete excessive amounts of cortisol (about twice the normal level), especially in the evening. Carroll (Carroll et al., 1981) has observed that whereas normals show a suppression of hydrocortisone secretion when given dexamethasone, about 40% of depressed people show no suppression at all.

The original hope that the Dexamethasone Suppression Test (DST) would reflect the severity of clinical illness has not eventuated, and indeed recent studies have shown that the metabolism of dexamethasone itself may be a better correlate of clinical outcome than baseline cortisol or the response of the hypothalamic-pituitary-adrenal axis to dexamethasone (Ball & Whybrow, 1993).

The brain thyroid axis has also been implicated in the biology of depression and the blunting of the thyroid-stimulating hormone (TSH) response to thyrotropin-releasing hormone and the elevation of serum T_4 are the most consistent findings (Bauer & Whybrow, 1988).

As yet the support for the monoamine hypothesis remains weak with little evidence for the notion other than the post-hoc justification provided by the fact that the TCAs, the SSRIs, and the MAOIs all work by their putative effect on the biogenic amines, and that there is clear disruption of the HPA axis in depressed individuals (Gold et al., 1988).

While little is known about the biology of depression, yet less applies in the case of the bipolar disorders. Wirz-Justice and Wehr (1983) have proposed that sleep deprivation precipitates escalations of the disease to more marked symptomatic manifestations. A similar observation has been made regarding activity levels, and in patients who are taken off lithium and then tracked in terms of their activity levels, the subjects who showed greater levels of motor activity were more likely to relapse (Klein et al., 1992). It is difficult in this context to determine whether this represents a cause or an effect.

Genetic explanations of the bipolar disorders have been proposed including the notion that schizoaffective disorder and bipolar I disorder are closely related at the genotypic level and that bipolar II and major recurrent depression are to some extent independent of bipolar I disorders, but this proposal is very much in its infancy and requires considerably more empirical support (Gershon, Hamovit & Guroff, 1982).

THE PSYCHOLOGICAL ORIGINS OF THE AFFECTIVE DISORDERS

Within the literature on the cognitive behaviour therapy of depression (Abramson, Seligman & Teasdale, 1978; Beck, 1967; Beck et al., 1979; Lewinsohn, 1974; Lewinsohn, Youngren & Grosscup, 1979; Seligman, 1974), it is postulated that depressive mentation is activated and maintained by internal self-talk. Beck (1967) maintains that depression is caused by particular stresses that evoke the activation of an internal scheme that screens and encodes the individual's subsequent experience in a negative fashion. As a consequence, depressed individuals perceive themselves, their future and their environment in a negative manner.

Kuiper and his colleagues (Kuiper, Derry & MacDonald, 1981; Kuiper, Olinger & MacDonald, 1984) have extended Beck's model and provided support for the notion that the cognitive schemata influence information processing in depression. Specifically they propose that self-schemata in depression consist of negative content and that these schemata facilitate efficient processing of schemata-congruent information. There is some empirical support for these notions provided by the cognitive biasing literature to be discussed in the attentional effects of the affective disorders presented below.

NEUROPATHOLOGY

The number of neuropathological investigations into subjects with the affective disorders is quite low. Nonetheless, they allow some useful insights into the nature of these disorders and to their possible clinical effects.

Young et al. (1994) have examined the turnover rates of serotonin, noradrenaline and dopamine levels in nine autopsied brains of patients with bipolar disorder. Their findings indicated an increase in turnover rates in the frontal, temporal and occipital cortices of the patients as compared to normal controls for noradrenaline, a decrease in serotonin turnover and a smaller decrease in dopamine turnover in the parieto-occipital cortex of the bipolars as compared to normal subjects. The authors maintain that the increase in NA turnover rates appears to be specific to bipolar disorder, and speculate that these increased turnover rates may be associated specifically with the manic phase. Little data seems available to date on pathological studies in the depressed state.

STRUCTURAL AND FUNCTIONAL IMAGING DATA

Abnormalities in brain structure and function have been observed in patients with affective disorders. CT scanning of these patients has revealed ventricular enlargement in the bipolar disorders (Nasrallah, McCalley-Withers & Pfohl, 1984; Pearlson, Garbacz, Breakey et al., 1984; Pearlson et al., 1985; Pearlson, Garbacz, Tompkins, et al., 1984; Schlegel & Kretzschmar, 1987), the unipolar depression (Scott et al., 1983) and the mixed affective disorders (Dolan, Calloway & Mann, 1985; Luchins, Lewine & Meltzer, 1984).

Numerous studies have noted that elderly depressed individuals possess imaging data more similar to those observed with irreversible dementia than they do with normal controls. Burns, Jacoby and Levy (1990) found that AD patients who had concurrent depressive symptoms had less cognitive impairment and less ventricular enlargement on CT scans compared to those without symptoms of depression. In a study conducted by Pearlson et al. (1989), CT scans revealed that patients with the dementia syndrome of depression had lower attenuation values and slightly higher ventricular to brain ratios (VBR) than cognitively normal depressed individuals.

MRI studies of bipolar patients have claimed to identify a common structural abnormality in this group. Dupont et al. (1990) in a study of 19 bipolar patients found subcortical white matter hyperintensities in 9 of these patients on blind evaluation of the images. Whilst the locations of these varied, 7 of the 9 subjects proved to have these areas localised to the frontal lobes. While the number of individuals noted to have deficits on the scans was only 47%, a similar level of deficit was identified in a subsequent study of 32 bipolar patients (Aylward et al., 1994). Of the pool, 11 (34%) were noted to have white matter hyperintensities, with the majority located in the frontal lobes or on the parieto-frontal junction. A similar result was also obtained by Figiel et al. (1991) who noted that 44% of their 18 bipolar patients showed deep white matter lesions, while only 6% of the normal controls did. The lesions were again all located in the frontal and parietal deep white matter.

Regional cerebral blood flow studies of 38 patients with major depression and 16 controls revealed that there were no mean hemispheric differences between the controls and the different subgroups of depressive (i.e. unipolar and bipolar) patients. There was, however, a lower level of blood flow in the left hemisphere of the bipolar as compared to the unipolar and normal groups (Delvenne et al., 1990).

Using a similar technique with 41 patients diagnosed with major depressive disorders and 40 matched controls, Sackheim et al. (1990) noted that the depressed group had a marked reduction in global cortical blood flow. The authors also noted that the depressed subjects had an abnormality in the topographical distribution of their blood flow such that there was a decrease in the flow in selective frontal, central, superior temporal and anterior parietal regions. They concluded that the deficit was consistent with a compromise in the distributed cortical network involving frontal and temporo-parietal polymodal association areas. Interestingly, the level of topographical abnormality correlated both with age and the severity of the depressive symptoms. Posner and Raichle (1994) have noted that depressed patients feature increases in blood flow to the frontal lobes as compared with controls, they also demonstrated decreased blood flow in the parietal and posterior temporal cortex, and increases in the amygdala. Whilst most of these changes were not susceptible to alteration of the depression by medication, the effect on the amygdala did appear to respond.

In an early positron emission tomography (PET) investigation of the cerebral functioning studies of bipolar disorder, Baxter et al. (1985) compared the profiles of bipolar manic, bipolar depressed, unipolar depressed and normal controls. Their results suggested a discontinuous bimodal distribution of metabolic rates with the bipolar manic phase at the hypermetabolic end of the spectrum, and the unipolar depressed phase at the hypometabolic end. Of particular interest in this study was the repeated scanning of the same rapid cycling bipolar patients as a function of phase of illness. The results of a single subject were presented with a marked decrease in glucose usage observed in the depressed phase, markedly increased glucose metabolism in the manic phase a day later and the return to the hypometabolic profile with the return of the depression a few days after that.

Buchsbaum (1986) also conducted a PET study with 20 bipolar patients (no details of the phase of illness were provided) but found no difference in global glucose metabolism between his unipolar and bipolar patients. The bipolar patients were, however, found to have reduced anterior posterior glucose gradients, hypofrontality and greater glucose metabolism in the left, as compared to the right, basal ganglia. Again a similar pattern of frontal as compared to occipital glucose hypometabolism was noted for bipolar patients with respect to controls (Buchsbaum et al., 1986).

Suhara et al. (1992) have examined D_1 receptor binding using PET and have noted decreased binding potential for the ligand in the frontal cortex of these subjects as compared to normal controls. The authors argue that the result may indicate a functional alteration of these receptors in the frontal lobe of these subjects.

Baxter et al. (1989) noted that there was marked reduction in glucose metabolism in the dorsal anterolateral prefrontal cortex of the left hemisphere but not in the right hemisphere of bipolar depressed phase patients, as compared to bipolar manic phase patients. The authors maintain that reduction in the left dorsal anterolateral cortex is common to three types of major depression: unipolar depression, bipolar depression, and obsessive–compulsive disorder with depression.

In a recent review, Steffens, Tuppler and Krishnan (1993) concluded that the basal ganglia, limbic system, frontal cortex and temporal lobes are each implicated in the clinical syndromes associated with major depression and bipolar disorder. In depression the metabolic rates of the caudate and the putamen are reduced. With Late Onset Depression (LOD) ventriculomegaly is more common. In bipolar disorder the temporal lobe volume is decreased, particularly in the right hemisphere. In both unipolar and bipolar disorder subcortical hyperintensities are prominent, particularly in association with late onset, suggesting that vascular changes may play an important aetiological role. The compelling nature of the data presented by Baxter et al. (1985) and that of Suhara et al. (1992) further indicate that during the manic phase of the bipolar disorder the likelihood of a hypermetabolic rate in the frontal regions is high, which stands in marked contrast to their hypometabolic rate during the depressed phase even within the same patient.

NEUROPSYCHOLOGICAL FEATURES

It is something of a pity that the approach to the neuropsychological assessment of individuals with the affective disorders has been so piecemeal. The principal issue of cognitive compromise associated with depression has been in the differentiation of this problem from the co-morbidity of dementia. As such the data base is somewhat inconsistent in terms of the nature of the effects of depression *per se* on cognitive functioning in otherwise intact individuals. A similar problem exists in the area of the bipolar disorders. While some neuropsychological studies have approached the problem directly, others have used bipolar patients as the control groups in investigations of the neuropsychological changes associated with schizophrenia. Although this provides some data about the performance of these subjects in clinical research studies, it undermines to a degree the quality of the data presented and also the nature of the data gathered as secondary to some other aim.

Attention and mental tracking

Using the Sternberg task and the Digit Symbol Substitution Task from the WAIS, Hart and Kwentus (1987) noted that reaction times in depressed subjects were significantly slowed. Interestingly, their incidental learning was unaffected by the diagnosis. Austin et al. (1992) similarly noted impairment on the Digit Symbol Substitution Task, and the subjects' level of slowing was correlated with their symptom scores on the Hamilton Rating Scale for Depression. Patients with affective psychoses (mania and depression), demonstrated impairments in digit span and block span, with the deficit in spatial span worse than that of the schizophrenic subject (Gruzelier et al., 1988).

Gnosis and praxis

One of the heartening things to note in affectively disordered subjects is that almost invariably the skills in the area of gnosis, praxis and language function are largely unaffected (Emery & Breslau, 1989). This is a most helpful observation particularly in that area of practice where the clinician is called upon to make a differential diagnosis from a dementing condition such as Alzheimer's disease. In Alzheimer's disease, the subject will always reflect deficits in memory, but in association with this will also feature associated problem with gnosis, praxis and language functions, particularly in confrontational naming. In contrast, the depressed subject will feature a similar if not quite so severe deficit in memory functions, but will not feature the associated deficits of gnosis, praxis, or language function. This allows a relatively strong decision rule for the differentiation of these two conditions.

Language and spatial cognition

In a study by Hoffman, Stopek and Andreasen (1986), assessing the semantic elements of discourse in the language of schizophrenic and manic patients, overall patterns of deficit in coherence in the discourse were noted for both groups, however the patterns of error differed between the groups. While the schizophrenic subjects showed poor discourse planning, the manic subjects demonstrated frequent loss of set.

Little investigation has transpired with the unipolar affective disorders in these domains. Sackheim et al. (1992) have noted that lowered Performance IQ on the Wechsler Scales is a characteristic finding.

Learning and memory

Caine (1986), in his summary of the literature regarding the effects of depression on memory functioning, noted that the primary effect of the disorder was to: (1) decrease attention on tasks which require effort; (2) decrease initial acquisition of stimuli; and (3) decrease retrieval of the information which has been encoded, but without affecting the encoding process itself. Weingartner and his colleagues (Weingartner et al., 1981) have noted that these subjects feature weak memory encoding and disrupted arousal and activation. This applies to both verbal and visuospatial recall, and the performance of depressed subjects is reflected on their performance on the Benton Visual Retention Test as well as on the Fuld Object Memory Evaluation (LaRue, 1989). Sternberg and Jarvik (1976) have noted that the observed deficits on memory functioning improved with the pharmacological treatment of the depression.

Another interesting finding to emerge in this area is that depressed patients tend to differ in their performance on meta-memory. Depressed subjects are more conservative in their decision criteria regarding recognition of memory items (Miller & Lewis, 1977; Whitehead, 1973) and they do not tend to actively organise material for recall (Lamberty & Beliauskas, 1993). When structure is placed on the material for them they tend to produce considerably better performances (Weingartner, 1986).

A neuropsychological investigation of 30 patients with bipolar disorder with psychotic features noted deficits on nonverbal but not verbal memory (Coffman et al., 1990). In a later study by Gruzelier et al. (1988), affective disordered subjects were reported to show greater impairment on spatial tasks, a finding supported by a study comparing the performance of schizophrenic, bipolar and normal subjects on the Rey Complex Figure Test. Yergelun-Todd et al. (1987) noted that in recall, both psychiatric groups showed a greater than control level of confabulation as defined by adding novel details to the drawings. They maintained that, in the recall condition of this task, right hemisphere frontal mechanisms of organisation and retrieval are involved in the performance as well as temporal memory processes. They thus maintained that the effect was consistent with a dysfunction of the right frontal area.

The conclusion that it is possible to draw from all of this data is that the depressed subjects perform on tests of memory in a manner between that of the normal condition and that observed in dementing subjects. The problem seems to be one associated with the effortfulness of the encoding and on tests of incidental learning no clear deficits have been observed.

Adaptive behaviour

Morice (1990), in a study comparing the performance of schizophrenic with bipolar subjects on the Wisconsin Card Sorting Test (WCST), found that both patients groups performed significantly worse than the control group on the task. The author noted that there was no difference between the performance on the WCST among the bipolar (manic) patients, between those recovering from an acute episode and those in remission. The results suggested that the subjects with bipolar disorder had problems shifting set. Morice interpreted these results as representing the fact that bipolar disorder was related to right pre-frontal functioning while schizophrenia was related to left pre-frontal functioning.

Gureje et al. (1994) conducted a study in which they compared a bipolar group to a schizophrenic and a normal group on a battery of tests including an adaptation of the Logical memory test, verbal and design fluency, and a selected sample of the WAIS Verbal (Digit Span and Similarities) and Performance (Object Assembly and Picture Completion). Whilst the principal thrust of the study was the comparison of the schizophrenic subjects with the normals, it was noted that the manic patients performed worse than the normal controls on picture arrangement, digits backwards and the similarities subtests.

Yurgelun-Todd et al. (1988) compared schizophrenic patients with psychotic bipolar patients and normal controls on the WCST. While the schizophrenic subjects made fewer correct responses on the first pack of 64 cards, the bipolar subjects showed no significant impairment. On the second pack, after the criteria had been explained, the schizophrenic subjects had a higher number of within-category perseverative errors. The bipolar subjects, however, demonstrated a significant difference from the normal subjects by demonstrating a significant decrease in the ability to sustain the appropriate sequence. The bipolar subjects did not significantly differ from the schizophrenic subjects. Qualitative analysis of the error patterns, however, indicated that the schizophrenic subjects demonstrated poor mental flexibility resulting in perseveration, while the bipolar group were unable to self-regulate and thus maintain set.

HEMISPHERIC CONTRIBUTION TO THE AFFECTIVE DISORDERS

In one of the earliest investigations of bipolar disorders, Flor-Henry (1974) reported that manic-depressive psychoses associated with temporal lobe epilepsy was significantly related to non-dominant temporo-limbic function, while schizophrenia associated with temporal lobe epilepsy was related to dysfunction in the dominant temporal lobe. In a later study comparing 54 schizophrenia patients with 60 patients with affective psychoses (mania, hypomania, unipolar and bipolar depression), he made the claim that the affective psychoses were associated with dysfunction in the non-dominant hemisphere with a strong association to the anterior limbic structures (Flor-Henry, 1976). In another study in 1979, Flor-Henry and Yuedall examined 60 bipolar patients and 54 schizophrenic patients on a neuropsychological battery. They concluded that depression was the result of non-dominant temporal and frontal dysfunction. Mania, on the other hand, was characterised by more extensive non-dominant temporal and frontal dysfunction with a more generalised bilateral dysfunction also apparent.

PSEUDODEMENTIA

The term pseudodementia is used to describe a state in which dementia is mimicked by functional psychiatric illness (Caine, 1981; Kiloh, 1961; Wells, 1979). Such illnesses include various personality disorders, schizophrenia and the affective disorders (McAllister, 1983). Although pseudodementia is predominantly a disorder of the elderly, it has been reported in individuals of various ages. There are a number of labels which have been recommended for this syndrome including depression-induced organic mental disorder, dementia syndrome of depression (Caine, 1981), dementia in depression, and depressive pseudodementia (Katzman, 1986). A number of complaints have been raised about the use of the term pseudodementia due to its misleading connotations, as such it is preferable, according to desRosiers (1992), to use the term 'depressive dementia'. A less controversial approach is afforded by the use of the term 'depression with cognitive impairment'.

Pseudodementia has been defined as: (1) intellectual impairment in patients with a primary psychiatric illness, (2) the features of the intellectual change resemble those caused by degenerative dementias, (3) the intellectual deficits are reversible, and (4) the patient has no identifiable neurological disease than can account for their mental changes (Caine, 1981). Pseudodementia accounted for approximately 8% of the patients referred for assessment in the sample assembled by Marsden and Harrison (1972), with the majority of subjects suffering from depression.

Four possible causes can be ascribed to patients presenting with an apparent dementing syndrome: (1) a pseudodementia due to psychiatric illness; (2) a focal neurological syndrome, rather than a diffuse one; (3) an acute confusional state; or (4) an actual dementia. Of the actual dementias Alzheimer's disease represents the lion's share of patients referred for evaluation of progressive intellectual deterioration.

Published data indicates that 10% to 20% of depressed elderly patients have substantial cognitive deficits (depressive pseudodementia) and that 3% to 57% of patients with dementia of the Alzheimer type (DAT) develop depressive symptoms (MacKenzie, Robiner & Knopman, 1989; Reynolds et al., 1988; Rovner et al., 1989). The differences in prevalence rates between studies may be due to a number of factors including inter-study differences, method of patient selection and diagnostic criteria. The picture of differential diagnosis is further complicated by dementia existing secondary to depression and dementia presenting as depression (Pearlson et al., 1990). Although the latter two conditions occur less frequently, it is important to consider them when making a diagnosis. Overall it appears that about 10% of individuals originally diagnosed as having dementia are subsequently rediagnosed as having depressive disorders (desRosiers, 1992).

Variation in estimates of the prevalence of significant depression in patients with DAT (i.e. 3% to 57%) can be accounted for by several factors. MacKenzie et al. (1989) found that interviewing patients with DAT yielded a depression rate of 13.9% using DSM-III criteria, whereas information from families gave a rate of 50%. Moreover, the measures used and the criteria set to make the diagnosis of depression differ between studies, and are often those designed to apply to a younger age group (Logie et al., 1992). Whilst somatic symptoms are a key to diagnosis of depression in the young, they are less useful in the elderly where, for instance, sleep disturbances are also common in the non-depressed elderly. Many examples of this exist including the normal decline of sexual functioning, constipation, and the aches and pains associated with arthritis and other ailments in the aged (Yesavage et al., 1983).

DIFFERENTIAL DIAGNOSIS

One of the primary challenges of the differential diagnosis of DAT from depressive dementia centres on the early distinction between these disorders. As DAT progresses and cognitive impairment becomes more severe, it can be distinguished relatively easily from depressive dementia on the basis of many cognitive abilities (Jones et al., 1992). Earlier in the evolution of these conditions, however, the clinical picture of the two disorders are quite similar, thus differentiating between the two can be quite difficult. A number of complicating factors impinge on this differentiation including the numerous clinical presentations of dementia due to their divergent cerebral pathology, the effects of personality and the interaction of psychological, educational, environmental, social and organic factors. A significant degree of overlap also exists between the various dementias themselves, making accurate differentiation difficult. The picture of dementia is further complicated by the similarity of the changes in dementia to those of normal aging. These common changes blur the boundary between the normal and abnormal. Similarly, many psychiatric disorders and medical conditions can present with a picture of cognitive impairment and alterations in behaviour and personality, thus masquerading as dementia. The absence of specific diagnostic markers poses diverse diagnostic problems. In particular, elderly patients with mixed symptoms of depression and dementia present complex diagnostic challenges.

Wells (1979) compiled a widely quoted list of features thought to differentiate between depressive dementia and progressive dementia (see Table 1 for an adaptation of this list). These original features were based on clinical impressions and case history studies and intended as clinical guidelines rather than discriminative criteria for the disorder. Many of these features have gained empirical support since they were originally proposed (Carney, 1983; Janowsky, 1982; Katzman, 1986; McAllister, 1983; Rabins, Merchant & Nestadt, 1984), however patient variability means that features such as acute versus insidious onset and rapid versus slow progression, lack predictive power. In addition, more recent evidence indicates that the likelihood of previous depressive illness is also increased in DAT (Agbayewa, 1986). Thus, whilst previous history of affective disorder may be a risk factor for depressive pseudodementia, this may also be the case for DAT, particularly if secondary depression exists.

The claim that affective symptoms in depressive pseudodementia are pervasive is erroneous, as it is not unusual for these patients to lack the usual signs and symptoms of depression (Cavenar, Maltbie & Austin, 1979; Good, 1981). Similarly, 'don't know' responses have been found as often in dementia patients as in those with depression (Jorm, 1986; McAllister & Price, 1982; Young, Manley & Alexopoulos, 1985). Moreover, research suggests that depressive pseudodementia is characterised by a deficit in recollecting stored information rather than encoding new material (Cummings, 1986; desRosiers, 1992). In comparison, the memory impairment in DAT is due largely to an inability to encode a sufficient number of stimulus features or attributes (Martin et al., 1986).

Whilst Wells reports normal CT results in depressive demented patients, some

Table 1 Clinical Features of Depressive Dementia and Dementia

Clinical Feature	Depressive Dementia	Dementia
Clinical Course and History		
Family is aware of dysfunction and severity	Usually	Rarely
Onset can be date with some precision	Usually	Rarely
Duration of symptoms before medical help sought	Short	Long
Progression of symptoms	Rapid	Slow
Previous history of psychiatric illness	Usual	Unusual
Complaints and clinical behaviour		
Nature of complaints	Cognitive	General
Quality of complaints	Detailed	Vague
Level of disability	Emphasised	Concealed
Achievements (of trivial day to day activities)	Devalued	Valued
Effortfulness	Weak	Dogged
Coping strategies (e.g. diaries, notes etc)	Minimal	Extensive
Level of distress about symptoms	Strong	Unconcerned
Affective changes	Pervasive	Shallow
Deterioration in social skills	Early	Retained
Congruence of behaviour and cognitive deficit	Incongruent	Consistent
Nocturnal confusion	Uncommon	Common
Intellectual dysfunction		
Attention and concentration	Preserved	Faulty
Responses to questioning	Don't know	Near misses
Recent and remote memory impairment	Equal	Recent worse
Memory gaps for specific periods	Common	Unusual
Performance on tasks of similar difficulty	Variable	Consistent

Source: Adapted from Wells, C. (1979) Pseudodementia. *Am. J. Psychiat.*, **136**, 895–900.

evidence suggests that elderly depressed individuals actually possess values more similar to those of irreversible dementia than to that of normals (Pearlson et al., 1989). One of the difficulties with using the CT scan is its lack of diagnostic specificity. Post-mortem gross anatomical studies of the normal brain document decrements in cerebral weight and volume as age increases from 60 years (Creasey & Rapoport, 1985). *In vivo* CT studies also reveal increases in ventricular dilatation and sulcal volume with age (Pearlson et al., 1989). Studies have consistently found more atrophy in patients with dementia than in age-matched controls, however, the overlap between the two groups may be as high as 20% (McLean, 1987).

The clinical utility of the Dexamethasone Suppression Test (DST) in differentiating depressive pseudodementia from DAT has not been conclusively established. McAllister, Ferrell, Price & Neville (1982) found it useful, whilst Georgotas and his colleagues and Spar & Gerner (1982) did not.

The efficacy of sleep deprivation as a way of differentially diagnosing depressive pseudodementia from DAT has received attention in recent years (Leibenluft & Wehr, 1992; Southmayd, 1989; Wu & Bunney, 1990). Sleep deprivation works by targeting the disruptions in circadian rhythms which occurs in depression (short REM latency and distribution of REM to the first half of the night). Wu and Bunney (1990) report that 67% of those designated as having endogenous depression responded to sleep deprivation. However, the relief from the depression is usually only transient (Southmayd, 1989).

Due to the lack of specificity of laboratory techniques in the differential diagnosis of dementia, they are generally used as ancillary aids only. Neuropsychological tests are considered the most sensitive way of determining the existence of cognitive deficit and the nature of that deficit.

The most valuable studies concerning the question of differential diagnosis of depressive dementia and DAT are those that closely resemble the clinical situation encountered by the neuropsychologist. That is, those that test subjects early in the course of the disorder when the diagnosis is uncertain. Such a study was carried out by Jones et al. (1992), who assessed the extent to which neuropsychological probes were predictive of cognitive course in patients with depressive pseudodementia and DAT. They found that patients with DAT demonstrated impairment on tests of temporal orientation (the Temporal Orientation Questionnaire), visuoconstructional skills (the Block Design subtest of the WAIS-R) and visual memory (the Benton Visual Retention Test). The patients with depressive pseudodementia showed intact abilities on these tests. Jones et al. (1992) hypothesised that these findings could reflect the different structural and biochemical underpinning of the two conditions.

A number of other clinical rules of thumb have been generated over the years as guides to determining the difference between depressive dementia and the degenerative disorders. Granick (1971) has noted that the 'hold tests' (i.e. those tests which have been observed to be relatively immune to cerebral insult) of the WAIS, including Information, Similarities and Vocabulary, show no differences between depressed and demented subjects. Post (1975) notes that near miss answers are more typical of DAT, while 'don't know' answers are more common in depression. This notion of the effortfulness of responding on cognitive tests is one which can prove a useful guideline to determining the basis of the observed cognitive deficit. Depressed subjects, as observed above in the discussion of the cognitive basis of the depression, may feel that their responses make no difference anyway so why should they care.

Hart, Kwentus, Taylor and Harkins (1987) have noted that the digit symbol performance of Depressed and mild DATS indicated similar performance on psychomotor speed, but the DATS recalled few digit-symbol items. The notion of a specific pattern of memory deficits which differentiates between the two disorders has also be proposed by Massman et al. (1992).

The possibility of differentiating these disorders on the basis of the cortical (i.e. DAT) versus subcortical patterns of performance has proven most interesting. The cortical dementing patterns are associated with deficits in gnosis, praxis and language function, whilst the subcortical ones are characterised by slowing of information processing and a dysmnesia (i.e. deficits in effortful memory functions such as recall as opposed to priming or recognition), rather than an amnesia. Both Caine (1981) and Cummings and Benson (1983), as well as our own recent study (Crowe and Hoogenraad, in press), indicate that the elderly depressed show deficits similar to subcortical dementia but not cortical features (apraxia, agnosia or aphasia). This seems one of the best available means of making the distinction between these disorders so far presented.

Nonetheless, it is possible to differentiate depression and dementia in the elderly on other grounds, the most consistent of which are the presence or absence of depressive symptoms and/or a previous history of affective disorder (Kiloh, 1961; McAllister, 1983; Rabins et al., 1984). Although caution must be exercised in applying this approach as 60% of presenile demented subjects feature depression early in the course of the disorder and in one quarter of cases affective disorder was diagnosed prior to a final diagnosis of dementia (Liston, 1977).

How are the deficits produced?

Broadly speaking, there are two possible ways in which the cognitive deficit associated with depression could arise. The first proposes that impaired cognition is a secondary effect of the depressive state. According to this view, depressed people have the capability for normal performance on cognitive tasks but are not able to use it. Miller (1975), in his review of the psychological deficit in depression, distinguished three hypotheses which fall into this category:

1. The cognitive interference hypothesis according to which depressive thoughts and worries interfere with and disrupt performance.

2.   The reduced motivation hypothesis which suggests that depressed people
      are insufficiently motivated to perform normally.
3.   The learned helplessness hypothesis, which states that depressed people
      expect that their responses will make no difference and so they give up
      trying.

The alternative viewpoint is that the cognitive deficit is intrinsic to the depression and not just a secondary effect. That is, the depressed elderly have a real
defect of cognitive function which is fundamental to their depression, rather
than an inability to use intact capacities. For example, Savard, Rey and Post
(1980) have suggested that depression may involve deficiencies in biogenic amines
which have influences on cognitive function. The neurotransmitter systems
involved could then share partially overlapping neural pathways with those related
to deficiencies of normal ageing and thus produce more severe cognitive
impairments in the elderly.

The corticotropin-releasing hormone and the locus-ceruleus-norepinephrine
systems, as well as the dorsal raphe and its neurotransmitter serotonin, are the
principal biologic effectors of the generalised stress response, first described by
Hans Selye more than 60 years ago (Selye, 1936). These pathways are set in
motion when the organism's homeostasis is threatened, to facilitate adaptive behavioural and neural response to the perceived 'threat'. The so-called fight/flight
response (see Chapter 4) sets in chain effectors within the CNS which promote
attention, arousal and aggression, while inhibiting non-adaptive ones which promote such vegetative functions as feeding, sexual behaviour and reproductive
behaviours. In the periphery, blood flow is directed towards the CNS to mobilise
for immediate action (Gold et al., 1988).

What, then, is it possible for us to conclude regarding the implications of
these disorders for neuropsychological functioning? The deficits associated with
depressive mentation seem to be mediated by diminution of activation of cortical
arousal systems which are themselves mediated by the noradrenergic and the
serotonergic system. As a consequence, the ability of the subject to motivate
himself/herself, to demonstrate drive and vigour and to 'get on with the job'
seems impaired. This manifests itself in the problems with effortful processing
noted with memory, attentional and other tasks of higher level adaptive behaviour.

The effect of the manic phase of the bipolar disorders is fascinating but our
interpretation here must be slightly more speculative. There seems good evidence
for the fact that mania is associated with heightened glucose metabolism in the
frontal regions as reflected by the PET studies. There may also be static lesions in

these disorders, again in the anterior regions. The over activation of the frontal regions results in two effects: (1) the generation of more behaviour, and (2) alteration in the tone and intensity of that behaviour. This seems to be consistent with the usually observed deficits of executive functioning associated with the diminished control of behavioural response. The behaviour is characterised by disinhibition and increased flow of responses with an associated decrease in rule governance. These subjects generate more behaviour, and the usual checks and balances which ensure that this is socially, morally and legally appropriate seem to be swept aside in the rush. The affective disorders are characterised by their interference with the absolute level of behaviour. The depressed subject is inert, immobile and poorly able to absorb his/her environment, the patient featuring mania is hyperactive, overstimulated and unable to screen himself/herself from the teeming array of his/her environment.

* * *

It seems worthwhile now to examine a man who features a marked depressive syndrome to allow an examination of the facets of the cognitive, emotional and personality related changes which are the effects of this disorder.

CASE REPORT

MP, a 68-year-old retired naval commander, first become psychiatrically ill some two-and-a-half years before I had seen him. At the time of his first problems he had become so depressed and controlling, that he had persuaded his wife to participate in a suicide pact with him. Fortunately, this attempt failed and he was admitted to a psychiatric hospital with a diagnosis of agitated depression with associated delusions of poverty. He was initially treated with a course of 16 ECT which relieved the depression, however the delusion of poverty remained.

Background

Prior to his retirement, MP was as an engineer and was in command of a large number of personnel. Premorbidly, he was described as domineering, obsessional, perfectionistic, self-critical, punctilious and emotionally withholding. It was said that he controlled his household in the same way that he had controlled his naval subordinates.

Upon retirement MP undertook a number of retirement investments, as well as engaging in a major renovation of the family home. The arrangements for some of these activities seem to have lacked his usual obsessional care; contractual arrangements, some even for many thousands of dollars, appear to have been scant, if existent at all.

By the end of his first year of retirement things seem to have gone awry. The renovations had run hugely over budget and the quality of the workmanship seems to have been poor. By the end of his eighteenth month of retirement, MP was in debt and very critical of his mistakes and could no longer cope with organising his financial dealings.

Following his admission to the psychiatric hospital his previously dominated wife had taken control of the finances and was luxuriating in the opportunity. Her first sale was that of his much prized prestige motor vehicle. She was attending regular personal growth seminars and was no longer prepared to accept his control over her activities.

Extensive medical investigation at that stage, including full physical and biochemical examinations and CT of the head, indicated no abnormality.

At the time of my assessment MP sat in the same chair in the hospital ward as he had sat in every day since his admission. He was uncommunicative and showed little interest in anything. He was poorly maintained and his finger nails were dirty and he had clearly not washed or selected clean clothes for many days. It was difficult to establish eye contact with him and his responses to questions were no more than one to two words. His affect was restricted, and he did not so much describe feeling depressed as feeling nothing at all. He admitted to no suicidal ideation and he denied nihilistic, guilty or other delusions.

Formal Assessment

His performance on the Minnesota Multi-phasic Personality Inventory (MMPI) indicated that his LFK profile displayed a pattern suggestive of an individual trying to present himself in the best possible light. He denied common foibles and tended to see the world in terms of extremes of good and evil. The clinical scales revealed marked elevations (>80T) on the depression (105T), hypochondriasis, and the hysteria scales. The performance on the MMPI was interpreted as a 2-1 profile. This was consistent with the notion that MP was experiencing self-deprecatory thoughts associated with feelings of withdrawal, guilt and hopelessness. On the Beck Depression Inventory he proved to have a score of 27 which indicates moderate to severe depression.

On neurobehavioural testing MP proved well oriented to time, place and person and he performed the serial addition of sevens without problems. His conversational level of knowledge regarding current affairs was good. He demonstrated no evidence of deficit in gnosis, praxis or language function and he could read, write, name, draw and copy in an exemplary manner.

Formal testing included the WAIS-R, WMS-R, and the Austin Maze Test. The performance on the Adult Wechsler Intelligence Scale Revised indicated that MP had a Verbal Intelligence Quotient of 117, a Performance Intelligence Quotient of 105 and a Full Scale IQ of 113. This indicates that his overall pattern of performance on the skills assessed by the WAIS-R were largely intact. He did feature somewhat attenuated performance on tests of high level attention functions in the form of the Arithmetic and Digit Symbol Substitution tasks.

Tests of memory functions using the WMS-R revealed that MP had a Verbal Memory Index of 68, a Visual Memory Index of 88, a General Memory Index of 73 and a Delayed Recall Index of 55. Clearly MP had great difficulty with all forms of new learning and recall and he demonstrated a moderately severe level of amnesia. It is interesting to note that his level of attention and concentration

VERBAL TESTS (Age Scaled Scores)

Information	16
Digit Span	12
Vocabulary	12
Arithmetic	9
Comprehension	13
Similarities	13
VIQ	117

PERFORMANCE TESTS

Picture Completion	13
Picture Arrangement	10
Block Design	11
Object Assembly	10
Digit Symbol	9
PIQ	105
FSIQ	113

WECHSLER MEMORY SCALE-REVISED

Verbal Memory Index	68
Visual Memory Index	88
General Memory Index	73
Attention/Concentration	117
Delayed Recall	55

AUSTIN MAZE TEST

Trial	1	2	3	4	5	6	7	8	9	10
Number of Errors	19	19	7	5	8	7	7	5	4	4

Trial	11	12	13	14	15	16	17	18	19	20
Number of Errors	3	3	3	1	2	1	2	2	2	2

Trial	21	22
Number of Errors	0	0

as assessed by the Attention and Concentration Index was appropriate to his level of intelligence. This indicates that this index does not really assess the ability to perform tasks of sustained attention or attentional shift, skills that seem to be particularly affected in these subjects.

On tests of the frontal executive functions MP had a great deal of difficulty learning the Austin maze and finally achieved the criterion after 20 attempts. This is a relatively poor performance but does illustrate that the skills requisite to learn the maze are not impaired, *but* the ability to use them in a flexible and timely way is.

Conclusion

The pattern of performance that MP presented on the assessment were consistent with a man of high average pre-morbid intelligence who, at that point in time, was showing attenuation of performance on tasks associated with memory and new learning and also in tasks which assess higher level attention. MP did not feature an intercurrent degenerative process such as Alzheimer's disease because his skills in language, naming, drawing and calculation on paper remained unimpaired.

This indicates one of the interesting aspects of the presentation of these individuals in so far as that his ability to reason arithmetically is extremely poor when he is asked to figure the problems out in his head, yet he could solve considerably more difficult tasks in arithmetic if he was allowed to work at them with a pen and paper. The problems with motivation and application adverted to in the discussion of how the affective disorders produce their effects on cognition are important here. It is clear that there are many cognitive operations that MP can still perform, however his ability to use these skills due to his disinterest, preoccupation or stubborn pride would not allow him to perform in the way he has previously been capable of. It is this inability to be able to use these intact skills that colours the cognitive performances of individuals with the affective disorders.

An interesting side note on the case of MP is why a man of such intelligence and skill could allow himself to fall into the financial and emotional mire that he finally found himself. Clearly the transition from having one's identity created by one's position, as enshrined in the military establishment, in association with the years of neglect in his relationship with his wife left him with virtually no external anchors to reality. Cast adrift by a minor upset or delay, the problems eventually added together until like a desperate gambler he placed all of his stake money on the possibility of the grand parting display, in the form of the suicide pact. Even this went awry.

SUMMARY

The affective disorders can be characterised by their interference with the emotional tone of the processing of information. From a neuropsychological perspective, depression results in a massive disruption of orderly information processing, which is characterised by relatively poor performance on tests of memory and higher level problem solving. These deficits are more by way of a loss of effortful processing rather than any intrinsic problems with the information processing *per se*. In the bipolar affective disorder there appears to be relatively good evidence that there are increases in the activation of the frontal areas during the phases of manic excitement. It seems reasonable to assume that associated with this is the overexpansive cognitive and emotional outlook characteristic of mania. It would appear that during the depressed phase a similar pattern of neuropsychological responding, as observed with unipolar depression, is noted.

CHAPTER 4

ANXIETY DISORDERS

Fear is one of our basic emotions and has clearly been a crucial mechanism for our survival, both as individuals and as a species. Taken to excess however, undue concerns about particular objects or situations and an overanticipation of the future become pathological, and are reflected in the various clinical states which will be surveyed in this chapter.

In nature, the response of an organism to a perceived stressor can be broken down into a number of steps which have become recognised as the fight/flight response. These steps consist of: (1) the initial recognition of the nature of the present situation; (2) an appraisal of this situation as threatening; (3) the development of a state of arousal proportional to the nature of the perceived threat; (4) preparation for reaction to the threat by way of activation of the muscles and increased alertness; (5) response to the threat either by avoiding it, confronting it or by psychological controlling either of these responses (i.e fight, flight or freeze); and finally (6) the resolution of the conflict, the dissipation of the arousal and return to the baseline state.

Anxiety is the normal reaction of an organism to a stressor which can either be external (e.g. a bully kicking sand into your face) or internal (e.g. the thought of Christmas with your family). The anxiety reaction has two components, one physiological and the other psychological. The gamut of these responses, both physiological and psychological, are largely mediated by the adrenergic neurotransmitter system. The changes associated with activation of adrenaline and noradrenaline in the acute stress response include increased heart rate, dry mouth, piloerection (hair standing on end), sweating or clammy palms, paraesthesia (sensory loss or numbness usually of the hands and feet), nausea and headache, increase in urinary frequency, and hypersensitivity to sensory stimuli.

A number of the physiological responses associated with the arousal response are similar to those resulting from an injection of adrenaline. From a physiological standpoint, our ability to distinguish one emotional state from another is quite poor. Each emotional state results in an undifferentiated acute stress response. Thus to the body, love is equivalent to fear. How then do we differentiate these states from each other?

This question gave rise to an interesting experiment undertaken by Schacter and Singer in 1962. These researchers argued that an injection of the drug adrenaline causes the physiological changes observed in strong emotional states. They further maintained that emotion is not determined by physiological factors alone, but also by cognitive factors. They suggested that a person identifies, interprets and labels his/her emotional state by analysing his/her immediate situation for the cause. The experiment that they undertook to illustrate this point involved injecting normal subjects with adrenaline. The subjects were either informed, not informed or were misinformed about the physiological effects that the drug would produce. The subjects were then placed in a room with an angry or a euphoric stooge. The results that they obtained revealed that a person in a physiologically aroused state for which he/she had a satisfactory explanation would not be likely to turn elsewhere for an interpretation of his/her feelings. However, if the subject found himself/herself in a state of physiological arousal for which no explanation could be located, he/she would label this state according to the cognitions that he/she had available. Thus, the subject housed with the euphoric stooge tended to share the euphoria while the subjects housed with the angry stooge reflected anger.

This study, although fascinating, has been criticised on the basis of a number of methodological flaws (Lader, 1982). Indeed in one attempt to replicate the study which tried to overcome the methodological problems, the experimenters found no support for the conclusions regarding the labelling of the unexpected emotional state (Marshall & Zimbardo, 1979). Nonetheless, it does seem that there is some overlap in these findings that is consistent with the idea that we tend to label unexplained arousal in terms of negative rather than positive emotional states (Marshall & Zimbardo, 1979). This observation may throw some light on the nature of anxiety, as rarely is the heightened state of arousal characteristic of the anxiety conditions labelled as a positive emotional state or an exhilarating experience by the sufferer.

NOSOLOGY

Anxiety consists of apprehension, tension and undue concerns about a perceived danger. It is usually accompanied by signs associated with the activation of the sympathetic nervous system, and is described as free-floating anxiety when there is no conscious recognition of the specific threat. Anxiety is regarded as the chief characteristic of all of the neurotic disorders, and can be differentiated from normal or adaptive fear in that: (1) it is not related to a perceived realistic threat or at least is out of keeping in degree with the level of threat that such an object or event actually would pose, (2) it results from some form of intrapsychic conflict, and (3) it is not relieved by the amelioration of the objective situation.

Spielberger et al. (1977) has divided anxiety into two distinct forms: trait anxiety and state anxiety. State anxiety is that level of anxiety that all individuals experience from time to time in response to a real or perceived threat. This anxiety is responsive to the presence of the perceived environmental cue which elicits the anxious state and varies as a function of time. State anxiety, on the other hand, is a dispositional pattern of responding to a variety of evoking stimuli which are typically associated with the anxiety disorders.

DSM-IV (American Psychiatric Association, 1994) divides the anxiety disorders into a series of subdisorders including panic attacks, agoraphobia, panic disorder with and without agoraphobia, the specific phobias, social phobia, obsessive–compulsive disorder, post-traumatic stress disorder, generalised anxiety disorder, anxiety disorder due to a general medical condition, substance-induced anxiety disorder and anxiety disorders not otherwise specified. (Consult DSM-IV for full details of the diagnostic criteria for each of the anxiety conditions.)

Each of the disorders is characterised by a pattern of anxiety inappropriate to the environmental cues elicited by the stimuli in normal individuals. Within the context of this discussion only the disorders of generalised anxiety disorder, panic disorder, phobia, post-traumatic stress disorder and obsessive–compulsive disorder will be considered in detail. This decision stems from the fact that these represent the only anxiety conditions that have been studied in any detail from a neuropsychological perspective. Nonetheless, there is a consistency in the nature of the physiological and behavioural manifestations of these disorders which gives them a predicability in effect at a behavioural and neuropsychological level.

Generalised anxiety disorder is characterised by excessive anxiety and worry occurring on more days than not for a period of at least six months. The person finds it difficult to control this worry and is distressed by it, and as a consequence is compromised in daily functioning. Panic disorder is characterised by the presence of recurrent, unexpected panic attacks followed by at least one month of persistent concern about having an attack. Phobias are characterised by a persistent fear of a clearly discernible circumscribed object or situation. Post-traumatic stress disorder is characterised by the development of characteristic anxiety symptoms following exposure to an extreme traumatic stressor. Obsessive–compulsive disorder is characterised by the presence of recurrent obsession or compulsions. Obsession are persistent ideas, thoughts or experiences that are experienced as intrusive and inappropriate, while compulsions are repetitive thoughts (for example praying, counting, repeating words silently) or behaviours (such as hand washing, checking, ordering or adjusting things), the goal of which is to reduce anxiety or distress as a result of their completion (American Psychiatric Association, 1994).

THE BIOLOGICAL ORIGINS OF ANXIETY

The mechanisms which result in the activation associated with the acute stress response appear to be largely mediated by noradrenaline. Acute stress results in an increased release of adrenocorticotrophic hormone (ACTH) from the anterior pituitary. This response occurs as a consequence of the release of corticotrophin releasing factor (CRF) from the hypothalamus. ACTH is then carried by the blood to the adrenal cortex where it stimulates the synthesis and secretion of glucocorticoids. The response is a biphasic one, beginning with the discharge of hormone followed by inhibition of release. The changes in the hormone levels are mediated by the activity of NA.

Whilst the implication of the last few statements may appear to indicate that the hypothalamic/pituitary/adrenal axis is the only system involved in the stress response, this is clearly not the case as the peripheral effects of these agents are crucial in their ultimate behavioural implication.

The secretion of a number of other hormones also occurs during stress, including increases in vasopressin, prolactin, and reductions in oestrogen and testosterone.

The association between stress (or arousal as it is sometimes called in the literature) and performance has been described by the Yerkes Dodson Law (1908). The law states that up to a certain level, performance improves with increasing levels of arousal to an optimal level. However, if the peak level is exceeded arousal interferes with the performance of a particular task. This observation still has explanatory power in our discussion of anxiety as many of the conditions we will survey feature levels of arousal which would be considered to be beyond the peak level.

Up to this point we have been discussing the notion of acute stress as a relatively rapid response much in the manner of the fight/flight response described above. The notion of a chronic stress condition is more in keeping with the sorts of conditions we are discussing in this chapter.

The concept of more chronic stress has largely developed from the work of Hans Selye, a Canadian medical practitioner (1976). As a young medical practitioner Selye noted that if foreign or toxic material was injected into rats their response resulted in a consistent set of changes which he labelled the general adaptation response (GAR). In the rat the introduction of the toxin resulted in enlargement of the adrenal cortex and discharge of the secretory granules, changes to the thymus, spleen and lymphatic structures, and deep bleeding ulcers of the stomach and duodenum. He maintained that the GAR took place in three stages, an initial alarm response, a stage of resistance and finally exhaustion.

As with the other psychiatric conditions considered so far, the serendipitous finding that a particular drug or group of drugs (i.e. drug X) is capable of inducing or reducing symptomatology in a given condition inevitably results in the drug X theory of anxiety. This has happened a number of times already in the history of these conditions.

The observation that the benzodiazepines (firstly chlordiazepoxide (Librium) in the early 1960s and later diazepam (Valium)) were capable of controlling anxiety states led to considerable speculation regarding the mechanism of these agents in producing their effects. The demonstration of the specific receptors for the benzodiazepines in the brain and spinal cord, and the close relationship of these with the inhibitory neurotransmitter gamma amino-butyric acid (GABA), has resulted in numerous studies. Many neurotransmitters appear to play a role in the development of the anxiety disorders, but noradrenaline and serotonin seem to be the ones which are most consistently implicated.

THE PSYCHOLOGICAL ORIGINS OF ANXIETY

Historically the explanation for anxiety has centred on learning theories. Mowrer's (1960) two-stage theory of avoidance learning proposes that a neutral thought, image or object (e.g. patting a dog) becomes associated with a fearful response due to classical conditioning (i.e. being informed that dogs bite). The second stage of symptom development occurs when the subject develops avoidance behaviours (e.g. crossing the road when he sees a dog) in order to reduce the anxiety experienced when confronting the conditioned stimulus. Thus the avoidance is reinforced and as a result increases in frequency.

NEUROPATHOLOGY

To date, little pathological study of the brains of anxiety sufferers has been reported. One exception to this rule is the observation of Bremner et al. (1995) who have reported an 8% decrease in the hippocampal volume on the right side in a group of combat veterans diagnosed with PTSD. This is somewhat surprising and clearly indicates that further investigation is warranted. From a neurochemical perspective the altered neurotransmitter balances would be the most interesting focus of study, but the possibility that the chronic activation of a particular neurotransmitter network resulting in alteration to the cortex would be a fascinating possibility if our techniques were sufficiently concise to be able to identify such changes.

STRUCTURAL AND FUNCTIONAL IMAGING DATA

The number of studies conducted with the anxiety states is low. However, of those undertaken the results are interesting. Bremner et al. (1997) have noted decrease in glucose metabolism in the prefrontal, temporal, parietal, and orbito-frontal cortices of a series of patients with a diagnosis of PTSD. In a study using PET, Baxter and his colleagues (1987) noted that patients with OCD demon-strated increased activity in the orbital gyri and the caudate nucleus. They interpreted these findings as support for the notion that the overactivation in these areas, which have direct links to the striatal and limbic areas, may explain why patients with OCD have difficulty in shifting the focus of their attention away from the obsession or compulsion.

In contrast, Machlin and colleagues using SPECT imaging (1991) noted el-evated perfusion rates in the medial frontal area but not in the orbital frontal cortex. Interestingly they also noted that in their control subjects who were highly anxious, the higher their level of anxiety the lower their medial frontal perfusion ratio.

In patients with an anxiety neurosis, Johanson and colleagues noted that if they were subjected to an anxiety provoking situation there was an elevation of cerebral blood flow in the frontotemporal areas (1986). Interestingly, this proved to be more so on the left orbital region in those subjects who reported feeling anxious. The authors considered that this effect occurred because the anxiety was verbally induced.

In a similar study, Gottschalk et al. (1992) noted that if they induced normal subjects to think about anxious and hostile situations that they had been in-volved in, significant correlations between medial, lateral and subcortical grey matter and white matter were noted, with the energy consumption strongly in-fluenced by the quality and quantity of the mentation.

Whilst the data is by no means comprehensive, it does seem that anxious thoughts do result in heightened levels of activation in the anterior frontal and temporal regions, and do so in a relatively specific way. The heightened levels of metabolism reflected in the PET activation studies seem to indicate that a generalised increase in anterior activation is the most reliable finding to date, and, as far as it is possible to ascertain, this does not appear to be a sided effect.

NEUROPSYCHOLOGICAL FEATURES

While almost every practicing neuropsychologist would immediately affirm that anxiety plays a crucial role in the neuropsychological assessment (e.g. Lezak, 1995), as well as in the everyday behaviour of individuals suffering from anxiety disorder, the lack of literature on the effects of anxiety on the performance of normal subjects, much less those with the anxiety states, continues to be astounding. Lezak (1995) has noted that high anxiety levels tend to result in mental inefficiency problems such as slow, scrambled or blocked thoughts and naming and memory failures. Much of the literature in the area of the neuropsychological effects of anxiety has been directed at the question of what the nature of the brain processes involved in anxiety conditions might be, rather than what is the effect of anxiety on the performance of a particular test or class of tests. We will now survey the available data on these conditions, assessing the effects of the pathological anxiety states, as well as the effects of anxiety induction in normal subjects, on each of the designated domains of cognitive processes.

Attention and mental tracking

Perhaps the most often employed, and to this day probably the least understood test of cognitive function used in the area of anxiety, is the digit span task. Lezak (1995) maintains that the forward digit span task is prone to the effects of anxiety, and as this effect dissipates across the assessment process, she suggests that if the task is failed or poorly performed early in the assessment, it may well be worthwhile to go back and attempt the task again later on, with a view to approaching the subject when he/she is more comfortable with his/her situation and surroundings. In examining the issue of whether performance on the digit span task is affected by trait or state anxiety, Spielberger and Hodges (1969) noted that digit span performance in male normals is diminished as a result of increase in state anxiety and is independent of the level of trait anxiety.

Other studies however, have questioned the reliability of the digit span task as a measure of the situational stress effect (Chavez et al., 1983). Markham and

Darke (1991), in a study comparing the performance of low versus high state anxious university students in an anxiety provoking experimental condition, found no anxiety-related effects on either digit or block (Corsi Blocks) span performance.

On other tasks of attention and working memory function in normal subjects, a variety of effects have been observed. Martin and Franzen (1989) randomly assigned university students to a stressful or a neutral situation, and found that anxiety produced a greater decrement in both the word and the colour-word conditions of the Stroop Test in male as compared to female subjects. Chavez and colleagues (1983) noted that the level of test anxiety had no effect on performance on the Trail Making Test for low versus high anxious subjects. They did, however, report a significant correlation between decrements in performance on Trail A in high trait anxious/high test anxious male but not female subjects. In the same study they did not note any effect of test anxiety on performance on the Digit Symbol Substitution Test of the WAIS.

The effects of pathological anxiety on tests of attention and working memory prove very interesting. To date much of this work has focused on the relatively recently described anxiety disorder of post-traumatic stress disorder. Dalton, Pedersen and Ryan (1989) noted a slight decrement in digit span performance in comparison to the published norms for one hundred Vietnam veterans diagnosed as showing PTSD. However, Uddo et al. (1993) noted no difference between 16 Vietnam veterans with PTSD and matched controls on digit span, but did note such a difference for the visual span task on the WMS-R. Sutker and colleagues (Sutker, Allain & Johnson, 1993; Sutker, Vasterling, Brailey & Allain, 1995), in a number of studies with veterans featuring PTSD, noted deficits with attention, mental tracking and executive functions in these subjects.

Dalton and his colleagues, in the study mentioned above, also noted an impairment on the Digit Symbol Substitution Test, the Stroop Test, as well as on Part B of the Trail Making Test, when compared to the published norms. This does present some problems with interpretation as no control group was used for comparison purposes, hence the results must be viewed with some trepidation. Gass and Daniel (1990) compared the performance of a number of Vietnam veterans on the TMT whilst correlating their performance with emotional factors (i.e. performance on the Psychasthenia and Depression scales of the MMPI) and concluded that Trails (B) was unaffected by anxiety or depression.

The performance of subjects with obsessive–compulsive disorder (OCD) represents an equally contradictory set of results. Flor-Henry (Flor-Henry, Yeudall, Koles & Howarth, 1979) noted that OCD subjects performed more poorly than age and education matched control subjects on the digit span and digit symbol substitution tests of the WAIS. The matching of the subjects, however, reflected a 10 point mean discrepancy between the treatment and control subjects. Zielinski, Taylor and Juzwin (1991) compared 21 subjects with OCD with a matched control group and found no difference on the Continuous Performance Test, concluding that attention is relatively unimpaired in anxiety disorder.

A number of studies have concentrated on the issue of whether anxiety results in a cognitive bias in attention towards threatening stimuli. Tucker and Derryberry (1992) noted that the tendency for high levels of anxiety to increase ventral limbic and orbital frontal activation may signal the heightened activation of the processes of vigilant attention and motor readiness. Both Mogg et al. (1990) and Mineka and Sutton (1992) noted that anxiety seems to be associated with an attentional bias for threatening material, a finding supported by Dalgleish and Watts (1990) in their earlier review of this topic.

What can we conclude from all of this? There seems at least some evidence on the basis of the available literature which suggests a specific deficit in attentional functions in normal subjects who are placed in conditions of acute stress, and this seems to be particularly the case for threatening stimuli. The pathological anxiety states seem to be consistently, although not unequivocally, characterised by attentional deficits, and these seem to be as a consequence of the disruption of functions by heightened levels of anxiety, that is disrupting cognitive functions by the informational overload.

Gnosis and praxis

Relatively little study of the function of the secondary association cortices has been undertaken with the anxious subject. Hence at this stage, for want of evidence to the contrary, it seems that these functions are left largely intact as a consequence of these conditions.

Language and spatial cognition

Little data is available on the nature of language specific deficits in anxiety disorders. However, there has been a deal of inquiry into the nature of visuospatial function in these individuals, particularly in subjects suffering from OCD.

In normal subjects, King, Hannay, Masek and Burns (1978) found that the completion time on the Minnesota Paper Form Board Test (MPFBT) increased significantly in response to higher levels of trait anxiety in females but not in males. Markham and Darke (1991) found that there was no effect for anxiety in studies manipulating the effects of trait and state anxiety using the MPBFT.

Zielinski and his colleagues (1991) noted visuospatial processing deficits in OCD sufferers on the Recurring Figures Test as well as the Corsi Block span. Behar et al. (1984) noted significant differences between their OCD group as compared to controls on the Money Road Map Test and on the Stylus Maze Learning Test. (The Road Map test measures directional orienting ability and the stylus maze measures trial and error learning and visuospatial memory.)

One confounding effect of the measurement of visuospatial functioning, particularly in subjects suffering from OCD, is the contribution of psychomotor speed to performance on these tasks. Checking and ritualisation inevitably must impinge on the performance of a timed task and purer measures of these skills would be useful for the further elucidation of this area.

Learning and memory

For such a crucial aspect of human cognition it remains a mystery why such little work has taken place in examining the neuropsychological consequences of anxiety disorders. In a study of 74 normal subjects aged over 60 years, Hill and Vanderwort (1992) noted that a subgroup of the subjects who featured higher levels of anxiety performed worse than a low anxious group on a task of delayed recall. Martin and Franzen (1989) randomly assigned university students to a stressful or a neutral situation and tested them on a number of measures, including those previously described as well as the Randt Memory Battery, and found no effect of anxiety in either condition.

A number of the studies surveyed so far have included memory testing in their protocols and it seems worthwhile to examine these results. In the previously described study by Dalton and colleagues (1989), they noted that the 100 PTSD sufferers performed in a similar manner to the published norms on both the Rey Auditory Verbal Learning Test and on the Serial Digit Learning Test. Again, in contrast to these findings, Uddo et al. (1993) noted that their 16 PTSD veterans performed worse than matched controls on the RAVLT; in particular the subjects recalled less across trials, recalled more on list B than they did on the first trial with List A, showed more pro-active interference and more perseverative errors. Sutker et al. (1992) note that both POW survivors and combat veterans displayed evidence of deficits on the WMS-R and the RAVLT, a similar finding to the work of Bremmer et al. (1993) who noted that their PTSD group displayed significant impairments on both immediate and delayed recall of a story. However, in a subsequent investigation Sutker et al. (1995) note that PTSD was associated with impairments in mental tracking, attention and executive functions, but not with disruption of leaning and memory functions to the same degree.

A more consistent pattern of results has emerged with OCD subjects, which seems to indicate a visuospatial memory deficit in these subjects. Zielinski et al. (1991) in their study of 21 patients with OCD, noted that they did not feature deficits on the California Verbal Learning Test when compared to controls, suggesting no deficit with verbal learning and memory. However, both Zielinski et al. (1991) and Boone et al. (1991) noted poorer performance by OCD subjects on tests of visuospatial memory as compared to Verbal IQ matched controls. The subjects did not differ on tests of attention, memory or executive functioning tasks including the Wisconsin Card Sorting Test (WCST).

Further support for the notion of memory deficits in OCD sufferers is found in the interesting study by Sher et al. (1989) who noted that their non-clinical sample of subjects who featured high levels of checking behaviour, had deficits in memory for recently completed actions. Visual memory is frequently used in the checking and reviewing of personal acts (Reed, 1977), and deficits in visual memory, and by implication, an inability to be able to recall the outcome of a previous investigation regarding an obsessive concern or the adequacy of a compulsive act, may well drive the subject to repeat these actions (Otto, 1992). It is interesting in this regard that subjects with OCD who are prone to checking (i.e. door locks, windows, iron, stove) find that carrying out their compulsion leads to less anxiety reduction than does washing for those with an obsession with contamination (Davidson & Neale, 1996).

Working Memory

MacLeod and Donnellan (1993) have noted that high trait anxious subjects were impaired on a grammatical reasoning task used as a measure of working memory capacity. Sorg and Wittney (1992) studied 30 high and low trait anxious subjects on a test of word and reading span, and found that the poorest recall on both tests was by low-anxious subjects in the non-stress condition and by high anxious subjects in the high stress condition. The authors claim their finding supports the conclusion that high trait anxious subjects have reduced working memory capacity when they are subjected to additional stress. Such a possibility is attractive in the context of the notion of the Yerkes Dodson Law, where unduly low arousal (i.e. low trait, low state anxiety) results in a poorly activated learning state, while unduly high arousal (i.e. high trait and high state anxiety) results in an equally poor performance, due to the heightened arousal impairing responsivity.

A number of studies with normal subjects looking at the issue of whether worry impinges on working memory functions have been conducted. Rapee (1993) has noted that in normal subjects induced to worry about a topic of importance to them, that the generation of random letters interfered signifi-cantly with the ability to worry. He consequently concluded that the process of worry primarily uses the phonological loop but not other aspects of working memory. A similar finding has also been reported by MacLeod and Donellan (1993) who note that high anxious subjects were more impaired in their functioning on a memory task when they were required to maintain a high simultaneous memory load whilst performing the task.

EXECUTIVE FUNCTIONS

In the context of impaired performance on tests of attention, concentration, working memory and memory functions generally it is quite difficult to make a case for a separate deficit in the area of executive functions. Due to the high probability of conflation of each of these deficits with each other in this context, deficits in each of these areas are referred to their more basic constituent. An interesting case study of the effects of PTSD on identical twin brothers was pre-sented by Sutker et al. (1993). One brother was a veteran with PTSD following incarceration as a POW while the other was not. The two brothers were assessed with the WAIS-R, WMS-R, RAVLT, Porteus mazes, Wisconsin Card Sorting Test, the Category Tests and the Trail Making Test. The veteran performed more inconsistently than his brother with particular deficits in the area of arithmetic calculation, visual memory (WMS-R Visual Reproduction) planning (on the Porteus Mazes) and in complex concept formation (on the WCST). They specu-lated that this represented acquired cerebral dysfunction particularly affecting the frontal lobe.

HEMISPHERIC CONTRIBUTIONS TO ANXIETY STATES

The notion of a hemispheric specialisation for a particular psychiatric state or condition really began the search for the neuropsychological insights into these disorders. For this we owe a great debt of gratitude to Flor-Henry for his numer-ous investigations into the hemispheric lateralisation of a number of the psychiatric disorders.

Anxiety has not missed out on this treatment and a number of investigations into the lateralisation of deficits in anxiety have been undertaken. In 24 high trait anxious and 36 low trait anxious subjects, Tyler and Tuck (1982) noted that if they were subjected to a right as opposed to a left hemisphere mediated task under conditions of stress-inducing white noise, the right hemisphere mediated task was affected by both state and trait anxiety. This effect was not observed with the digit span task. The authors concluded that nonverbal tests which tap into right hemisphere functions are particularly sensitive to the effects of anxiety, while tasks which are processed by the left hemisphere are not. In studies of eye movement data, Tucker and his colleagues (Tucker et al., 1978; Tucker et al., 1977; Tucker & Williamson, 1984) have noted that increased levels of stress result in an increased probability of right hemisphere activation and a proportional decrease in performance. Otto et al. (1994) have noted a similar finding in patients with panic disorder. These authors noted that memory biases for threat stimuli were associated with patients who had a greater right ear (left hemisphere) advantage, whereas patients with lower right ear advantage scores avoided the material.

A complementary finding has been observed by Heller, Etienne and Miller (1995) who studied depressed and anxious students using a chimeric faces test. These tests present a particular image to only one hemisphere whilst presenting an opposite or complementary stimulus to the opposite hemisphere. The investigators noted that anxious students demonstrated a significantly greater attentional bias to the left rather than the right, whilst the depressed students had the opposite effect. The authors concluded that state anxiety is characterised by higher levels of right temporoparietal activity resulting in the observed bias.

HOW ANXIETY DISORDERS PRODUCE THEIR COGNITIVE DEFICITS

Whilst the literature concerning the effects of the anxiety related conditions on neuropsychological functioning could not in any way be considered to be either elegant or comprehensive, it is possible for us to say some things regarding the effects of these conditions on neuropsychological and cognitive functions. Under conditions of high anxiety it appears that the tasks which are most susceptible to the disruption caused by these conditions are measures of attention and concentration, more than tests of spatial, language or memory related phenomena. This observation is supported by studies which have implicated heightened activation in the frontal lobe in states of pathological anxiety as well as in normal subjects subjected to heightened levels of anxiety. This is further supported by the research which indicates that during anxiety states, attentional functions are directed towards the focus on threatening stimuli. These issues are clearly illustrated in the case of DT in his dealings with what he perceives to be an increasingly threatening world.

CASE REPORT

DT was referred to me by his solicitor due to problems associated with his inability to return to his work as a schoolteacher due to his heightened levels of anxiety. At that time, DT's complaints included a poor ability to cope with everyday situations, situations in which he felt sure he could have coped with before the emergence of his problems. He became upset if he forgot something, and his wife had to continually check that he had attended to things that previously he would have been quite capable of attending to. DT became anxious very easily over minor things and during these phases lost control of himself. He had become increasingly impatient with everyone and everything in contrast to descriptions of his premorbid personality as a composed sort of chap.

Background

DT had always been a perfectionist and now found himself unable to complete almost any purposive action. He tired very easily and found himself in an almost constant state of exhaustion. Though still capable of reading, according to his admission, he found he read the same book repeatedly and had not attempted to read any new books.

DT complained of a visual problem, particularly with close visual work or when he was agitated. This included an inability to focus on particular items, and on a number of occasions during the testing I had to stop and allow him respite. He also featured numbness and pain over his eye. Subsequent investigation indicated that the visual problems were organic in origin and related to his heightened stress response. DT also proved to be very distractible and had a moderately severe memory deficit according to his own report. He found himself frustrated and lost when he attempted almost anything, for example shopping for groceries in the supermarket.

DT was prone to panic in almost every situation in which he found himself, often waking in panic through the night. Both he and his wife could not plan anything ahead because of the fact that he might find himself unable to manage the constraints of the forthcoming situation. His standard response during these episodes was to put his wife off, saying 'I can't talk about it now, I can't do it now'.

DT's mother and father both died of cancer and he has never been a drinker or a smoker. He has blood pressure problems and atrial fibrillation as stated by other medical opinions. He slept about seven hours per night and had a tendency to nap through the day. I asked DT about his present state of mind and he admitted being depressed with concerns about his security and inability to cope.

DT informed me that he has never been suicidal. He eats adequately but in a nervous manner, and there has been a longstanding change in the DT's sex life with diminished interest on the part of DT.

DT completed a three-year university degree and a diploma of teaching, and worked as a secondary schoolteacher. He enjoyed listening to classical music.

Formal Assessment

Formal testing revealed that DT had a Full Scale IQ of 97, a Verbal IQ of 106 and a performance IQ of 90. On the basis of the performance of well learned information DT premorbidly was probably performing in the high average to superior range on such an intelligence test, and his scaled scores of 14 and 15 on well learned information indicates that he has shown considerable deterioration in his ability to be able to flexibly use the information that he has available to him. DT performed considerably below expectation on a number of tests, including the repetition of digit spans, the solving of problems in arithmetic, determining the similarity between apparently dissimilar things, the construction of block designs, the construction of jigsaw type puzzles, and perhaps most seriously of all his ability to be able to recode digits into symbols on the Digit Symbol substitution test. Overall, this pattern of performance indicates attenuation of speed of information processing, concreteness in his ability to be able to determine the similarity between notionally dissimilar things and poor problem solving skills, as determined by his performance on the Block Design and Object Assembly tasks.

Tests of memory indicated that DT was well oriented for time, place and person and had good control over counting backwards from 20, saying the alphabet and the serial addition of 3s. His performance on counting backwards from 20 was very measured and controlled in an unusual sort of way, in that appeared he was checking on himself every step of the count backwards. This seems to be as a consequence of his anxiety and the inward focus on his own mental processes. DT had a digit span of 6 digits forwards and 3 digits backwards which is quite a poor performance for someone with a premorbid IQ in the high average to superior range.

I read DT two passages of prose each containing 25 items of information and he only recalled 6 and 9 items respectively from each passage. This is a very poor performance for a man of DT's level of premorbid function. A similar observation could be made about his new learning in both the audioverbal and visuospatial domains. He learned poorly on a test of recall of previously presented figures and he demonstrated an impoverished learning curve of the Paired Associate Learning Test of the Wechsler Scale. Taken together this pattern indicates an attenuated performance on all tests of memory function and, in DT's case, indicate a moderately severe amnesia.

Tests of the frontal executive functions indicated that DT could not demonstrate improvement on the complex learning test of the Austin maze which requires the subject to negotiate a 10×10 button maze over a series of trials. After 10 trials DT was still making seven errors per trial, again a very poor performance for a person of DT's level of functioning premorbidly. DT should have been capable of learning the task to a criterion of two error-free trials within about this many trials. On a test of verbal fluency DT demonstrated some rule breaking and impoverished responding on the task.

DT did not demonstrate word finding difficulty, agnosia or apraxia and his poor arithmetic functions were as a consequence of poor attention rather than due to an anarithmetria *per se*. This indicates that DT's deficits are not associated with the pattern usually observed in a dementing illness such as Alzheimer's disease.

VERBAL TESTS (Scaled Scores)	
Information	14
Digit Span	7
Vocabulary	15
Arithmetic	8
Comprehension	15
Similarities	8
VIQ	112
PERFORMANCE TESTS	
Picture Completion	11
Picture Arrangement	6
Block Design	6
Object Assembly	5
Digit Symbol	3
PIQ	90
FSIQ	101
WECHSLER MEMORY SCALE-REVISED	
Verbal Memory Index	79
Visual Memory Index	100
General Memory Index	85
Attention/Concentration	81
VERBAL FLUENCY TEST	
Items Produced (Low Normal)	28
Number of Errors	1

AUSTIN MAZE TEST

Trial	1	2	3	4	5	6	7	8	9	10
Errors	18	12	15	9	7	7	7	7	6	7

Conclusion

DT is a 62-year-old man with a past history of anxiety disorder and atrial fibrillation, who at this point in time features marked deficits in almost all modes of information processing, including slowing of information processing, poor problem solving, deficits in problem solving in arithmetic tasks, a moderately severe memory deficit, and a poor ability to be able to plan and execute programs for the solution of complicated problems.

Overall, DT's pattern of performance indicated severe disability and I felt quite convinced that these would invalidate any attempt that he would make to be able to seek or maintain employment of any description. DT did not feature any alternative cause for such a pattern of cognitive disturbance that could be determined, and does not feature a pattern consistent with dementia of the Alzheimer type or a past drinking history. The pattern observed is quite consistent with the effects of a very disabling stress syndrome, which is producing a pseudodementia, and the basic deficit underlying the problems on each of the cognitive domains seems to be the hyperaroused state that he continually experiences. This results in disruption of his processing of information in many of the higher level domains, including his difficulties with repeating digit spans, solving problems, recalling information, using information flexibly, and in higher level problem solving.

SUMMARY

Whilst considerable caution must be exercised in the analysis of the data arising regarding anxiety related conditions, it is possible for us to come to some tentative conclusions. The anxiety conditions can be characterised by their disruption of attentional processes at all levels. This results in a heightened focus on threatening stimuli and a generalised hyperaroused state in all aspects of cognition and purposive behaviour. As a result, the cognitive profile of these individuals is characterised by the inability to take information on, to be able to work with it flexibly or to be able to screen out interfering cognitive input. This has an impact on the performance of tasks as diverse as the repetition of digit spans to the ability to be able to screen out the multiplicity of inputs in going to the supermarket. At lower levels of anxiety however, little can be said and it appears that the usual stresses associated with assessment procedures in non-clinical subjects result in negligible changes to cognition.

CHAPTER 5

SOMATOFORM, FACTITIOUS AND DISSOCIATIVE DISORDERS

At some point in the evaluation of every individual referred for assessment the clinician must ask himself/herself: Are the responses and the behaviour of this individual in this circumstance consistent with an actual psychiatric or neurological disorder or are the observed deficits due to some other cause? It is the issue of what this something else might be that is addressed in this chapter.

This issue occurs most frequently in the context of medico-legal disputation in which considerable periods of incarceration, or sizeable sums of money, are at stake on the basis of a clinician's evidence. This issue culminates when the barrister asks: 'Tell me doctor, is it not possible that people can either consciously or unconsciously fake brain damage?' Whilst one would like to be able to instantly reply that any competent clinician should be able to, the literature and most experienced clinicians are aware that the problem is not quite so simple. As Guilmette and Guiliano have observed, 'regardless of the assumptions or convictions that neuropsychologists may have about their ability to detect malingering, at the present time the expert witness must concede that, at best, there is little to no scientific evidence that supports a clinician's ability to detect malingering with traditional measures of neuropsychological functioning' (1991, p. 208).

Caution must be exercised in the interpretation of all material obtained during the assessment, including the history and presentation of the client, and most importantly of all, the testing. This issue has been succinctly put by Miller who observes that:

> If damage in structure X is known to produce a decline on test T it is tempting to argue that any new subject, or group of subjects, having a relatively poor performance on T must have a lesion at X. In fact the logical status of

> this argument is the same as reasoning that because a horse meets the test of being a large animal with four legs then any newly encountered large animal with four legs must be a horse. The newly encountered specimen could of course be a cow or a hippopotamus and still meet the same test. Similarly new subjects who do badly on T may do so for reasons other than having a lesion at X (1983, p. 131).

Failure on tests of cognitive functioning may occur as a consequence of a number of factors and the clinician must be constantly alert to the various causes of poor performance. In psychiatric patients this caution is doubly appropriate due to the effects of medication, compliance, motivation and preoccupation. Neuropsychological assessment of psychiatric patients is a difficult task even for well experienced clinicians, and this problem is multiplied if there are extramural forces at work in the form of compensation or evasion of criminal responsibility.

NOSOLOGY

A number of definitional issues surround this area and it is worthwhile clarifying a number of these before we go further. DSM-IV (American Psychiatric Association, 1994) describes somatoform disorders as those conditions in which the physical symptoms suggest a general medical condition but are not fully explained by that general medical condition. The manual draws a distinction between somatoform disorders and factitious disorders, and malingering in that in the former case, the symptoms are not intentional or under voluntary control. The manual suggests that there are a number of entities under the umbrella of somatoform disorders, including somatization disorder, conversion disorder, pain disorder, hypochondriasis, body dysmorphic disorder, and those somatoform disorders not otherwise specified. (Consult DSM-IV for a full description.)

Conversion disorder is of particular interest as these conditions affect voluntary motor or sensory functions which suggest a neurological or other general medical condition. One of the interesting features of the conversion disorder is that the symptoms typically do not conform to the usual anatomical or physiological patterns. For example, a paralysis may be in the form of a glove or stocking distribution and may be delimited by perceived boundaries rather than anatomical ones (the wrist for example), whilst the distribution of the anaesthesia and their responsivity to particular forms of sensory stimulation do not accord with anatomical reality. The patient may also show little anxiety or concern about the apparently massively debilitating nature of their presented problems, a situation which Charcot referred to as *la belle indifférence* (beautiful indifference).

Factitious disorders are characterised by either psychological or physical symptoms which are intentionally produced with a view to fulfilling a sick role. Chronic factitious disorder with physical symptoms has been referred to historically as Munchausen's syndrome, named after the legendary Baron Munchausen who undertook fantastic travels and celebrated extravagant tales of his own prowess. Chronic factitious disorder with psychological symptoms has been historically referred to as Ganser syndrome, which is characterised by a strange pattern of cognitive impairment and associated 'approximate answers' (e.g. 2 + 2 = 5). This syndrome was originally described in 1898 by Ganser after attending three patients who featured the characteristic 'Ganser' response. These responses are sometimes referred to as answers past the point or approximate answers. The patient's responses to questions are markedly inaccurate and often absurdly so. However, they betray a knowledge as to the purpose of the question, and by their close approximation to the correct answer imply that this too is at some level available. In an attempt to prevent massive overdiagnosis, the proviso that the false response although wrong is never far wrong and bears a definite and obvious relationship to the question, indicates clearly that the question has been grasped by the patient. The apparent dementia that accompanies the approximate answers is usually incomplete, inconsistent and often self-contradictory. Disorientation is invariably present, but the apparently gross disturbance of intellect fails to be reflected in the patient's overall behaviour.

The factitious disorders are distinguished from malingering in which the individual is producing symptoms intentionally and has a clear goal in mind (e.g. financial gain, evading imprisonment), in contrast to factitious disorders where obvious incentives are absent.

Dissociative disorders are characterised by the disruption of the flow of consciousness, memory, identity or perception of the environment, including such patterns of disorder as dissociative amnesia, dissociative fugue, dissociative identity disorder and depersonalisation disorder. (Consult DSM-IV for a full description.)

Dissociative fugue is one of the more interesting conditions in this group in which there is sudden unexpected travel away from one's home and general activities with an associated inability to recall some or all of one's past. This is the Hollywood amnesia of Ronald Coleman in *Random Harvest* who takes on a new identity in a new environment with no knowledge of or reference to his past.

The notion of malingering refers to a voluntary production or exaggeration of symptoms with a view to presenting oneself as worse than one is with a view to a demonstrable and predictable gain.

Gain has generally been divided into primary versus secondary in the psycho-analytic tradition. Primary gain is considered to represent the reduction in anxiety and relief generated by the unconscious emotional conflict. Secondary gain de-scribes the psychosocial benefit of the sick role including such things as release from unpleasant responsibility, increased personal attention and sympathy, and financial reward. Cullum, Heaton and Grant (1991) propose that the distinction between primary and secondary gain is somewhat artificial, and they prefer the notion of merely gain irrespective of whether the benefit is conscious or uncon-scious. It follows from their suggestion that all psychologically determined symptoms involve gain. In somatoform disorders this involves anxiety reduction and a symbolic statement of the disorder that is unconsciously determined. In the case of factitious disorders there is a conscious attempt to adopt the sick role to avoid an emotional conflict. In malingering the activity is again under con-scious control and is directed towards a demonstrable and tangible benefit.

BIOLOGICAL ORIGINS

A number of theories of the biological origins of conversion reactions have been proposed but to date none of them could be considered to clearly elucidate the mechanism of the disorder (Jones, 1980; Miller, 1984). As discussed above, the analytic tradition is replete with a number of characterisations of the problem. A more biological model of hysteria has been proposed by Ludwig (1972). This theory is based on the assumption that an underlying cortical inhibitory state, triggered at the level of the reticular activating system, is the principal cause of the various clinical manifestations of the disorder. Some support for this model has been claimed on the basis of EEG evidence (e.g. Levy & Mushin, 1973), and on the specificity of the memory related effects of conversion hysteria (Bendefeldt, Miller & Ludwig, 1976). However, considerable evidence to the contrary exists and at this point the value of the corticofugal inhibition model is unclear.

The somatoform, factitious and dissociative conditions are characterised by the fact that they do not have a biological origin. The malady is by definition a misinterpretation or embellishment of the usually observed pattern of disorder associated with a given diagnosis. The tendency for the invocation of the notion of the subconscious or the unconscious tends to be popular in explanations of these phenomena. It is difficult to ascertain how informative these approaches actually are, as rarely does this area result in extensive research, exploration or theory generation.

NEUROPATHOLOGY AND STRUCTURAL AND FUNCTIONAL IMAGING

Clearly the evidence obtained in the areas of neuropathology and structural and functional imaging results in diagnosis by exclusion. It is the X-ray, CT, MRI or SPECT scan which indicates no abnormality in the subject who is, to all intents and purposes, severely demented that raises the index of concern in these cases.

One matter on which all investigators do agree about these conditions is that conversion symptoms occur much more frequently in women than they do in men (Boffeli & Guze, 1992). Whether this observation occurs as a consequence of sex differences at a biological, psychological or social level is difficult to ascertain.

NEUROPSYCHOLOGICAL FEATURES

Few studies of the neuropsychological status of subjects suffering from the somatoform, factitious or dissociative disorders have been published, thus it is difficult to say much about these conditions from a neuropsychological perspective. In one of the few studies undertaken on somatization disorder, Flor-Henry et al. (1981) compared ten subjects with a diagnosis of somatization disorder with 10 controls using a battery of neuropsychological tests. Ninety per cent of the clinical patients were classified as showing evidence of neuropsychological impairment in comparison to none of the controls. The authors interpreted their result as supporting the notion that dominant hemisphere dysfunction is associated with compromise in hysteria. Some concerns regarding the sample size, the subjects-to-variables ratio and the sampling procedures have been raised (Cullum et al., 1991), making this result suspect.

Matthews, Shaw and Klove (1966) conducted a study using a pseudo-neurological group (paraesthesias, visual difficulties, motor weakness or dyscoordination or pseudoseizures) in a comparison with 32 demographically matched brain impaired. Their brain impaired group scored worse than the pseudoneurological group on 17 of the 26 measures from the Halstead-Reitan Battery. Only 6% of the pseudoneurological group was classified as having brain disorder on the basis of the Impairment Index.

In a more recent study, Liebson, White and Albert (1996) sought to distinguish abnormal illness behaviour from cognitive impairment secondary to neurological disease. Thirty patients with hysteria or malingering were compared with age matched neurological controls. A battery of tests aimed at measuring impairments in motivation and cognitive functions were employed. The results of the study revealed that there was no sign or symptom which was specific to the abnormal illness behaviour group. Motivational and cognitive impairments occurred equally as often in the neurological sample and the authors emphasised caution in the diagnosis of abnormal illness behaviour.

It seems that the neuropsychological finding in this group of patients is anything but consistent. Clearly the likelihood of neuropsychological deficits in this group is largely contingent on how much they are capable of creating the appearance of neuropsychological disorder, either at a conscious or unconscious level. The observation of Leff regarding the expression of hysteria is of particular note. Increasingly, according to Leff (1988), the expression of hysteria has shifted over the last one hundred years from the bodily mode to the psychological mode. As a consequence the likelihood of the increasing presentation of the psychological equivalent of the glove and stocking anaesthesias will become more prevalent.

Due to the fact that the somatoform, factitious and dissociative disorders are each due to an interpretation on the part of the patient of what neurological and neuropsychological symptoms should look like, they do not conform in any consistent way to the usual patterns of neuropsychological disorder. Descriptions in the literature have indicated a tendency by patients to focus on particular aspects of cognitive functioning.

In the case of placebo-induced conversion reaction described by Levy and Jankovic (1983), a patient with an alleged idiosyncratic response to phenytoin (Dilantin) was assessed and monitored under strict laboratory conditions in a cross over design in which she was led to believe that she was being given Dilantin when in fact she was given saline, and was then given saline under the impression that it was the active agent. The authors noted that after a 200 mg injection of saline (which she believed to be Dilantin) the patient's right hand finger tapping speed slowed from 49 taps in 10 seconds (at baseline) to 37 taps in 10 seconds. Similarly her left hand speed dropped from 41 to 30 taps in 10 seconds. Her speech became laboured and slow, moderately slurred and reduced in volume. She became prone to paraphasic errors and pseudoagrammatic speech in repetition and spontaneous speech, and demonstrated overgeneralisations and circumlocutions on confrontational naming. As the session progressed she became gradually more unresponsive to verbal commands eventually slipping into a pseudocoma.

During this phase she proved unresponsive to even quite painful stimuli, and when it was announced that the dose of Dilantin had reached 900 mg she had a pseudoseizure. All electrical activity recorded by the EEG at this period revealed no abnormality. Ten to 15 minutes after the 'fit' the patient was readministered the neuropsychological tests battery which revealed no abnormality.

During the Dilantin administration condition (the patient believed that the injection was inert) the 10 second finger tapping rates were (right/left) 52/52, 53/54, 59/54, 56/56. She also proved capable of recalling in the minutest detail the contents of the morning session including a perfect recall of a visuospatial figure that had been represented to her only minutes before the pseudocoma.

The variety of responses the patient produced during the hysterical episode were classified into three categories: language disturbance, unresponsiveness and seizure-like phenomena. The language disturbance was characterised by dysfluencies, slurring, reduced volume, agrammatism, paraphasias, anomia and circumlocution.

Bendefeldt, Miller and Ludwig (1976), in their assessment of 17 patients with conversion hysteria, noted that their hysterical subjects displayed a greater tendency towards suggestibility, a greater field dependency, greater impairment of recent memory, and poorer performance on test of vigilance and attention than did their psychiatric controls.

In the case of Ganser Syndrome described by Heron, Kritchevsky and Delis (1991), a full neuropsychological examination was conducted which revealed deficits in a number of cognitive spheres. The patient was a 54-year-old white male with an extensive history of forensic, histrionic and medical complaints. On formal testing his performance suggested the presence of severe dementia, but as Heron et al. note 'this diagnosis contrasted sharply with his fluent, complex and grammatically accurate speech, his finding his way around a large medical centre, his ability to remember follow up appointments and his highly communication-dependent "vocation" '(1991, p. 656).

Whilst the patient indicated no difficulty with language functions during conversation, on formal testing with the Boston Naming Test he made semantic errors, circumlocutions, misperceptions, phonemic errors, and foreign language substitutions. On the Wisconsin Card Sort he ignored the feedback and failed to successfully complete a single category. On the Rey 15 item Test (a test of malingering; Lezak, 1995), the patient reproduced only seven items correctly.

HOW ARE THE DEFICITS PRODUCED?

To understand the mechanism of the action of these disorders, it is necessary to understand the knowledge and the sophistication of the subject who suffers from them. Clearly the more experienced and knowledgeable the subject, the more that their symptomatology will look real. The subject who has had previous exposure to a friend or relative with Broca's aphasia is likely to present with agrammatism and halting speech, the client who has seen Alzheimer's disease at close quarters is more likely to present amnesia, apraxia and agnosia.

Regarding the issue of the tendency of clients to embroider their clinical symptomatology, the techniques of assessment, reassessment and assessment yet again, which are characteristic of our adversarial legal system, almost beg the client to overpresent and embroider his/her symptoms. Most assessors will ask the same set of questions, and generally as the assessor has asked the questions so often before, the answers are virtually written down before the client has responded. The traumatically brain injured subject invariably complains of problems with memory, attention, irritability, tiredness and vague depressive mentation. The assessor is astounded if the subject does not complain of these and if he or she does not, the assessor asks why not. In this context it is quite easy for the injured subject to learn how to play the game and present the most 'convincing' set of symptoms.

As noted above, the likelihood of an increase in the presentation of psychologically based factitious disorders is a growing clinical reality. If we consider these symptoms a cry for help, the fact that a glove or stocking anaesthesia can be immediately dismissed by the general practitioner as a clear attempt at attention seeking, will result in the lessened likelihood of the presentation of such a symptom. The presence of chronic unremitting tiredness, ongoing pain or the presence of migraines may result in a more sympathetic hearing on the part of the general practitioner, and as a consequence validation of the problem by the world.

Heron et al. (1991) noted that their patient with Ganser syndrome only produced his ludicrous replies when directly questioned by the clinicians, never in the context of spontaneous speech. They interpreted the presentation of the patient as indicating a condition intermediate between malingering and hysteria. They note that individuals who are poorly able to cope with stress, seem to be those most vulnerable to the development of these symptoms. Butcher (1995), in his extensive review of the psychological processes involved in psychogenic voice disorders, notes a similar observation, in that the research findings in this area suggest that the most likely individual to present with this condition is a woman who is experiencing high levels of stress, has heightened musculo-skeletal tension, and who has difficulty in voicing her feelings and views.

It seems that the instances in which this pattern of responding is most likely to occur will be in stressed individuals or in those who do not have the resources to adequately cope with stress, and who do not feel that they have an acceptable means to present their disquiet about their situation. The more experienced and exposed they have been to the actual clinical phenomena that they would hope to mimic, the harder they will be to distinguish from the real thing.

In the case report we will examine a woman who presents with a series of problems that we have discussed in the context of a minor head injury.

CASE REPORT

MD worked as a solicitor and had a fall at work with a brief loss of consciousness. Neurological and physical investigations were negative including the CT scan. Her psychiatrist, who referred her to me, felt that the problem was a post-concussional syndrome and post-traumatic stress disorder following the accident which was now grafted on to a previous diagnosis of manic depressive illness. He noted that she was very fragile, depressed and feeling depersonalisation. She was vague and disoriented on occasions and was having pseudo hallucinations.

Background

MD had slipped and fallen down 22 cement stairs. There was no retrograde amnesia and her loss of consciousness was probably for a few seconds or so during which she felt quite dazed. She remembers the accident took place at 5.00 p.m. and she got home at about 6.30 p.m. She drove home and could remember the drive following the accident. She lived about 40 minutes away so the post-traumatic amnesia was at most about one hour in duration.

MD was married and had been working for a large multinational company as a solicitor but was terminated from this work twelve months after the accident. MD had noted a couple of changes since the accident including the fact that she 'did not have any coordination'. She also noted lapses of concentration and periods of disorientation. She noted that her concentration was poor. She had drooping on the right side of her mouth and problems handling things with her right hand. She also had a droop of the left eye which she noted was continuously black. She has trouble remembering where she lived and noted that she walks backwards and perhaps to the side. She also observes some change in her sense of smell.

MD completed the matriculation, went on to university for four years and following that did two years as an article clerk. Following her studies, MD started work in a bank where she worked for about 12–14 years. She then emigrated to Australia and worked for 5 years in a legal department of a bank.

There has been no subsequent return to work since the accident due to the problems previously noted. She has no history of fits, faints, falls or funny turns.

She did not use alcohol, nor did she smoke. And at the time of the assessment MD was taking a sedative (Rohypnol), lithium for the treatment of her bipolar disorder, and Amitriptyline for the treatment of her depression. The observation of a bipolar disorder, MD noted, was first made when she was a little girl.

Formal Assessment

I conducted a number of tests with MD with a view to determining her present level of function. On the Wechsler Adult Intelligence Scale Revised she proved to have a Verbal Intelligence Quotient of 79, a Performance Intelligence Quotient of 66 and a Full Scale Intelligence Quotient of 71. This result places her performance in the borderline intellectually disabled range.

Her performance on a test of memory revealed that she had a Verbal Memory Index of 65, a Visual Memory Index of 51, a General Memory Index of 50 and a Delayed Recall Index of 51. This pattern indicates massive deterioration in performances on all cognitive skills including well learned information, as well as in her ability to be able to solve problems, to be able to remember audio-verbally or spatio-visually presented material, and an inability to be able to solve problems in arithmetic.

The pattern of the performances was one of approximate answers, where by in presenting an answer to the question seemed to indicate that at some level the correct answer was known to her. For example, when I asked her in which direction the sun rose, she indicated that it rose in the West. When I asked her who was Ned Kelly she stated that he was a poet, and when I asked her how many weeks there are in a year she suggested that there were 48. When I asked her to solve problems in arithmetic she indicated that if you had $10 and you spent $4 that you would have $7 left and if you had $4 and then were given another $5 that altogether you would have $8.

Tests of higher level problem solving were equally poorly performed, as indexed by her poor performance at less than the 10 percentile on the Trail Making Test part A. She proved incapable of conducting the alternation between numbers and letters on the Trail Making Test part B. She performed in the defective range on the Controlled Oral Word Association Test and produced numerous errors.

The pattern of performances revealed marked attenuation in all cognitive skills on the tests that I conducted; they seemed to be far out of keeping with the nature of the injury that she had sustained; and I could not help but think that the problem was one of a decompensation subsequent to the accident in the form of a pseudodementing syndrome with a Ganser-like pattern to it. I had her

complete the Beck Depression Inventory which revealed that she had a total score of 54, indicating massive endorsement of depressive symptomatology, including numerous, very marked disturbances of thoughts and behaviour. For example, she indicated she would kill herself if she had the chance, that she has lost all interest in other people, and that she blames herself for everything bad that happens.

VERBAL TESTS (Age Scaled Scores)		
Information		3
Digit Span		2
Vocabulary		8
Arithmetic		2
Comprehension		4
Similarities		6
VIQ		79
PERFORMANCE TESTS		
Picture Completion		3
Picture Arrangement		4
Block Design		5
Object Assembly		4
Digit Symbol		4
PIQ		66
FSIQ		71
WECHSLER MEMORY SCALE-REVISED		
Verbal Memory Index		65
Visual Memory Index		51
General Memory Index		50
Delayed Recall		51
TRAIL MAKING TEST	Time	Centile
Part A	77 secs	< 10th
Part B	incomplete	—
COWAT	22 words	
	4 errors	

Conclusion

The pattern of performances that we see with MD seems to indicate a woman who has had a massive decompensation following a minor head injury with perhaps a few seconds of loss of consciousness and something like less than an hour of post-traumatic amnesia. This exists in association with a history of affective illness and a tendency to somatise concerns. The issues that sensitise to a diagnosis of a factitious disorder are the relatively minor nature of the injury in the first place, the marked discrepancy between her 'life' performance and her test performance (an individual performing so poorly on so many aspects of cognitive functioning could not live independently in the community), and the fact that she reveals a variety of approximate answers which indicate that at some level she does have the correct answer available to her.

SUMMARY

The patterns of neuropsychological deficit in the somatoform, factitious or dissociative disorders are characterised by their larger than life pattern. The nature of the disorder can be fairly unpredictable, but the flavour of presentation that alerts the clinician to the problem is the tendency for them to be out of keeping with the ability of the patient in situations other than the testing situation. If a person who scores zero on the block design proves capable of finding his or her way to your office on time unassisted, then the likelihood that they are attempting to appear worse than what they are, for whatever reason, must be high on the list of differential diagnoses.

CHAPTER 6

DISORDERS OF SLEEPING AND EATING

In this chapter we will examine disorders of neurovegetative functioning in the form of the sleeping and eating disorders. Whilst the data available on the neuropsychological performance of subjects featuring these disorders is relatively scant, some data does exist and this will be examined with a view to elucidating the neuropsychological effects of these conditions. The conditions that will be surveyed in the chapter include anorexia and bulimia nervosa, primary insomnia and breathing-related sleep disorder.

DISORDERS OF SLEEPING

Sleep and waking are two opposite states of being which compete for consciousness. Wakefulness is maintained by the activity of the reticular activating system (RAS) assisted by the activity of the catecholaminergic and cholinergic transmitter systems which convey the activation of the RAS via the thalamus to the cortex. Sleep is promoted by the activity of the dorsal raphe, which acts in accord with other brain stem nuclei to deactivate the RAS. Serotonergic neurons dampen down sensory activity and inhibit motor activity during sleep promoting slow wave activity of the cortex (Culebras, 1992).

Nosology

The sleep disorders represent a complex set of conditions, few of which have resulted in neuropsychological investigation. Nonetheless, two of the conditions in this group deserve consideration: primary insomnia, a complaint of difficulty initiating or maintaining sleep or of non-restorative sleep that lasts for at least a month, and breathing-related sleep disorder, a condition in which there is sleep disruption leading to excessive sleepiness that is judged to be due to abnormalities of ventilation during sleep. (DSM-IV should be consulted for a comprehensive listing of these conditions.)

Neuropsychological Features

Chronic sleep deprivation occurs as a consequence of insufficient sleep and is characterised by chronic tiredness and fatigue. More extreme levels of sleep deprivation (i.e. 100 hours without sleep) may cause numerous physical and psychic manifestations including hallucination, microsleep, lapses of attention and impairment of motor coordination (Culebras, 1992).

Little information is available on the issue of chronic sleep deprivation, and it is surprising that such a simple and ever present issue has resulted in little investigation. Lingenfelser, Kaschel, Weber, and Zaiser-Kaschel (1994) tested young hospital doctors either after a night off duty, following at least 6 hours of uninterrupted sleep, or after a night on call which involved being in the hospital for 24 hours. The tests they employed included the Trail Making Test, a reaction time test and the Stroop Test. In the on call condition, the doctor's neuropsychological function and mood status deteriorated significantly through the shift.

The finding alerts the clinician to the issue that sleep loss of itself can contribute significantly to impairment in measures of attention in as little as 24 hours of sleep deprivation.

Breathing-related sleep disorder or Obstructive Sleep Apnoea Syndrome (OSAS) is characterised by loud snoring, irregular breathing whilst asleep, restlessness whilst asleep, daytime sleepiness and mental dullness. OSAS increases with age, is more common in men and may contribute to cardiovascular disease. Sleep apnoea occurs in virtually every male past the age of 45 (Culebras, 1992). In sleep apnoea, the upper airway typically occludes and diaphragmatic expansion still persists, creating a negative pressure in the thorax. As a result of these processes, oxygen desaturation of the blood occurs. Management of this condition has become possible by the introduction of nasal continuous positive air pressure (CPAP) treatment, whereby a continuous flow of air is maintained at low pressure through a facial mask during sleep which acts to 'splint' the airway maintaining it open during sleep.

Cognitive deficits in people with sleep apnoea have been demonstrated at a number of centres (Berry et al., 1986; Bliwise, 1989; Findley et al., 1986). The data so far also seems to indicate that the severity of the apnoea and, as a consequence, the level of hypoxemia (lower blood oxygenation), contribute significantly to the level of impairment (Bedard et al., 1991). Reductions in general intellectual measures, as well as in executive and psychomotor tasks, have been attributed to the severity of hypoxemia, while deficits of attention and memory were ascribed to an impairment of vigilance (Bedard et al., 1991).

Attention and mental tracking

A number of deficits in the area of attention, mental tracking and psychomotor speed and agility have been noted with this population. OSAS subjects performed more poorly on a test requiring sustained attention while subjects with chronic obstructive airway disease performed more poorly on a test requiring motor skills. The authors interpreted these results as reflecting the fact that deficits in psychomotor and attention functions appear to be specifically related to OSAS, while the other deficits found in complex reasoning and memory are nonspecific (Roehrs, Merrion, Pedrosi, & Stepanski, 1995). A similar result was noted by Greenberg, Watson, and Deptula (1987) who observed that severity of the hypoxemia was significantly correlated with deficits on measures of motor and perceptual-organisational ability. Treatment with CPAP resulted in a number of effects, including a statistically significant improvement in problems correctly solved on the Wilkinson Addition Test from pre- to post-CPAP by non-hypoxemic subjects. The hypoxemic subjects, however, showed only a marginal increase (Valencia-Flores et al., 1996).

The literature seems relatively consistent in indicating that sleep apnoea interferes with attention and motor responsivity. The problem also seems to indicate a dose response effect, in so far as the lower the levels of oxygenation, the more profound the deficit.

Language and spatial cognition

Little data on the issue of language dysfunction in this group has been noted, although Berry et al. (1986) have noted deficits on the level of response on tests of verbal fluency with these subjects. Kajaste and Partinen (1985) noted deficits on visuoconstructive abilities and visual memory drawings in subjects with sleep apnoea, which they contended was a consequence of the increased levels of hypoxemia.

Learning and memory

Treatment with CPAP has resulted in a number of interesting effects including the fact that performance on the recall trial of the Rey Auditory Verbal Learning Test increased from pre- to post-CPAP for an increased alertness group but decreased significantly for subjects with decreased alertness (Valencia-Flores et al.,

1996), an observation supported by the findings of Ferber, Taillard, and Dealberto (1992).

Adaptive behaviour

Bedard, Montplaisir, Malo, Richer, and Rouleau (1993) note that following CPAP treatment most of the neuropsychological deficits observed prior to CPAP resolved subsequent to the treatment with the exception of planning abilities and manual dexterity. The authors note that these are the deficits which have been reported to be most highly correlated with the severity of nocturnal hypoxemia.

Summary

It appears that there is consistent data to support the notion of compromise in a number of cognitive spheres following decreased sleep and in the context of OSAS. These effects are commonly observed in the areas of attention and tasks of high level integration such as the solution of problems in arithmetic. The findings with OSAS clearly indicate that there is a dose response relationship between the level of hypoxia and the neuropsychological deficits. The effects of CPAP seem to be helpful in improving both oxygenation and neuropsychological functioning following treatment.

DISORDERS OF EATING

As we approach the millennium, we stand at a most unusual point in history at which thinness has become intimately interlinked with the notion of beauty. Interestingly, as the media depiction of women has become thinner, the average weight of women has gone the other way (O'Dea, 1995). These issues have resulted in the development of entirely new patterns of behaviour in which control over eating has become maladaptive. The first of these disorders, anorexia nervosa, appeared for the first time in the bible of psychiatric disorders, the *Diagnostic and Statistical Manual of Mental Disorders* (DSM, for short; American Psychiatric Association), in 1980.

Nosology

Two diagnoses specifically apply to disorders of eating. These are: (1) anorexia nervosa, the essential features of which include that the individual refuses to maintain a minimally normal body weight, is afraid of gaining weight and exhibits a significant disturbance in the perception of the shape or size of the body; and

(2) bulimia nervosa defined as binge eating in association with compensatory methods to prevent weight gain.

The defining feature of anorexia nervosa is not so much that these individuals lose their appetites but that they fear gaining weight (Achenbach, 1982). In association with the fear of weight gain is an associated distortion of the way that they perceive their bodies. Despite their appearance to the world as bony, debilitated and thin, they view themselves as still too fat or of only having just achieved an attractive weight. The other physical features associated with the condition include cessation of menstruation, dry cracked skin, downy hair of the face (lanugo hair), brittle fingernails, yellowish discolouration of the skin, weakness and fatigue. These individuals also often have an unusually avid preoccupation with food, often collecting recipes and preparing elaborate meals for others (Davison & Neale, 1996).

Bulimia nervosa has been recognised as a separate disorder for the first time in the DSM-IV (American Psychiatric Association, 1994). It is characterised by a pattern of gross overeating followed by induced vomiting or laxative use in the attempt to rid the body of the large bolus of food just ingested. These bingeing and purging episodes must occur at least three times per week for the diagnosis to be made. The condition is also often associated with frenetic exercising. These individuals do not necessarily have abnormally low weight but do have a preoccupation with body size.

The biological origins of the eating disorders

Whilst a number of biological theories of the eating disorders have been proposed there seems little objective data at this point in time to either support or exclude them. The most popular theory is that there is some abnormality in the hypothalamus which disrupts the eating, sexual and menstruation function of these individuals. Clearly there is a multifaceted interaction between the weight loss, the altered cognitions and the emotional state of these individuals which make causative links very difficult to establish, and the data gathered in support of the hypothesis remains flimsy (Garfinkel & Garner, 1982).

The psychological origins of the eating disorders

Numerous theories of psychological causation of the eating disorders have also been propounded (Davison & Neale, 1996), and to this point in time they too remain largely unsubstantiated. Freudian theories suggest sexual repression is reflected as suppression of eating, while the striving towards individuation and control, by controlling what one ingests, has also been proposed. Learning theories have suggested that anorexia nervosa may be a weight phobia or alternatively a desire to assume the image of the slim and svelte image of the idealised beauties of magazines and the movies. What it is possible to conclude from these suggestions is that we are still a long way from a well-reasoned testable explanation of the intrapsychic and biological phenomenon that underlies these conditions.

Structural and Functional Imaging Data

Whilst the number of studies examining the imaging status of individuals suffering from the eating disorders has been small, some studies do exist. Using computerized tomography, Palazidou, Robinson, and Lishman (1990) noted that their 17 female patients with anorexia nervosa had enlarged external cerebrospinal fluid (CSF) spaces compared to their controls. Interestingly, the subjects also performed abnormally on the symbol digit test, the scores of which displayed a significant negative correlation with the CT scan changes, implying worse performance in the presence of larger external CSF spaces relative to controls. In contrast, Laessle et al. (1989) noted, again using CT data, that whilst the anorexic and bulimic subjects performed significantly more poorly in the cognitive task, patients with ventricular dilatation did not perform any worse on the cognitive test than did patients with normally sized ventricles. They also noted that other clinical characteristics such as symptom severity or duration of illness were also not correlated with ventricular size. In contrast to Palazidou et al. (1990), they observe that cerebral atrophy does not seem to have severe consequences on the neuropsychological or psychopathological status in eating disorder patients.

Clearly, insufficient data is currently available to make an informed decision about the status of eating disordered individuals on the basis of their CT data, other than to say that at very low body weights CT evidence will indicate changes but the permanence of this effect and its correlation with cognitive disorder remains unclear.

Neuropsychological Features

The difficulty that arises as a consequence of the eating disorders occurs due to the deficiency in the numerous vitamins, amino acids and electrolytes associated with a balanced diet. A number of conditions which have well-established neuropsychological sequelae associated with prolonged failure to eat or dietary insufficiencies have been noted. These include the Wernicke Korsakoff syndrome which is often, although not exclusively, associated with alcoholism. The syn-

drome is characterised by an almost complete inability to learn new material in the context of a normal short-term memory. There is also often a retrograde amnesia associated with the memory deficit which has a temporal gradient, such that information closer to the present in time is remembered worse than information from the more distant past. The performance is improved by direct questioning and there tends to be preservation of early established skills and habits, for example language, gesture, well-practised skills, and procedural memory. Confabulation can also occur with the tendency to fabricate memories when asked questions about the past. These individuals are also characterised by decreased initiative and spontaneity, together with blunting of affect (Victor, Adams & Collins, 1989).

Vitamin B_{12} (cyanocobalamin) plays a fundamental role in metabolic processes throughout the body including the synthesis of nucleic acids and the metabolism of carbohydrates and lipids. The most common manifestations of vitamin B_{12} deficiency in humans are megaloblastic anaemia (usually pernicious anaemia) and/or neurological impairments. Mental disturbances including irritability, memory loss, moodiness, agitation, depression, confusion, hallucinations, delusions and paranoid psychosis (Zucker et al., 1981) have been noted. Vitamin B_{12} deficiency appears to also result in cognitive disturbances as evidenced by impaired performance on the Halstead-Reitan Categories Test, the Weschler Memory Scale (Goodwin, Goodwin, & Gary, 1983) and the Mini-Mental State Examination (Bell et al., 1990). Memory impairment has also been reported by Shulman (1967) to be apparent in three quarters of his patients with pernicious anaemia. Most returned to normal following treatment.

Folate deficiency is one of the most common avitaminosis in humans, and has been implicated in a number of specific cognitive impairments. Patients with low folate levels have been reported to perform poorly on the Halstead-Reitan Category Test, the Weschler Memory Scale (Goodwin et al., 1983), and the Mini Mental State Examination (Bell et al., 1990). Of particular significance is a study by Botez and colleagues (1984) which found significant improvement in each of the ten subtests of the Ottowa-Weschler Scale (WAIS) following 7–11 months of folate administration.

The other problematic condition arising for these individuals is the possible development of delirium associated with their compromise in electrolyte status, particularly in the form of hyponatraemia (low levels of sodium) and hypokalaemia (low levels of potassium), both of which constitute acute medical emergencies.

In the context of the deficits associated with the eating disorders it is difficult to be able to point to a clear and consistent deficit which has been observed by all investigators. Opinions swing from the observations of Jones, Duncan, Brouwers and Mirsky (1991) who observed that underweight anorexic subjects show compromise in the areas of focusing and execution, verbal, memory and visuospatial cognition, whilst bulimics only feature deficits on focusing and execution, through to the study of Touyz, Beumont, and Johnstone (1986) who noted no significant differences between the anorexia nervosa and the bulimia nervosa subjects on any of the intellectual, neuropsychological, or academic-related tasks they conducted. In the latter study there was no evidence of cognitive deficit in the patient groups as compared with theoretical norms.

Clearly the truth probably lies somewhere between these two poles of opinion. In the case of the Jones et al. (1991) study, the level of impairment reported on each of the tests administered was at best small, suggesting that the effects of the condition are subtle and are, as would be expected, dependent upon the severity of the weight loss.

Attention and mental tracking

A number of the studies in this area have noted deficits in the area of attention functions. Hamsher, Halmi and Benton (1981) noted that nine of their 20 subjects performed poorly on two or more of their cognitive measures which included tests of reaction time, short-term memory or retrieval efficiency. Szmukler et al. (1992) noted that, in their low body weight anorexic subjects, impairment was evident on the Trail Making Test. Interestingly, these researchers noted that refeeding resulted in significant improvements in performance.

Language and spatial cognition

No deficits have been noted for these subjects on tests of formal language functions, but a number of findings in tests of visuospatial cognition have been noted. Szmukler et al. (1992) noted significant deficits on the Block Design and Austin maze tasks, and a similar observation has been made by Witt and her colleagues (1985). These investigators noted that their subjects featured impaired design copying as a consequence of compromise in organisation and planning of their reproductions.

Within the context of the research in the area of anorexia nervosa little research seems to have as yet taken place into the neurocognitive basis of the marked distortions in body image which characterise the disorder. The findings regarding the level of this problem seem to indicate that the identification of the correct size and shape of the body is profoundly disturbed in these subjects (Cooper &

Fairburn, 1992; Huron & Brown, 1986; Waller & Hogson, 1996) and it would appear that these deficits are probably independent of the distortion of other visuospatial and visuo-perceptive functions (Smeets & Panhuysen, 1995). Clearly psychological factors are not irrelevant here, but specific investigation of this fascinating 'autosomagnosia' would be most illuminating.

Learning and memory

In their study Witt and colleagues (1985) noted that their subjects did not feature deficits in the area of tests of attention, speed or cognitive efficiency, but did feature deficits in the area of verbal learning and memory. A similar finding has been made by Beatty et al. (1990) in their study of 32 patients with bulimia nervosa and patients with major depression. Both groups were impaired in learning and recalling a list of unrelated words and in generating the names of famous people, and both groups showed elevated scores on the Beck Depression Inventory and the State Trait Anxiety Inventory. The former finding was opposite to that made by Szmukler et al. (1992) who observed no deficit on tests of learning or recall.

Deficits in memory would certainly not be unexpected in this group who are prone to the effects of the avitaminosis which characterises the WKS. It would appear likely that such deficits would occur in populations of subjects with anorexia nervosa, particularly those in the most emaciated state.

Adaptive behaviour

Bowers (1994) in a comparison of anorexia nervosa and bulimia noted that a significantly greater number of the anorexia nervosa subjects had deficits on neuropsychological testing, as compared to bulimic subjects (62.5% versus 30%). However, neuropsychological testing showed that some subjects in the bulimic group were also impaired. Bulimic, but not depressed, subjects made more rule violations than controls on a design-fluency task. The authors further contend that bulimia, but not depression, may be characterised by a previously unrecognised cognitive impairment: the tendency to violate task rules (Beatty et al., 1990).

Deficits in executive functions would be likely to be observed with the subjects due to their compromise in a variety of aspects of cognition.

Hemispheric contribution to the affective disorders

In their comprehensive review of the evidence for the CNS and cortical aetiology of anorexia nervosa and its restrictive and bulimic eating behaviour subtypes,

Braun and Chouinard (1992) note that there is evidence for the suggestion of an aetiological role of a right hemispheric disturbance in the syndrome. This hypothesis is supported by Casper and Heller (1991) who observed that at a lower body weight and more pronounced anorexic symptomatology were associated with increased left hemispheric activation. Weight gain, greater awareness of negative affect, and overestimation of body part size were correlated with an increase in right hemispheric activation. The findings also supported a correlation between the degree of weight loss and the rightward attentional bias. Braun and Chouinard's review (1992) should be consulted for a more detailed analysis of this fascinating hypothesis.

* * *

The case report we will examine in this discussion of the disorders of eating and sleeping is that of a young woman of 20 years who has had a several year history of anorexia nervosa which has been largely untreatable.

CASE REPORT

At the time of the assessment, MD was a 20-year-old woman living at home with her parents and had recently deferred from her first year of study in a Bachelor of Arts degree at university.

Background

MD had had a two-and-a-half year history of anorexia nervosa, with the onset of the condition in her senior year in high school. She became preoccupied with her weight and fearful of failure during the time of her final examinations. Around that time, MD commenced food restriction and laxative abuse (6–7 Coloxyl per day). Her weight dropped from 45 to 35 kg, and at that stage she was admitted to a private psychiatric hospital in a large regional centre. The admission coincided with the onset of her amenorrhoea.

MD had four subsequent hospital admissions, the second again precipitated by examination stress during the first year of her BA. Each of the subsequent admissions was characterised by an exacerbation of the disorder with a progressively decreasing body weight with each admission. On the admission in which I saw her, her body weight was 27.5 kg.

Psychiatric examination revealed schizoid and obsessional personality traits, and a poor ability to cope with stress. The Beck Depression Inventory indicated a score of 32 consistent with the notion of moderately severe depression. The CT indicated prominence of the ventricles, out of keeping with the age of the patient, and the physical examination revealed signs of severe emaciation including muscle wasting.

During the assessment MD appeared flattened in her affect, but warmed and became animated as the assessment progressed. Once the formal assessment had begun, she appeared to enjoy the intellectual challenge and proved eager to do well. By way of recent patterns of cognitive functioning MD noted that recently her concentration had become somewhat worse and she could not read (previously her greatest pleasure) for more than a few minutes at a time.

Formal Assessment

Formal testing revealed that MD had a Full Scale IQ of 111, a Verbal IQ of 125 and a Performance IQ of 90. On the basis of the performance of well learned information MD premorbidly was probably performing in the high average to superior range on such an intelligence test, her scaled scores of 14 and 15 indicating that she has shown considerable deterioration in her ability to be able to flexibly use the information that she has available to her. MD performed considerably below expectation on a number of the WAIS-R subtests. These included the repetition of digit spans, the solving of problems in arithmetic, the construction of block designs, the construction of jigsaw type puzzles and in her ability to be able to recode digits into symbols on the Digit Symbol substitution test. This pattern of performance overall indicates attenuation of speed of information processing, and poor visuospatial problem solving skills as determined by her performances on the Block Design and Object Assembly tasks. The notion of a decrease in the speed of information processing was also supported by her slower level of responding noted on the Paced Auditory Serial Addition Test and on the Trail Making Test.

Tests of memory indicated that MD was well oriented for time, place and person and had good control over counting backwards from 20, saying the alphabet and the serial addition of threes. MD had a digit span of 7 digits forwards and 4 digits backwards which is a relatively poor performance for someone with a premorbid IQ in the high average to superior range.

On the prose passages of information MD could only recall 10 and 6 items from each passage respectively. This is a very poor performance for a young woman of MD's level of premorbid function. A similar observation could be made about her new learning in both the audio-verbal and visuospatial domains. She did, however, manage to learn material after a series of presentations, as reflected by her relatively well preserved performance on the Rey Auditory Verbal Learning Test and her maintenance of material on the recall index of the WMS-R.

Tests of the frontal executive functions indicated that MD could not demonstrate improvement on the complex learning test of the Austin maze which requires the subject to negotiate a 10×10 button maze over a series of trials. During the test MD became frustrated and lost her concentration. Frequently, she would increase her rate of key pressing in an attempt to rapidly reach the end resulting in more errors. The performance was characterised by impulsivity, poor error utilisation and failure to plan.

VERBAL TESTS (Scaled Scores)

Information	14
Digit Span	10
Vocabulary	15
Arithmetic	11
Comprehension	15
Similarities	15
VIQ	125

PERFORMANCE TESTS

Picture Completion	12
Picture Arrangement	10
Block Design	6
Object Assembly	10
Digit Symbol	8
PIQ	90
FSIQ	111

WECHSLER MEMORY SCALE-REVISED

Verbal Memory Index	79
Visual Memory Index	103
General Memory Index	84
Attention/Concentration	85
Delayed Recall	91

AUSTIN MAZE TEST

Trial	1	2	3	4	5	6	7	8	9
Number of Errors	16	8	4	10	8	8	3	4	14

Trial	10	11	12	13	14	15	
Number of Errors	6	4	9	4	12	4	ABANDONED

TRAIL MAKING TEST

	Time	Centile
Part A	34 secs	50th
Part B	90 secs	25th

PACED AUDITORY SERIAL ADDITION TESTS

Speed (secs)	% correct	Norms (% correct)
2.4	47	82
2.0	30	73
1.6	25	66
1.2	22	51

Conclusion

MD is a 20-year-old woman with an extensive past history of hospitalisation for the management of anorexia nervosa. She clearly suffers from a number of neuropsychological deficits in the present including marked slowing of her speed of information processing, as illustrated by her poor performance on the Trail Making Test, the Digit Symbol Substitution Test and the Paced Auditory Serial Addition Test. She also features a problem with complex problem solving in the visuospatial sphere, as assessed by the Block Design and Austin Maze Tests, and a moderate level of compromise on measures of memory. These deficits are consistent with the notion of a compromise in the ability to attend to and concentrate on newly incoming information, in association with a mild level of compromise in executive skill. Unfortunately, it was not possible to reassess MD after refeeding which may well have indicated improvement on a number of these indices.

SUMMARY

The disorders of eating and sleeping provide useful insights into the effects of disruption of the neurovegetative functions on cognition. However, it is not possible to contend that these conditions are specific in their effects. Nonetheless, there are a considerable number of commonalities in their neuropsychological sequelae. The first neuropsychological sign of each of these conditions seems to be the disruption of attention and mental tracking. These deficits are found consistently with each of the conditions surveyed in this chapter. As the level of hypoxemia, sleep deprivation or failure to maintain balanced nutrition increases in severity, more deficits seem to emerge in the areas of executive functions, visuospatial functions and memory disorder. These deficits seem responsive to restoration as reflected by refeeding in the eating disorders or the use of CPAP in the case of the sleep apnoea syndrome.

CHAPTER 7

PHYSICAL TREATMENTS OF THE PSYCHIATRIC DISORDERS

Before the advent of modern pharmacotherapy in the mid to latter half of the 20th century, the principal modality of intervention in the psychiatric disorders was with physical treatment. This includes the litany of barbaric techniques that dot the history of the mistreatment of the mentally ill including isolation, physical restraint, immobilisation, dieting and starvation, heating, chilling, burning, bleeding, abdominal and cranial surgery, beating, water immersion, and the administration of various purgatives, emetics, opioids, sedatives and stimulants (Gregory & Smeltzer, 1977). The outcome of these treatments was invariably poor and the barbarity of the approaches occasionally lead to public outcry. Nonetheless the commitment to the notion that the mental disorders were indeed physical diseases persisted and as a consequence attempts at new therapeutic approaches persisted.

The twenties and thirties were replete with a number of these new approaches including Julius Wagner von Jauregg's transfusion of the blood of patients suffering with malaria into patients with general paresis (tertiary syphilis) for which he ultimately earned the Nobel prize in 1927, Jacob Klaesi's prolonged sleep therapy, Manfred Sakel's insulin coma treatment, Laszlo von Meduna's pharmacological convulsive therapy and Egas Moniz's prefrontal lobotomy. The issues to be addressed within this chapter will be the surviving two physical treatments: psychosurgery and electoconvulsive therapy (ECT).

PSYCHOSURGERY

The notion of modification of the personality by modifying the structure of the brain is by no means a new one (Valenstein, 1986). The discovery of skulls dating back to prehistory which have been trepanned (i.e. had holes cut into them to release evil spirits) clearly indicates that the attempt to tamper with the cerebral substance has a long history. The modern (if modern is the right term to use) resurgence of psychosurgery begins with the observations of Fulton and Jacobsen (1935) that destruction of the frontal lobes of primates resulted in increased placidity in these beasts. Moniz (1936, 1994) having heard of these results decided that such an approach would work well with humans, and his report of three cases in which he attempted to sever the connections between the prefrontal areas and the remainder of the brain by sectioning the subcortical white matter lead to a wildfire of application and approbation for the technique which culminated in Moniz receiving the Nobel prize in 1949. To Moniz the rationale for the application of the technique was the attempt to produce the same level of placidity in the agitated and disturbed patient suffering from schizophrenia as had been observed in the earlier experimentation with primates. Moniz's first three patients had a variety of presentations including paraphrenia (late onset psychosis) and depression, schizophrenia and dementia praecox, in which the gains noted after surgery were maintained at follow-up. Interestingly, Moniz eventually was shot by one of his patients resulting in paraplegia (Pinel, 1997).

Freeman and Watts (1947) developed a standard leucotomy technique. In the original operation, large sections of white matter were destroyed with the icepike-like leucotome which was repeatedly inserted through either a burr hole, although subsequently the leucotome was applied through the eye socket.

Freeman is perhaps one of the most curious characters that has ever strode the stage of brain behaviour relationships. Whilst in the initial phases it would appear his approach was both circumspect and appropriate, as time went by his approach to psychosurgery and the indications for its application became increasingly cavalier. Freeman ended up driving from town to town throughout the US in a vehicle he affectionately called his 'lobotomobile' (Kalat, 1998) plying his treatment with messianic zeal. Eventually he decided that he would dispense with the notion of anaesthesia and he would do his inductions with the use of ECT as anaesthesia. His criteria for application of the technique also became more flexible. Whilst initially the treatment was considered only in cases of severe untreatable schizophrenia, as time went by it was used for a variety of other major and minor complaints many of which would be considered normal by today's standards (Kalat, 1998). Through its reign the lobotomy was administered to no less than 40,000 individuals in the US (Shutts, 1982), with possibly an equivalent number throughout the rest of the world.

Among the common sequelae of lobotomy were an increase in apathy, a loss of planning and foresight, as well as a lack of initiative, and in association with these changes were distractability, blunting of the emotions and loss of facial expression (Stuss & Benson, 1984). Obviously the clinician who was seeking remission of an agitated schizophrenia gratefully welcomed the more sedate, composed, less tortured patient following the surgery. However, producing adynamia in a subject is not equivalent to producing amelioration, much less a cure of his or her symptoms, much less a cure of the disorder. Unfortunately, the logical inconsistency of this approach took a number of years to emerge. As the procedure is no longer in use it seems futile to further discuss the effects of the sequelae. There are several excellent reviews on this matter in the literature including Stuss' work on 16 patients with schizophrenia assessed more than 25 years after their initial surgery on attention (Stuss et al., 1981), language (Stuss et al., 1986), memory (Stuss et al., 1982), motor function (Benson & Stuss, 1982) and general cognitive abilities (Stuss et al., 1983). In the final analysis, lobotomy or leucotomy produces a disruption of the major connections or substance of the frontal lobe resulting in a marked frontal lobe syndrome, which is characterised by diminution of drive and activity leading to a marked adynamic syndrome in most patients but occasionally leading to a markedly disinhibited syndrome in some others.

Whilst the brutish procedure of the lobotomy and leucotomy have gone the way of the dinosaurs, the notion of interruption of the circuitry of the brain by surgical means itself has progressed. We are presently in a new wave of surgical intervention in the area of Parkinson's disease with the resurgence in the use of the pallidotomy procedure, particularly for the treatment of the dyskinesias associated with this disorder.

The procedures currently employed as psychosurgical interventions include cingulotomy, subcaudate tractotomy, limbic leucotomy and capsulotomy. The indication for surgical intervention have now been considerably refined and the principal focus of approach to the disorder surrounds the symptom of tortured self-concern. This pattern of behaviour can arise as a consequence of a number of psychiatric conditions including obsessive–compulsive disorder (OCD), the other anxiety disorders and depression. The role for the treatment in schizophrenia is now virtually non-existent.

In a long-term follow up of 33 patients given cingulotomy for refractive OCD, Jenike and colleagues (1991) noted that 48% of their sample indicated improvement following cingulotomy after having unsuccessfully attempted one or two other proven treatments for the disorder. They further noted that other treatments such as pharmacotherapy and behavioural intervention are more likely to be successful after the application of the cingulotomy than they would of been before the surgery.

Neuropsychological Features

The neuropsychological effects of the stereotactic procedures used to treat tortured self-concern have yielded little data. This is probably as a consequence of the fact that psychosurgery remains a treatment of last resort and the community response to the proposal of psychosurgery causes a marked negative reaction. The changes associated with psychosurgery largely centre on the functions of the executive and of attention.

Cumming, Hay, Lee and Sachdev (1995) noted that in their 17 patients with OCD subjected to cingulotomy, the patients showed no impairment of intelligence or memory functions in comparison to age and severity matched OCD controls who had not received surgery. The subjects themselves did not indicate deterioration of their performance from before as compared to after the operation. The investigators did note, however, that the subjects did show deficits in the area of idea generation and in shifting of response sets.

In a fascinating study looking at PET changes as a consequence of cingulotomy, Janer and Pardo (1991) looked at the selective attention processes of 10 normal subjects with a view to developing tasks which activated the cingulate in these subjects. Having established the parameters of interest they applied the task to a woman with OCD in order to determine the specificity of the effect of bilateral cingulotomy. The OCD subject proved to have an impaired performance on attentional tasks in the subacute postoperative period which resolved spontaneously several months after surgery. Another study by Cohen, Kaplan, Meadows and Wilkinson (1994) studied habituation responses in cingulotomised subjects. The cingulotomy subjects indicated slower rates of habituation and greater variability across trials. They attributed this change to subtle changes in attentional functions in these subjects.

Summary

The data on the stereotactic procedures for the treatment of OCD seem to indicate that there is a subtle but nonetheless pervasive effect of the lesions. This is only to be expected, as the rationale for the procedure is to attempt to interrupt ruminative patterns of mentation which repeat continually.

ELECTROCONVULSIVE THERAPY (ECT)

Several investigators became interested in the induction of epileptic seizures in the 1930s. Manfred Sakel, a psychiatrist in Vienna, began treatment using insulin injections as a means of reducing the withdrawal reactions associated with morphine addiction. In one patient he noted that the induction of low blood sugar caused a coma, subsequent to which the patient was noted to be less confused. He continued his experimentation with the technique and later maintained that it could significantly reduce psychotic symptoms. Problems emerged with the treatment due to the long duration of the inductions (4–5 hours per treatment over a period of several months), and that the patients were subjected to considerable weight gain due to the disruption of the blood sugar levels.

Von Medusa's clinical experience led him to the spurious conclusion that there was an antagonism between epilepsy and schizophrenia, as a consequence of which he concluded that induction of seizures in patients with schizophrenia would result in amelioration of the deficits. He used metrazol (a variant of the agent camphor, which had been known to induce seizures for many years before) as his principal means of induction.

Cerletti and Bini (1938) are credited with the introduction of electroconvulsive therapy (ECT). Bini was very interested in epilepsy and was seeking a means of inducing artificial seizures. He attended a local slaughterhouse and observed that the pigs before they were slaughtered were stunned by a shock to the head. He found that he could reproduce this effect in man and he attempted the treatment on the first schizophrenic patient in Rome in 1938.

The electrical means of induction due to its speed, accuracy and lesser level of untoward side effects quickly became the preferred method and has remained essentially the same up to the present. Bilateral ECT employs electrode placement, usually in the frontotemporal position, and unilateral ECT applies the electrode only to the non-dominant hemisphere. The current is applied for a fraction of a second until a generalised seizure (i.e. a tonic/clonic seizure) is observed. A period of electrical silence in the patient's brain follows, and slowly the pattern returns to generalised theta and delta activity (i.e. slow wave activity signalling low levels of neural activation) which becomes more persistent as successive treatments are given. After 3–4 treatments spaced at a 2–3 day intervals are given, the abnormal rhythm may persist in between the treatments, and it often has a preponderance in the frontal region. As the course progresses the disturbance becomes more widespread and of higher voltage, and α-activity (high-level electrical activity) may disappear altogether. Individual patients differ in the severity of these effects and in the time taken to return to normality. Shagass (1965) has reported that most patients return to a normal pattern 1 to 3 months after the termination of a standard course of treatments. Patients are usually given a pretreatment of atropine, and an anaesthetic of a short acting barbiturate, oxygenation during the procedure and a depolarising muscle relaxant.

The current place of ECT in the clinical armamentarium has been reviewed a number of times over the last 10 years due to the resurgence in its application. The indications for ECT were formalised in the US National Institute of Health Consensus Development Conference in 1986 which stated that: 'ECT is demonstrably effective for a narrow range of severe psychiatric disorders in a limited number of diagnostic categories: delusional and severe endogenous depression and manic and certain schizophrenic syndromes.'

ECT has also been subjected to an interesting form of reverse discrimination with the treatment being reserved as one of 'last resort'. This approach implies that the patient could not be treated with ECT until he or she had been subjected to repeated attempts at drug therapy. The 1990 American Psychiatric Association Task force have reflected a change in this attitude with a series of guidelines which provides for initial treatment with ECT in those cases where there is a need for a rapid, definitive response on medical (inanition, i.e. failure to eat), psychiatric (uncontrolled excitement; severe drive to suicide), or where a poor response to drug or a good response to ECT or patient preference occurs (Weiner et al., 1990). The treatment may also be considered in those cases of major depression with delusions or conditions with prominent catatonic features (Zervas & Fink, 1991).

It is interesting that the pattern of ECT use has varied over the years more as a consequence of its public perception than as a consequence of its efficacy. Use of the treatment increased by 16% from 1980 to 1986 (Prudic & Sackheim, 1996). One of the more fascinating issues to arise from treatment rates with ECT is to whom it is administered. Whilst the treatment has a reputation in line with *One Flew Over the Cuckoos Nest* as being a treatment of repression of the lower classes by the upper ones, in 1980 no nonwhite patient received ECT in a state run facility in the US (Prudic & Sackheim, 1996). In 1986 in the US, ECT was used primarily in private settings and 91% of the patients who received it were white. As Prudic and Sackheim conclude: 'In contrast to depictions of ECT as a method of behavioral control inflicted on the indigent, evidence indicates that ECT in the USA is most readily available to the affluent' (1996, p. 35). The same state of affairs also applies in the Australian context.

ECT continues to be one of the last lines of action in the treatment of the affective disorders. It has often been suggested that psychotic depressive patients respond better to ECT than to any of the more usual medication-based approaches. On average however, psychotically depressed individuals are more severely depressed than individuals without psychotic features, thus differences in treatment outcome may well come as a consequence of differing initial severity. Kocsis and his colleagues (1990) has reported that of his 38 severely depressed non-psychotic patients, the response to treatment was as poor as that observed in his 19 psychotically depressed individuals treated with tri-cyclic antidepressants (TCAs) (i.e. 39% and 31% respectively). On this basis he suggested that poor response to the TCAs may be a characteristic of severe depression irrespective of the presence of psychotic features. In deluded depressed patients the response rate was much higher (83%) than the comparably ill non-psychotic depressives (58%) (Pande & Gruhaus, 1990). It seems then that, in general, ECT may prove a more effective treatment than the SSRIs or the TCAs in psychotic depressive illness, at least in the short term.

The biological basis of ECT

Despite considerable speculation and armchair philosophy on the mechanism of ECT's action, the basis of its efficacy remains a mystery. The changes in brain functioning associated with ECT evolve over time, in line with the common clinical practice of administration of the treatment two to three times weekly. The effect of a course of ECT seems to be cumulative which has resulted in speculation regarding the duration of the time in seizure as a means of determining efficacy. Maletsky (1978) suggests that no response will be noted if the total seizure time from a course of ECT is less than 201 seconds, and that most individuals usually respond after 1,000 seconds.

At least six hypotheses have been put forward as the proposed mechanism of ECT's efficacy. These include:

1. Kindling: Kindling is used to describe the increases in excitability reflected in brain tissue following repetitive, fixed intensity, electrical stimulation of the brain which in its initial application would appear to have no effect (Goddard, 1967).
2. ECT can act as an anticonvulsant by increasing seizure threshold (Sackheim, Decina, Portnoy, Neeley & Malitz, 1987), thus extinguishing possible sub-ictal discharges associated with depression.

3.   Sensitisation has also been proposed as a mechanism in that a prior seizure results in increased responsivity to seizure activation (Antelman & Chiodo, 1984).

4.   Diencephalic stimulation has also been viewed as the basis for the effect (Abrams, 1986).

5.   A hemispheric dysfunction hypothesis based on the observations of Flor-Henry (1986), who contended that affective disorders are due to right hemisphere dysfunction. ECT may well stabilise this deficit.

6.   A variant of the hemispheric hypothesis proposed by Abrams, Taylor and Volavka (1987), who contend that a positive therapeutic response in depressed patients receiving bilateral ECT was related to asymmetrical EEG slowing on the left side but not on the right.

On balance the latter two hypotheses have been the ones which have received most support in the literature, with transient EEG slowing on the left side closely associated with a positive ECT response. It has been contended, therefore, that ECT acts to restore the electrical disequilibrium between the two hemispheres by enhancing the activity of the right hemisphere and dampening the activity of the left (Small et al., 1988).

ECT also has numerous effects on neurochemical and neuroendocrine functioning including a direct effect on adrenocorticotrophic hormone, cortisol, prolactin, and thyroid stimulating hormone levels (Aperia, 1985), and a diminution of the inhibitory neurotransmitter GABA one hour after ECT (Prudic & Sackheim, 1996).

Whilst some interesting data regarding ECT has been gathered, we remain a long way from a clear view of how ECT works and even of what parameters we should be measuring in investigating this issue.

NEUROPATHOLOGY AND STRUCTURAL AND FUNCTIONAL IMAGING DATA

The evidence from the numerous neuropathological and imaging studies with ECT both in animals and humans has recently been reviewed by both Devenand et al. (1994) and Coffey (1994). This literature supports the notion that no structural changes occur as a consequence of the current techniques of ECT administration as assessed by CT, MRI or post-mortem examination. Similarly animals exposed to equivalent levels of current as employed in ECT do not result in detectable cell loss in blind comparison regimes. Cell loss does occur in animal studies, but not until seizure durations of approximately 30 minutes which do not occur in standard ECT administration.

Transitory changes in the level of signal relaxation times for MRI have also been noted following ECT and the idea that there may be an increase in brain water content subsequent to ECT (due to its effect in disrupting the action of the blood brain barrier) has been proposed. This effect may be the cause of the observed anterograde memory deficit invariably noted with the treatment (Diehl et al., 1994). PET studies have also been employed with the treatment and it would appear that changes in uptake of tracer after the treatment occur principally in the inferior anterior cingulate cortex (Scott et al., 1994).

NEUROPSYCHOLOGICAL FEATURES

The literature on ECT indicates that there are transient neuropsychological deficits which occur during the first 30 minutes or so following each ECT. These changes include dysphasia (Clyma, 1975) and Pratt and Warrington (1972) have developed a protocol of hemispheric dominance testing based on a unilateral regime of ECT administration. Tactile and visual inattention (Kriss, Blumhardt, Halliday & Pratt, 1978) and constructional dyspraxia are also commonly observed after unilateral non-dominant ECT.

The longer term data regarding ECT administration to non-memory functions indicate that little if any ongoing disability occurs as a consequence of ECT administration, and indeed due to the amelioration of the depression many are noted to improve. As regards the time course of this improvement, Calev et al. (1995) have noted that non-memory effects of ECT usually progressively improve following the administration. At one week to seven months after the treatment, performance is better than before the treatment. They note that the time course of these changes parallels that observed with the memory-related effects. This pattern of changes has been noted on the WAIS (Small, Small & Milstein, 1986), and the Halstead Reitan Battery (HRB; Malloy, 1982), although Taylor and Abrams (1985) noted that no substantive change was noted on the HRB or the Luria Nebraska Battery before therapy as compared to shortly after the sixth seizure. This may be due to the lagging effects of the treatment and also to the fact that by the sixth treatment an appropriate antidepressive effect of the treatment may not of been obtained.

The issue of whether there might be deficits in non-memory cognitive functioning following a large life time dose was addressed by Devanand, Verma, Tirumalasetti and Sackheim (1991) who noted that of eight patients who received more than 100 bilateral treatments each, there were no measurable cognitive impairments in comparison to controls at follow-up.

Language and spatial cognition

As noted above, brief aphasic symptoms are associated with the immediately postictal period but there does not appear to be any long-term language related effect associated with the treatment.

A number of the older studies have noted that 'right hemisphere' functions were compromised before ECT and that this deficit has improved to normal levels after treatment. The tests employed included Benton's Judgement of Line Orientation and Facial Recognition Tests (Kronfol, Hamsher, Digre & Waziri, 1978) and the HRB (Goldstein, Filskov, Weaver & Ives, 1977). More recently assessment of dichotic listening performance indicated normalisation of impaired performance after ECT (Williams, Iacono, Remick & Greenwood, 1990).

Learning and memory

Both unilateral and bilateral ECT cause anterograde amnesia. Squire (1977) notes that bilateral ECT produced greater anterograde memory loss than did right unilateral ECT. Reactivating the memories before the application of ECT did not result in substantial amnesia for the material. Squire notes that recovery of new learning capacity was substantially complete by several months after ECT, and memory complaints were more common in individuals who received bilateral ECT. The degree of anterograde amnesia depends upon the distance of the ECT from the new learning. Squire, Chance and Slater (1976) note that recognition memory for material learned three hours after bilateral ECT was significantly better than for material learned one hour or less after ECT. Calev et al. (1991) note that memory for verbal, visuospatial and retrograde material was impaired at the end of a course of ECT, and the performance had improved to pre-ECT levels by one month after the course and exceeded these levels by six months after the course.

With regard to retrograde memory impairment effects it has been reported that ECT can cause retrograde amnesia for events that occurred close to the time of treatment. This effect seems to become more pronounced with an increasing number and frequency of ECT, particularly bilateral applications. The retrograde memory disruption occurs for both public and personal events, including those temporally close to the treatment as well as those for years (i.e. up to 20 years) before treatment. The traditional explanation for this retrograde deficit was that the ECT had somehow disrupted consolidation of this material, however the long periods of retrograde disruption seem more consistent with the notion of interference with retrieval of previously learned material.

One of the better studies of the retrograde memory disruption effect is that of Squire who asked his patients to recognise the names of TV programs broadcast for a single season from 1957 to 1972. The bilateral ECT patients could not remember programs broadcast one to three years before ECT (as compared to pre-ECT measures), whilst programs broadcast from 4–17 years before the treatment were remembered as well as previously. Interestingly, after five bilateral ECT treatments the patients developed marked impairment of their ability to make temporal judgements about the material.

Improvement in mood has been established to be independent of the effects of performance on formal tests of memory functioning, although a subjective perception of memory performance was correlated (Zervas & Jandorf, 1993).

HEMISPHERIC CONTRIBUTIONS TO THE EFFECT OF ECT

The notion of a hemispheric contribution to the action and efficacy of ECT has been addressed above. Nonetheless, viable hypotheses to the effect that the efficacy of the treatment may be hemispheric still exist in the tradition of the work of Flor-Henry. Clearly the ability of ECT to stabilise the intrinsic electrical patterns of the respective hemispheres following a course of ECT, in association with the noted improvement on tests of spatial cognition, support the notion of a hemispheric pattern of response.

SUMMARY

A number of generalisations about this curious treatment can be made (Squire, 1977). These include the following:

1.   ECT causes both anterograde and retrograde memory deficits;
2.   bilateral ECT causes greater anterograde amnesia that does unilateral ECT;
3.   anterograde amnesia severity depends on the temporal distance from ECT of the new learning;
4.   bilateral ECT causes greater retrograde amnesia than unilateral dominant or non-dominant ECT for both verbal and non-verbal material;
5.   the retrograde amnesia is characterised by a temporal gradient and recall of when events occurred in time is more sensitive to impairment than are other aspects of recall;

6. ECT does not normally cause enduring memory deficits beyond one to three months after the procedure;

7. ECT causes immediate post-treatment confusion which may accumulate over a course of treatment (this confusion appears to be less profound with unilateral as compared to bilateral ECT);

8. ECT would not appear to cause lasting impairment to non-memory functions; and

9. transient deficits in non-memory functions can occur but these resolve completely within two to eight weeks.

* * *

This chapter's case report is that of an individual who maintains that as a consequence of her treatment with ECT she has been left with a memory deficit for the entire period of her life before the procedure. Due to the marked community ambivalence to ECT, it has become a notable target for individuals who have become disgruntled as a consequence of their treatment at the hands of the mental health professionals. ECT becomes a repository of the anger and frustration felt by these folk and, in association with the perceived community disquiet, presents an appropriate vehicle for the venting of this anger.

CASE REPORT

CC was referred to me by her psychiatrist as a consequence of complaints that a past series of ECT had resulted in brain impairment as well as the emergence of epileptic seizures. CC was an unusual sort of woman and indicated when I first saw her that she had had a lot of shock treatments, and noted that ever since the shock treatments her head had been pounding. She noted that when she was really stressed this problem was even worse, and noted that the pounding was there all the time. She also indicated that she had developed epilepsy from the shock treatments. She believed that the ECT had slowed down her life in every way. She notes that her movements were slower, her eating was slower and she couldn't do things as fast as she used to. She had an electro-encephalograph two weeks previous and, according to the report of the neurologist, the record was within normal limits and demonstrated no focal or diagnostic paroxysmal activity.

Background

The last ECT that CC had undertaken was 10 years before I had seen her and had been administered as a result of a breakdown. She could not think of the name of her psychiatrist at that time. She indicated that she was gathering medical evidence for a possible medico-legal disputation regarding the long-term effects on her of the ECT.

CC had completed third form at high school (Year 9) and following this had worked in a supermarket, which she did for five years. She briefly worked for a shoe factory for about six months and then she went to work again for the supermarket for the following nine years. After nearly 14 years of service, CC walked out of the supermarket one lunchtime and noted that she 'sat in the sun for six months at home with her mother'.

Over the following few months, she noted that everyone was very worried and concerned about her and two days after her birthday she noted that she had 'never lived up until then', and from that time on all she did 'was cry and be upset'. She noted that at about this time she met someone who 'started opening her up' in the form of a counselling psychologist. She has had no return to work since. She had a breakdown and noted that her psychologist then became her 'adopted father'. She went to a Christian psychiatrist who admitted her to a 'Christian Psychiatric Hospital' which was the 'beginning of her problems', according to her report.

Three years later she attempted suicide. She indicated she 'met God and became a Christian that night' and following this she noted that she was very physically tired. She was then admitted to a psychiatric hospital for three weeks. She indicated that she felt as if she had gone to hell and was petrified by the staff and patients of the hospital.

Formal Assessment

I conducted a number of tests with CC in order to determine her present level of functioning. I completed the Wechsler Adult Intelligent Scale Revised which indicated that she had a Verbal Intelligence Quotient of 89, a Performance Intelligence Quotient of 79, and a Full Scale Intelligence Quotient of 84. This places her intelligence in the low average range. She performed reasonably consistently across the tests of the scale and her best performances were on the Information and Vocabulary subtests. Her weakest performance was on the identification of anomalies in line drawn pictures.

Tests of memory function revealed that she had a Verbal Memory Index of 93, a Visual Memory Index of 103, a General Memory Index of 95 and a Delayed Recall Index of 103. This pattern of performances clearly indicates that CC does not have anything by way of residual memory disorder as a consequence of the ECT and at this point in time she seems to be performing at a superior level in comparison to her overall intellectual functions on memory testing.

Tests of the frontal executive functions revealed that she was capable of performing the Trail Making Test parts a) and b) at about the 25th percentile for the population, at about the expected levels for her intellectual function and the performance on the Controlled Oral Word Association Test indicated she was at the low normal level.

VERBAL TESTS (Scaled Scores)		
Information		9
Digit Span		6
Vocabulary		10
Arithmetic		7
Comprehension		8
Similarities		6
VIQ		89
PERFORMANCE TESTS		
Picture Completion		4
Picture Arrangement		5
Block Design		6
Object Assembly		5
Digit Symbol		5
PIQ		79
FSIQ		84
WECHSLER MEMORY SCALE-REVISED		
Verbal Memory Index		93
Visual Memory Index		103
General Memory Index		95
Delayed Recall		103
Trail Making Test	*Time*	*Centile*
Part A	55 secs	10–25th
Part B	98 secs	25th
COWAT		
31	No errors	Low normal

Conclusion

The pattern of performances that CC indicates on this occasion shows no residual deficits as a consequence of the ECT and the fact that her memory functions are much better than estimates of her level of premorbid intellectual activity attest to this conclusion. The pattern overall reveals a woman with a poorly controlled pattern of mentation. She strings her history together in a haphazard way but does not feature anything consistent with the notion of any residual brain impairment, even from the perspective of cognitive compromise as a consequence of her psychiatric diagnosis.

SUMMARY

The physical treatments of the psychiatric disorders represent a fascinating and sometimes arcane view of where psychiatry has come from. The two surviving treatments, ECT and psychosurgery, yield a number of discernible neuropsychological effects. The effect of ECT seems to be to produce a transient amnesic syndrome which resolves following a few weeks to months after the treatment. Psychosurgery, particularly the stereotactic approaches, seem to leave some sequelae in the form of subtle deficits in attention and executive functioning, but these would appear to be minor in comparison to the massive frontal lobe syndromes associated with the traditional lobotomy.

CHAPTER 8

PHARMACOLOGICAL TREATMENT OF THE PSYCHIATRIC DISORDERS

The approach of investigators who have attempted to unravel the mystery of the neurochemical basis of the psychiatric disorders has focused on two principal research strategies: (1) the quest for abnormal biochemical products or pathways specific to a particular disorder, and (2) investigation into the common modes of action of agents which ameliorate or exacerbate the disorder. The often serendipitous finding that particular pharmacological agents influence particular psychiatric disease states has been the most productive approach to the formation of models of the biological basis of these disorders. Clearly, the dopamine hypothesis of schizophrenia and the monoamine theory of depression stand as salutary cases in point.

Perhaps one of the most fantastic stories to arise out of the early work in the exploration of the pharmacological study of mind altering drugs was the observations of Dr John Cade in his discovery of the action of lithium. During his time as a prisoner of war, Cade had thought at great length about the possibility of biological agents causing psychiatric disorders. His first approach to these problems was the attempt to identify toxic substances in the urine of patients suffering from the psychiatric disorders. He injected the urine of patients with mania and schizophrenia into the abdominal cavities of guinea pigs, and found that the urine of the manic patients killed his subjects far more readily than did that of the non-manic subjects (Copolov, 1995).

Cade later found that he was able to replicate the effects of the urine using urea, a constituent of urine. The next step in the saga began when Cade attempted to investigate the effect of uric acid, a breakdown product of the digestion of DNA molecules. Uric acid is relatively insoluble (in fact crystals of uric acid forming in the joints is the cause of the painful effects of gout), so Cade attempted to produce a salt of uric acid with a view to injecting it into his subjects. The salt that Cade chose was lithium urate. Unexpectedly, Cade found that the salt had a calming effect on the otherwise excitable guinea pigs. Cade quickly determined that the tranquillising effects were due to the lithium, and after attempting a regime of safe dosage using himself as subject he attempted treatment of 10 manic patients with the drug. His study (Cade, 1949) indicated that the agent had an appreciable calming effect on patients with manic excitement, opening the door way to perhaps the most effective treatment for bipolar disorder (Copolov, 1995).

Unfortunately due to a combination of circumstances, Cade's finding was virtually ignored for the ensuing 15 years. It was only in the mid 1960s that clinical trails were re-initiated, and finally in 1970 lithium was approved for use in the US as an anti-manic agent.

This chapter will survey the various effective drug treatment regimes that are currently applied in the psychiatric disorders and will then attempt to analyse their unwanted effects on various aspects of cognitive functioning.

TREATMENT FOR SCHIZOPHRENIA

During the latter course of the Second World War a number of chemists in France working at the Rhône-Poulenc laboratories became interested in the derivatives of phenothiazine, a compound which had been well known for some time. The original action of this agent was as an antihistamine and anti-emetic but these effects became less interesting after a crucial observation was made in 1952. The researchers used a compound synthesised some time earlier and labelled RP 4560 for the development of anaesthesia. Laborit (a surgeon) and his team noted that in a dose of 50–100 mg intravenously that there was an unusual sedative action of the drug without loss of consciousness or alteration in cognition.

The subsequent work of Delay and Deniker (1956) systematically studied the agent including naming it chlorpromazine, in 1952. These original observations opened the floodgates of the investigation into this group of drugs which became known as the major tranquillisers and later on as the antipsychotics or neuroleptics.

There are four main classes of antipsychotic agents: (1) the phenothiazenes (with a piperazine side chain, e.g. trifluoperazine; with piperidine side chain, e.g. chlorpromazine, thioridazine), (2) the butyrophenones (haloperidol, droperidol), (3) the thioxanthenes (e.g. flupenthixol), and (4) the new generation of atypical antipsychotic agents (including clozapine, sulpiride, remoxipride and respiridone). Most of these agents act by decreasing the level of dopamine at the synapse. Different types of drugs have different effects on the various dopamine receptors, and the traditional antipsychotic agents are considered to produce their action by decreasing the level of actuation by dopamine at the D_2 receptors in the mesolimbic and mesocortical pathways. (See Chapter 1 for a discussion of the neurotransmitter pathways.)

The atypical antipsychotic agents seem to be more effective at blocking D_1 and D_4 receptors, perhaps explaining their difference in action to the traditional antipsychotics (i.e. D_2 receptor blockers), and possibly accounting for their effects on the negative symptoms of schizophrenia (Smith & Darlington, 1996).

Due to the fact that the level of dopamine is effectively decreased with these agents, a major undesired effect is the production of extrapyramidal side effects in the form of movement disorder. This effects seems to be as a consequence of the action of these agents on the nigrostriatal pathway and indeed the effective reduction of dopaminergic neurotransmission in this pathway results in the development of Parkinsonism with the principal features of bucco-lingual masticatory movement, rigidity, tremor and motor restlessness (akithisia) in about 15% of patients treated with these agents. This result is most common with the butyrophenones and those agents with a piperazine side chains, and interestingly their ability to produce movement disorders is roughly proportional to their antipsychotic effect.

TREATMENT OF THE AFFECTIVE DISORDERS

There are three effective pharmacological treatments for unipolar depression: the serotonin-selective re-uptake inhibitors (SSRIs), the tri-cyclic antidepressants (TCAs), and the monoamine oxidase inhibitors (MAOIs). Nowadays the SSRIs are considered the drug of first choice. Generally speaking, one can classify all of the currently available antidepressant medications as either inhibitors of monoamine oxidase or as blockers of re-uptake of the biogenic amine neurotransmitters (Richelson, 1993).

The site of action of these drug agents seems to be at the synapse and involves either blocking the uptake (re-uptake) of neurotransmitters or inhibiting the mitochondrial enzyme monoamine oxidase which breaks the neurotransmitter down. Most antidepressants are more potent at blocking the uptake of noradrenaline than of serotonin, however selectivity cannot be equated with potency as it is the balance of the ratios of the effects of these agents on noradrenaline, serotonin and dopamine which contributes to their ultimate effectiveness.

The most potent effect of antidepressants, particularly the classical TCAs, is at the histamine H_1 receptor; followed by their action on the muscarinic acetyl choline receptors; followed by their effects on the α_1-adrenoreceptor; and then finally on the dopamine D_2 receptors (Richelson, 1993). The newer generation of agents, e.g. fluoxetine (Prozac), sertraline (Zoloft), and paroxetine (Paxil), are labelled the SSRIs due to their increased selectivity on the uptake of serotonin, but they continue to have an effect on the previously mentioned receptor types.

The first tricyclic, imipramine, was released in 1957; this group of drugs are called tricyclics as they have a three ringed structure. Developments of these drugs have produced heterocyclic and tetracyclic forms but an emphasis on function rather than chemical structure seems more appropriate for a discussion of this type. These drugs were found to inhibit the re-uptake of neurotransmitter by the terminal buttons of monoaminergic neurones. By retarding the re-uptake the drugs keep the neurotransmitter in contact with the post-synaptic receptor, thus prolonging the post-synaptic potential.

Iproniazid was the first MAOI to emerge, and its activity is attributable to its ability to inhibit monoamine oxidase which destroys excess monoamine neurotransmitters within the terminal buttons. The drug thus increases the release of dopamine (DA), noradrenaline (NA), and serotonin (5HT). MAOIs also have untoward side effects in inhibiting the breakdown of the pressor amines, substances similar to the catecholamines. MAO usually breaks down these pressor substances, which occur in cheese, chocolate and red wine, but in subjects receiving MAOIs a sympathetic reaction to these substances occurs resulting in increased heart rate and blood pressure and the medical complications associated with these problems. The MAOIs can be divided into two forms: those affecting the MAO-A enzyme and those affecting the MAO-B enzyme. A number of agents specific to MAO-B have been developed (selegiline and meclobemide) which do not alter the sensitivity to the pressor amines; however at higher doses this selectivity may be lost (Zajecka & Fawcett, 1991).

Bipolar affective disorders are best treated with lithium carbonate, carbamazepine and valproate (Gerner, 1993). Recently a large scale, placebo-controlled study of acute manic patients was published (Bowden, Brugger, Swann et al. 1994). One hundred and seventy nine patients were randomly assigned to a three-week regime of valproate, lithium or placebo, and the proportion of patients improving by at least 50% on a mania rating scale was significant for both valproate and lithium.

During the depressed phase of bipolar disorder, Zornberg and Pope (1993) noted that lithium, the tricyclic antidepressants, and ECT proved to be the most effective, however at present only limited data is available on the use of MAOIs, SSRIs, bupropion and other medications. They noted that tricyclic antidepressants may be of less benefit than other agents, and that few investigations of the condition have so far been conducted.

THE TREATMENT OF ANXIETY DISORDERS

There are two main categories of drugs employed to treat the anxiety disorders: the anxiolytic drugs and the sedative hypnotics. The role of the anxiolytics is to reduce anxiety while the role of the latter group is to induce sleep. The anxiolytics fall within a large class of agents each of which is thought to depress activity in the central nervous system, the CNS depressants. This includes agents as diverse as drugs with a selective action in the CNS such as the benzodiazepines, to those which are more global in their effects such as alcohol.

The benzodiazepines were developed by the American Laboratories of Roche Pharmaceuticals in the early 1960s. The observation that the benzodiazepines (firstly chlordiazepoxide (Librium) and later diazepam (Valium)) were capable of controlling anxiety states gave rise to considerable speculation regarding the mechanism of these agents in producing their effects. The demonstration of the specific receptors for the benzodiazepines in the brain and spinal cord, and the close relationship of these with the inhibitory neurotransmitter γ-amino-butyric acid (GABA), has resulted in numerous studies. The benzodiazepines act through a complex involving the benzodiazepine and GABA receptors associated with a chloride ionophore (Braestrup & Nielsen, 1980).

DRUG EFFECTS ON COGNITION

Many of the patients with a psychiatric diagnosis who are referred for neuropsychological assessment are either presently maintained on a drug regime or will be subjected to one when the final diagnosis is made. As a consequence it is useful to know what can be reasonably expected in terms of cognitive effects of these drugs, and whether the changes in cognition observed in the psychiatric disorders are attributable to the effect of the drug on cognition or whether they are attributable to the diagnosis of itself. The distinction between acute versus chronic effects of treatment with the agents is also important, as these may differ as a function of drug regime.

Neuroleptics

Studies of drug toxicity effects with anti-psychotic agents have come from two principal sources: their effects of normal subjects treated with these agents and the action of these drugs on schizophrenic subjects. In addition to their direct effects on dopaminegic neurotransmission, the antipsychotics are also capable of inducing long-term iatrogenic conditions in the form of the tardive (delayed onset) movement disorders including (tardive dyskinesia (abnormal involuntary movements), tardive dystonia (abnormal posturing)) and, akathisia (motor restlessness); and the life threatening condition of neuroleptic malignant syndrome (Reilly, Crowe & Lloyd, 1991).

With normal subjects, Chlorpromazine (CPZ) only slightly impaired serial adding speed at higher doses, whilst trifluoperazine (TFP) improved this performance at moderate doses (Heaton & Crowley, 1981). CPZ also significantly reduced finger tapping speed 4 hours after a 200 mg oral administration causing a 16% decline from pre-drug levels. A similar effect was noted with performance on the Pursuit Rotor at high doses. Of the piperazines trifluoperazine significantly improved coordination on the rotor, but not steadiness (DiMascio, Havens & Klerman, 1963).

Performance on Digit Symbol, symbol copying and cancellation tasks were all impaired after high doses of thioridazine in comparison to placebo. Moreover there was a significant correlation between Digit Symbol performance and blood levels of TDZ (Heaton & Crowley, 1981). CPZ decreased reaction time and steering accuracy in a driving simulator (Loomis & West, 1958). CPZ (three weeks, 400–600 mg orally) caused significant decreases in Digit Symbol performance and on prorated Performance IQ (Legg & Stiff, 1976).

Drugs with significant anti-cholinergic properties, e.g. TDZ or CPZ in higher doses, impair performance on a variety of motor and cognitive tasks. Phenothiazenes and haloperidol, which have little anticholinergic activity, do not seem to impair motor speed. However, these agents are more likely to produce extra-pyramidal side effects (EPS) and may thereby cause decreases in motor speed and coordination.

It is possible, on the basis of this data, to conclude that the performance of normal subjects is likely to be affected by the administration of the antipsychotic agents. In the case of patients with a diagnosis of schizophrenia, however, the matter becomes much more difficult to disentangle. At the very least it is difficult to ascertain how much of the neuropsychological changes, if there were any, were attributable to the diagnosis, as opposed to the independent effect of the medication (Sweeney et al., 1990).

Studies in clinical populations reveal that subjects with schizophrenia who received CPZ showed significant improvement on reaction time tests and other tests of attention and simple information processing. The drug-related improvements of attention tended to correlate with measures of clinical improvement

(Spohn et al., 1977). CPZ-treated schizophrenic patients improved significantly on associative learning, suggesting again that modest improvement in neuropsychological functioning can be observed in treated schizophrenics (Daston, 1959).

Longer term treatment with the antipsychotics and higher doses of these agents results in an additive effect. Klonoff, Fibiger and Hutton (1970) have noted that patients who received more medication demonstrated more deficits on the Halstead Reitan Battery, but clearly the fact that a patient warrants higher doses of neuroleptic indicates that the nature of the condition is more severe. Grant et al. (1978) noted that subjects with a longer lifetime incidence of medication use indicated higher levels of neuropsychological impairment, but again the intervening factor of the duration and severity of the psychosis makes the correlation less clear.

In a recent review of literature from the 1950s to the late 1980s analysing the effects of neuroleptics on neuropsychological functioning in chronic schizophrenic patients, Cassens et al. (1990) noted that acute administration of neuroleptics impairs performance on some tasks requiring vigilance and attention and on some tasks requiring motor behaviour. However, chronic administration of neuroleptics improves performance on some tasks requiring sustained attention and visuomotor problem solving. The authors concluded that there is consistent evidence to indicate that chronic administration of neuroleptics does not impair neuropsychological function independent of motor function.

Whilst the atypical antipsychotics have not been anywhere near so extensively surveyed in terms of their independent impact on cognition, it appears that some conclusion can be drawn from this literature. Mortimer et al. (1995) noted that following a six-month period of treatment with clozapine that their subjects showed improvement on cognitive functioning and on personal social variables. Lee, Thompson and Metzer (1994) also noted that clozapine was capable of improving several areas of cognitive functioning including measures of attention and verbal fluency. Buchanan, Holstein and Breier (1994) noted similar positive effects on attention, response speed, and verbal and category fluency, but little evidence of an effect on memory functioning.

In short, the continuing administration of antipsychotics to schizophrenics results in few significant changes in neuropsychological test performance, with the possible exception of the tendency to see improvement in attention and concentration, visuospatial cognition and possibly memory functions after medication. Clearly, whilst this may be a direct effect of the agents on cognition, the more likely explanation is that the tranquillising effects of the agents diminishes the level of positive symptomatology thus allowing the subjects to concentrate on the task in hand. The atypical antipsychotics seem to have a further beneficial effect on measures of attention and fluency in addition to their ability to ameliorate positive symptoms. Longer term treatment may well result in a higher level of impairment; it is impossible to discern on the basis of the available literature, however, whether these differences exist as a consequence of the treatment effect or as a result of the nature of the disorder that they would aim to treat.

Antidepressant and anti-manic drugs

The side effects of the tricyclic antidepressants relevant to the neuropsychologist include fine tremor and mild visual blurring. Normal subjects treated with a single dose of tricyclic are reported to show no effect (Heimann, Reed & Witt, 1968). However, I recently was prescribed amitryptiline for a shingles infection in my ear and after a single dose I felt like I was wrapped in cotton wool for at least the ensuing twenty-four hours.

With clinical subjects, Sternberg and Jarvik (1976) noted that the performance of depressed subjects before treatment were impaired on all tests of initial learning but not on measures of forgetting. However, imipramine-related deficits in STM have been reported. Three weeks of treatment impaired the depressed subjects performance on the BVRT (Benton Visual Retention Text), logical memory, Digit symbol and prorated Performance IQ (Legg & Stiff, 1976). Caution, however, must be exercised in the interpretation of this effect. As most psychoactive medications seem to require two to three weeks before they become clinically effective, the deficits noted by Legg and Stiff (1976) may well be as a results of this effect (Carlin, 1991).

There have been relatively few studies concerning the neuropsychological effects of the drugs used to treat affective disorders. Generally a single dose of imipramine does not affect attention, steadiness, or spatial analysis, while several weeks of imipramine has minimal effect on various tests of intelligence.

Normals subjects dosed with lithium indicated a significant decrement on a number of neuropsychological functions (Judd et al., 1977). Toxicity associated with lithium can occur and this results in tremor, muscle weakness, twitching and confusion. Lithium appears to have some negative effect on test performance (Ananth, Ghadirian & Engelsmann, 1987), but largely this would not be noted to cause marked deficits in individuals with a diagnosis of bipolar disorder, and are probably not great enough to cause false positive diagnoses of brain damage. Individuals treated with lithium who do not feature a diagnosis of bipolar disorder may be mildly affected by the drug.

The anxiolytics

The use of the barbiturates and other sedative hypnotics including valium have also lead to surprisingly little neuropsychological research. Bergman, Borg and Holm (1980) studied 55 long-term abusers of these agents (i.e. greater than five years) and noted that the abusers were significantly more impaired both on clinical judgement and by test scores (IQ, TMT, Memory for Designs). Performance decrements on tests considered to be 'hold' tests did not occur. A number of differences in leisure activities, living situation and employment stability was also made with this sample although this may well have been modulated by premorbid status or by depression.

The benzodiazepines impair the ability to learn new information in both the audioverbal and the visuospatial modality. These agents do not appear to interfere with the ability to retrieve material previously learned. These effects are dose dependent and although differences exist in the effectiveness of various benzodiazepines to induce memory deficits (i.e. lormetazepam and clobazam less than traizolam and midazolam), they all have this action. The differences may well be due to the pharmacokinetics of the various preparations (Stephens, Duka & Andrews, 1991).

The benzodiazepines also impair the performance on tasks of psychomotor integration, such as the digit-symbol substitution task of the WAIS-R, letter cancellation tasks, tasks requiring sustained attention, or attentional switching, as well as in simple measures of attentional capacity such as critical flicker fusion frequency (Stephens et al., 1991).

It is clear on the basis of this review that the benzodiazepines are reliably and consistently noted to affect both memory functions and attention and vigilance functions. These effects are dose responsive and the reporting of these types of deficits in individuals treated for anxiety states may well indicate a drug rather than a condition effect in those cases.

* * *

A number of the issues related to the effects of drugs on cognition and specifically the issue of how much of the change associated with the drug regime is as a consequence of overcoming the condition that is to be treated is surveyed in the following case report.

CASE REPORT

OG was referred to me by her medical practitioner as she had suffered from a past history of anxiety and depression and had a history of work related stress. In his referral the doctor noted that OG had had to defer her present course of advanced study due to her problem. A CT scan performed in 1992, one year before I first saw her, was normal; however the doctor noted that OG still complained of impairment of memory and concentration. Her medication was an antidepressant and a minor tranquilliser in small doses. OG had particular difficulties in coping with driving and banking. She was pessimistic about her future and felt oversensitive.

Background

OG had been subjected to quite an extensive series of assessments and disputations with the Worker's Compensation Authority, and at the time that I saw her was facing the possibility of an enforced return to work. She considered that she was not up to this due to her continuing disorganisation and memory problems, and the very thought of return to work evoked a marked anxiety response.

OG had also recently been assessed by a psychiatrist who noted that she was suffering from a chronic anxiety state and reactive depression of a moderately severe degree. The psychiatrist suspected that she had 'always been rather an obsessional person', but noted that she was able to cope with her duties up until 1987. He also indicated that he had little doubt that her emotional problems were and still are the result of difficulties that she encountered in the course of her work. He thought it unlikely that she would recover completely and saw little prospect of her ever returning to work.

On interview OG noted that she had a 'breakdown' and had been on worker's compensation since 1989. She had gone back to light duties in 1990 but her stress levels had built up and she discontinued in 1992. She indicated that she suffered from work related stress, high levels of anxiety and depression and that the anxiety appeared to interfere with her concentration and attention. OG noted that she cannot remember her past life, including much of her childhood, and that she can successfully recall material while she is reading it but cannot remember it after a brief delay.

OG had no previous history of loss of consciousness and drank only an occasional glass of wine. Her mother died from cancer of the breast and her father from a heart attack. It does not appear that there is any family history of progressive degenerative disorder.

She noted that she was actually upset at the moment and had a great deal of difficulty performing her usual functions. OG presented with a very common feature seen with the anxious and depressed subject: constant telephone calling to organise the appointment beforehand, and numerous inquiries to ensure that she was in the right place at the right time.

Formal Assessment

My assessment of OG included the Wechsler Adult Intelligence Scale Revised, the Wechsler Memory Scale Revised, the Verbal Fluency Test and the Austin maze test.

The performance on the Adult Wechsler Intelligence Scale Revised indicated that OG had a Verbal Intelligence Quotient of 120, a Performance Intelligence Quotient of 98 and a Full Scale IQ of 110. This indicated that OG's verbal functions were in the superior range whilst her performance functions were somewhat lower than this. She had the greatest difficulty with timed tasks and tasks requiring visuo-motor integration of information.

Tests of memory functions using the WMS-R revealed that OG had a Verbal Memory Index of 66, a Visual Memory Index of 98, a General Memory Index of 73 and a Delayed Recall Index of 73. OG had particular problems with verbal information processing and recall and less so with visual material. Her General Memory Index and her Delayed Recall Index indicate a moderately severe level of amnesia.

On tests of the frontal executive functions OG had a great deal of difficulty learning the Austin maze and after 10 trials was still making 10 errors per pass through the maze. This is a very poor performance indeed, and indicates poor ability to be able to learn from prior experience as well as probable memory difficulties. Her performance on the Verbal Fluency Test was interesting and she performed in the superior range, but had a marked tendency to break the rules on the task which is consistent with some level of compromise in frontal executive functions and inability to be able to learn from previous errors.

The pattern of performance that OG presented at that point in time was consistent with compromise in attention and concentration, learning, memory, particularly of verbal material, and in tests of the frontal executive functions. The pattern was quite consistent with the notion of an anxiety induced pseudo-dementing syndrome, and at that point in time I considered it very unlikely that OG would be unable to organise herself to be able to successfully undertake any return to work or study.

I saw OG again approximately eight months after my initial assessment. The problems that OG continued to observe at that point in time included problems with memory and concentration, sleeplessness, irritability, anxiousness and depression. She also forgot things halfway through. She found herself disorganised, and noted that she couldn't read road maps, and had to check on things all the time. She noted that her feet 'jump at night'. She also featured migraines, frustration and some suicidal ideation. She noted that she couldn't make decisions or manage her finances. She may have paid bills twice or forgotten to pay them altogether. She noted that she wrote down wrong numbers and has to check things over and again. OG's husband had by that stage taken over a major part of the household chores and this had caused some degree of family friction. OG also noted that she could not keep still and could not remember the past. She also noted that she reads but cannot retain the material that she has read.

Her treatments at that stage included Prozac daily and Zanax if terribly agitated. She had been attending a psychiatrist and was attending a clinical psychologist for stress management and relaxation.

My reassessment of OG included a number of the tests that I had previously administered, and the most heartening things noted about this performance was the considerable amount of improvement that had taken place from that of her first assessment.

On the Naylor Harwood Adult Intelligence Scale (a parallel form of the WAIS) OG had a Verbal score of 114, a Performance score of 111 and a Full Scale score of 113. The previous assessment indicated particular difficulties with the performance tests of the scale and on this occasion OG was performing considerably better on a number of aspects of the scales. Her weakest performances were still on the Arithmetic subtest and on the Letter Symbol subtest both of which required high levels of concentration and attention and a considerable flexibility in processing information. Nonetheless they do indicate some level of improvement and this was most heartening to note.

On the Wechsler Memory Scale Revised, her Verbal Memory Index was 83, her Visual Memory Index 93, her General Memory Index 85 and her Delayed Recall Index 98. This pattern of performance, although still somewhat lower than would be expected on the basis of OG's premorbid intelligence, clearly indicates that she has undertaken some improvement in her ability to be able to learn and remember information in both the audio-verbal and visuo-spatial domains.

Tests of the frontal executive functions indicated that OG performed quite well on a Verbal Fluency Task and in an appropriate and rule governed manner on the modified Wisconsin Card Sorting Test.

Whilst there is some possibility that the improvement noted in OG's case may have been due to practice effects on the tests, rarely, in my experience, is such a marked level of improvement noted from test one to test two on the basis of practice alone. The other aspect of this matter is that practice effects are essentially measures of learning from the previous exposure to the material. If OG's improvement is an indication of practice, it reflects the very point that the assessment seems to underline—improvement in concentration and new learning.

The pattern of performances that OG presented on this assessment indicates moderate improvement in her performances on a number of tests of cognitive function, indicating that in fact her overall performances were much better than they were eight months before. In discussions with her it would appear that she was much more calm and sedate although both she and her husband were still observing marked difficulty in her performance at home. Much of the improvement seemed to be as a consequence of the application of the Prozac which had resulted in considerable benefits in terms of her cognitive function as well as in her ability to cope on a daily basis.

VERBAL TESTS (Scaled Scores)	*Time 1*	*Time 2*
Information	14	13
Digit Span	11	11
Vocabulary	11	12
Arithmetic	12	9
Comprehension	13	13
Similarities	15	13
VIQ	120	14
PERFORMANCE TESTS		
Picture Completion	11	12
Picture Arrangement	6	10
Block Design	8	10
Object Assembly	9	10
Digit Symbol	7	8
PIQ	98	111
FSIQ	110	113
WECHSLER MEMORY SCALE-REVISED		
Verbal Memory Index	66	83
Visual Memory Index	98	93
General Memory Index	73	85
Attention/Concentration	109	95
Delayed Recall	73	98
VERBAL FLUENCY TEST		
Items Produced	48	44
Number of Errors	5	4

AUSTIN MAZE TEST (Time 1 only)										
Trial	1	2	3	4	5	6	7	8	9	10
Number of Errors	28	8	30	17	10	10	10	15	9	10

Conclusion

The conclusion to be drawn from this case is probably necessarily ambiguous. The problem in the investigation of cases in which there is an intercurrent psychiatric illness or illnesses, such as in the case of OG, further clouds an already cloudy picture. Nonetheless, it is clear that the aspects of OG's case which do show responsivity to the agent would appear to visuospatial information processing, verbal memory, and tests of higher order attention and concentration. Clearly much of the improvement here is attributable to the amelioration of the anxiety state, rather than as a direct effect of the agents themselves on the cognitive processes.

SUMMARY

The nature of the effects of the drugs used to treat the psychiatric disorders on cognition is in, to say the least, an imperfect state of knowledge. Nonetheless, it is possible to conclude that the effects, such as they are, do not present a massive impairment, and rarely would it be the case that an individual would incorrectly be diagnosed as having brain impairment on the basis of the effects of these agents on the cognitive profile (with the possible exception of benzodiazepine abusers). Care must be taken, however, in the elicitation of information regarding drug status at the time of assessment with a view to ensuring that a false positive diagnosis is not made.

CHAPTER 9

CONCLUSION

The study of the neuropsychological effects of the psychiatric disorders that we have just surveyed allows us to make some overall formulations of the implication of these disorders to the neuropsychological functioning of the individual. Let us review these conclusions for each of the clinical states.

Positive symptom schizophrenia may only be associated with the distortions of reality associated with hallucination, delusion and thought disorder and probably not much else by way of disruption of higher level cognitive functions. The negative state on the other hand is associated with a disruption of attention, memory and executive functioning. This results in a marked avolitional state which is characterised by lack of effort and an overall diminution of drive and direction.

Depression results in a disruption of orderly information processing which is characterised by relatively poor performance on tests of memory and higher level problem solving. These deficits are more by way of a loss of effortful processing rather than to any intrinsic problems with information processing *per se*. In the bipolar affective disorder there are increases in the activation of the frontal areas during the phases of manic excitement. During the depressed phase, a similar pattern of neuropsychological responding, as observed with unipolar depressions, is noted.

The anxiety conditions cause disruption of attentional processes at all levels. This results in a heightened focus on threatening stimuli and a generalised hyperaroused state in all aspects of cognition and purposive behaviour. As a result, the cognitive profile of these individuals is characterised by the inability to be able to take information on board, to be able to work with it flexibly, or to be able to screen out interfering cognitive input. This impacts on the performance of tasks as diverse as the repetition of digit spans to the ability to be able to screen out the multiplicity of inputs in going to the supermarket.

The patterns of neuropsychological deficit in the somatoform, factitious or dissociative disorders are characterised by their larger than life pattern. The nature of the disorder can be fairly unpredictable, but the flavour of presentation that alerts the clinician to the problem is the tendency for them to be out of keeping with the ability of the patient in situations other than the testing situation.

The disorders of eating and sleeping provide useful insights into the effects of disruption of the neurovegetative functions on cognition. However, it is not possible to contend that these conditions are specific in their effects. The first neuropsychological sign of each of these conditions seems to be the disruption of attention and mental tracking. As the level of hypoxemia, sleep deprivation or compromise in nutritional status increases in severity, more deficits seem to emerge in the areas of executive functions, visuospatial functions and memory disorder.

The effect of ECT seems to be to produce a transient amnesic syndrome which resolves following a few weeks to months after the treatment. Psychosurgery, particularly the stereotactic approaches, seem to leave some sequelae in the form of subtle deficits in attention and executive functioning, but these would appear to be minor in comparison to the massive frontal lobe syndromes associated with the traditional lobotomy.

The nature of the effects of the drugs used to treat the psychiatric disorders on cognition do not present a marked impairment and rarely would it be the case that an individual would incorrectly be diagnosed as having brain impairment on the basis of the effects of these agents on the cognitive profile (with the possible exception of benzodiazepine abusers).

It seems that we can conclude on the basis of this data that all the psychiatric conditions that we have considered in this book seem capable of interfering with the functions of attention, concentration, memory functions and the executive domain. The psychiatric disorders are thus consistently impinging on higher levels of cognitive functioning.

FRONTAL LOBOLOGY: A CAUTIONARY NOTE

In a marvellous paper which appeared in the *British Journal of Psychiatry* in 1992, Anthony David cautioned against the overzealous application of cognitive neuropsychological models in psychiatry. In describing the supposed association of almost all aspects of clinical psychiatry, including personality disorders, obsessions, delusions, depression, mania, hyperkinesis/conduct disorder, schizophrenia, catatonia, thought disorder, anorexia nervosa and hysteria to frontal lobe pathology. He then posed a question that is crucially important to the success of this discussion:

> Psychiatric disorders are, by definition, problems at the highest level of thought, so how does it help us to state that they are, by analogy and implication, the surface manifestations of frontal lobe neuropathology? Such a statement is tautology. (p. 244)

He went on to answer it.

> The attempt to construct a neuropsychology of psychiatric disorders is an exciting venture. If it is to be successful, it must go beyond crude localisationism and instead define psychiatric phenomena in terms of a breakdown or malfunction of psychological processes. (p. 246).

The phenomena of psychiatric disorders do not occur as a consequence of altered experience on the part of those individuals affected with these disorders. It seems very unlikely that individuals who hallucinate have access to the devil and the Holy Ghost on a regular basis. Similarly individuals with an overemphasis on what will happen (anxiety disorders) or what has previously happened (depressive disorders) seem to have had not too dissimilar experiences to those of us who have not yet suffered from a psychiatric illness. Therefore, there must be something about the way in which they have processed that reality that distinguishes them from those of us who are so far unaffected. The thrust of this book has been to attempt to examine this processing difference, with a view to a new synthesis of the ancient art of psychiatry with the relatively new discipline of clinical neuropsychology.

A CLUE FROM MODULARITY

At present in neuropsychology a debate is taking place over the issue of modularity. The original notion of modularity comes to us from the work of Gerry Fodor (1983, 1985). The basic premise of the theory is that there exist functionally isolated, specific cognitive processing systems in the brain. These components are independent of the other components of the operating brain and they can be selectively impaired by brain damage.

Fodor (1983, 1985) contends that there are two types of informational systems in the brain: (1) informationally specific bottom-up modules (such as some of the perceptual systems), and (2) diffuse nonspecific central systems. These latter systems are not associated with either top-down or bottom-up processing as the information flows 'every which way' (Fodor, 1985, p. 4). Fodor contends that modular processing is genetically hard wired and the action of these modular systems is characterised by their rapid, automatic and domain-specific processing. The central systems on the other hand are slower, nonspecific, cognitively penetrable and not fixed in their cognitive architecture. Fodor contends that modules are special purpose devices suitable for obtaining specific information within their cognate domains, processing it rapidly and automatically, and then delivering the results of that processing for interpretation by the central processing systems. The modules are characterised by the fact that top–down processes, such as the executive, cannot interfere with their circumscribed functions with opinions, beliefs or motivational factors. It is the responsibility of the central system to take the output of these processing systems, and interpret this information, and to relate it to the store of general knowledge (i.e. sematic memory; Fodor, 1983, p. 209).

Whilst Fodor's theory has been very influential in contemporary brain science, not everyone is a firm adherent. Elkhonon Goldberg (1995; also a major critic of the notion of double dissociation as evidence of cognitive specificity) contends that modularity theory has become popular because of its seductiveness and illusory appeal of instant explainability. Goldberg contends that each time the modularist encounters a new observation he can create a new module to explain it. As a result, modularity theory is not economical in that it increases rather than reduces the number of units of explanation. 'Like the belief systems of antiquity, it merely relabels its domain by inventing a separate deity for every thing' (Goldberg, 1995, p. 194).

A second problem for modular theory arises because of its apparent ability to conveniently explain double dissociation evidence. Double dissociation exists when two cognitive functions can be established to be independent of each other such that one individual may have a deficit in function X but not in function Y, while another individual has the reverse pattern of deficit. Modular theory is often considered to imply the existence of separable cognitive components. Shallice (1988) nicely points out the problem with this logic. If modules exist, then double dissociation is an excellent way of uncovering these. As the extensive neuropsychological literature can attest, double dissociations do exist, therefore modules exist. The latter inference is only valid if modular systems are the only systems that could produce double dissociations. However, a number of recent studies (e.g. Kimberg & Farah, 1993) clearly indicate that parallel distributed processing networks are equally capable of producing and explaining double dissociations.

Despite its imperfections, and no one can deny they exist, the model proposed by Fodor's modular theory can be of use in our discussion of the issues of interest to this book, the implications of psychiatric disorder to neuropsychological functioning.

THE TOP AND THE BOTTOM OF PSYCHIATRIC DISORDERS

As we can clearly see none of the psychiatric disorders seems capable of impairing in any consistent and enduring way the functions or operations of the basic modules of the brain. The sensory and perceptual functions, the motor functions, and language all seem intact in these individuals. It is at the top of the hierarchy, the attention, concentration, memory and executive functioning levels that each of the psychiatric disorders produces its resultant cognitive compromise. How can this come about?

In our discussion of the neurotransmitters of the brain in Chapter 1, much was made of the notion of the fact that a number of nuclei in the brain stem are responsible for the innervation of the entire cortex through a variety of the neurotransmitters including dopamine, noradrenaline, acetylcholine and serotonin. Each of these agents has been implicated in a variety of the psychiatric conditions that we have discussed in this book. One way we might view the implications of the psychiatric disorders on cognitive functioning is that they impinge on the integrity of the functioning brain by their disruption of these pathways, resulting in the relatively characteristic neuropsychological pattern of each of the conditions discussed in this book—deficits in executive systems.

Thus from a neuropsychological perspective, at least at this point in time, the variety of the psychiatric disorders does not manifest a variety of cognitive profiles. They are each almost indistinguishable from each other. Perhaps the only index we can reliably apply to these issues is the issue of intensity rather that specificity. Major endogenous depression results in more serious disruption of function that does a less intense manifestation of this disorder. The more chronic and the more pervasive the disorder of schizophrenia the more chronic and pervasive are its neuropsychological manifestations.

Is it possible now to say that we have not fallen into the traps outlined by David in his discussion of frontal lobology? Unfortunately, I fear at this stage of the enterprise the answer is no. Whether we like it or not, psychiatric disorders are disorders of higher order cognitive functioning. Whilst the search for specific cognitive dysfunction in conditions such as schizophrenia still continues, we still have a long way to travel, and as yet the road is long and craggy.

THE ROAD AHEAD

What sort of information, then, do we need to accurately determine a specific neuropsychology of the psychiatric disorders? The answer to this question lies in the specificity of the conditions themselves. We need to find disorders which are specific to a given condition and to that condition only. These specific deficits also need to be relevant to the psychiatric symptomatology, in so far as they explain the observations of the symptom by its cognitive underpinning. If the voice talking to me inside my head is not my own, then there must be a concise and identifiable cognitive basis for this failure of recognition. The task for the future is to find these problems and to characterise them clearly and concisely from both their cognitive and their anatomical perspectives. Only then will we be able to give frontal lobology a frontal lobotomy.

REFERENCES

Abrams, R.A. (1986) A hypothesis to explain divergent findings among studies comparing the efficacy of unilateral and bilateral ECT in depression. *Convulsive Therapy*, 2, 253–257.

Abrams, R.A., Taylor, M.A. and Volavka, J. (1987) ECT-induced EEG asymmetry and therapeutic response in melancholia: relation to treatment electrode placement. *American Journal Psychiatry*, 144, 327–329.

Abramson, L.Y., Seligman, M.E. and Teasdale, J.D. (1978) Learned helplessness in humans: Critique and reformulation. *Journal of Abnormal Psychology*, 87, 40–47.

Achenbach, T.M. (1982) *Developmental Psychopathology* (2nd edn). New York: Wiley.

Agbayewa, M.O. (1986) Earlier psychiatric morbidity in patients with Alzheimer's disease. *Journal of American Geriatrics Society*, 34, 561–564.

Altshuler, L.L., Conrad, A., Kovelman, J.A. and Scheibel, A.B. (1987) Hippocampal pyramidal cell orientation in schizophrenia: A controlled neurohistologic study of the Yakovlev collection. *Archives of General Psychiatry*, 44, 1094–1098.

American Psychiatric Association (1994) *Diagnostic and Statistical Manual of Mental Disorders* (4th edn). Washington, DC: American Psychiatric Association.

Ananth, J., Ghadirian, A.M.. and Engelsmann, F. (1987) Lithium and memory: A review. *Canadian Journal of Psychiatry*, 32, 312–316.

Anderson, S.W., Damasio, H., Jonas, R.D. and Tranel, D. (1991) Wisconsin Card Sorting Test performance as a measure of frontal lobe damage. *Journal of Clinical and Experimental Neuropsychology*, 13, 909–922.

Andreasen, N.C. (1983) *Scale for the Assessment of Negative Symptoms*. Iowa City: University of Iowa.

Andreasen, N.C. (1984) *Scale for the Assessment of Positive Symptoms*. Iowa City: University of Iowa.

Andreasen, N.C. and Olson, S. (1982) Negative versus positive schizophrenia: Definition and reliability. *Archives of General Psychiatry*, **39**, 789–794.

Antelman, S.M. and Chiodo, L.A. (1984) Stress-induced sensitization: A framework for viewing the effects of ECS and other antidepressants. In *ECT: Basic Mechanisms*, edited by B. Lerer, R.D. Weiner and R.H. Belmaker, pp. 28–32. Washington, DC: American Psychiatric Press.

Aperia, B. (1985) Effects of electroconvulsive therapy on neuropsychological function and circulating levels of ACTH, cortisol, prolactin, and TSH in patients with major depressive illness *Acta Psychiatrica Scandinavica*, **72**, 536–541.

Archer, J., Hay, D.C. and Young, A.W. (1992) Face processing in psychiatric conditions. *British Journal of Clinical Psychology*, **31**, 45–61.

Armitage, S.G. (1946) An analysis of certain psychological tests used for the evaluation of brain injury. *Psychological Monographs*, **60**, (Whole Number 277).

Army Individual Test Battery (1944) *Manual of Directions and Scoring*. Washington, DC: War Department, Adjutant General's Office.

Arnold, S.E. (1994) Investigations of neuronal morphology and the neuronal cytoskeleton in the hippocampal region in schizophrenia. *Neuropsychopharmacology*, **10**, 634S.

Austin, M.P., Ross, M., Murray, C. and O'Carroll, R.E. (1992) Cognitive function in major depression. *Journal of Affective Disorders*, **25**, 21–29.

Aylward, E.H., Roberts-Twillie, J.V., Barta, P.E., Kumar, A.J., Harris, G.J., Geer, M., Peyser, C.E. and Pearlson, G.D. (1994) Basal ganglia volumes and white matter hyperintensities in patients with bipolar disorders. *American Journal of Psychiatry*, **151**, 687–693.

Ball, W.A. and Whybrow, P.C. (1993) Biology of depression and mania. *Current Opinion in Psychiatry*, **6**, 27–34.

Bauer, M.S. and Whybrow, P.C. (1988) Thyroid hormones and the central nervous system in affective illness: Interactions that may have clinical significance. *Integrative Psychiatry*, **6**, 75–85.

Baxter, L.R., Phelps, M.E., Mazziota, J.C., Guze, B.H., Schwartz, J.M. and Selin, C.E. (1987) Local cerebral glucose metabolic rates in obsessive–compulsive disorder. *Archives of General Psychiatry*, **44**, 211–218.

Baxter, L.R., Phelps, M.E., Mazziota, J.C., Schwartz, J.M., Gerner, R.H., Selin, C.E. and Sumida, R.M. (1985) Cerebral metabolic rates for glucose in mood disorders. *Archives of General Psychiatry*, **42**, 441–447.

Baxter, L.R., Schwartz, J.M., Phelps, M.E., Mazziota, J.C., Guze, B.H., Selin, C.E., Gerner, R.H. and Sumida, R.M. (1989) Reduction of prefrontal cortex glucose metabolism common to three types of depression. *Archives of General Psychiatry*, **46**, 243–250.

Beatty, W.W., Jocic, Z., Monson, N. and Staton, R.D. (1993) Memory and frontal lobe dysfunction in schizophrenia and schizoaffective disorder. *The Journal of Nervous and Mental Disease*, 181, 448–453.

Beatty, W.W., Wonderlich, S.A., Staton, R.D. and Ternes, L.A. (1990) Cognitive functioning in bulimia: Comparison with depression. *Bulletin of the Psychonomic Society*, 28, 289–292.

Beck, A.T. (1967) *Depression: Clinical, Experimental and Theoretical Aspects*. New York: Harper and Rowe.

Beck, A.T., Rush, A.J., Shaw, B.F. and Emery, G. (1979) *Cognitive Therapy of Depression*. New York: Guilford Press.

Bedard, M.A., Montplaisir, J., Malo, J., Richer, F. and Rouleau, I. (1993) Persistent neuropsychological deficits and vigilance impairment in sleep apnea syndrome after treatment with continuous positive airway pressure (CPAP). *Journal of Clinical and Experimental Neuropsychology*, 15, 330–341.

Bedard, M.A., Montplaisir, J., Richer, F., Rouleau, I. and Malo, J. (1991) Obstructive sleep apnoea syndrome: Pathogenesis of neuropsychological deficits. *Journal of Clinical and Experimental Neuropsychology*, 13, 950–964.

Behar, D., Rapoport, J.L., Berg, C.J., Denckla, M.B., Mann, L., Cox, C., Fedio, P. and Wolfman, M.G. (1984) Computerised tomography and neuropsychological measures in adolescents with Obsessive Compulsive disorder. *American Journal of Psychiatry*, 141, 363–368.

Bell, I.R., Edman, J.S., Marby, D.W., Satlin, A., Dreier, T., Liptzin, B. and Cole, J.O. (1990) Vitamin B$_{12}$ and folate status in acute geriatric inpatients: Affective and cognitive characteristics of a vitamin nondeficient population. *Biological Psychiatry*, 27, 125–137.

Bendefeldt, F., Miller, L.L. and Ludwig, A.M. (1976) Cognitive performance in conversion hysteria. *Archives of General Psychiatry*, 33, 1250–1254.

Benes, F.M. and Bird, E.D. (1987) An analysis of the arrangement of neurons in the cingulate cortex of schizophrenic patients. *Archives of General Psychiatry*, 44, 608–616.

Benes, F.M., Davidson, J. and Bird, E.D. (1986) Quantitative cytoarchitectural studies of the cerebral cortex of schizophrenics. *Archives of General Psychiatry*, 43, 31–35.

Benes, F.M., Sorensen, I. and Bird, E.D. (1991) Reduced neuronal size in posterior hippocampus of schizophrenic patients. *Schizophrenia Bulletin*, 17, 597–608.

Benson, D.F. and Stuss, D. T. (1982) Motor abilities after frontal leukotomy. *Neurology*, 32, 1353–1357.

Benton, A.L. (1968) Differential behavioral effects in frontal lobe disease. *Neuropsychologia*, 6, 53–60.

Benton, A.L. (1981) Focal brain damage and the concept of localisation of function. In *Studies in Neuropsychology*, edited by L. Costa and O. Spreen. New York: Oxford University Press.

Bergman, H., Borg, S. and Holm, L. (1980) Neuropsychological impairment and exclusive use of sedative hypnotics. *American Journal of Psychiatry*, 137, 215–217.

Berman, K.S. and Weinberger, D. (1990) Lateralisation of cortical function during cognitive tasks: regional cerebral blood flow studies of normal individuals and patients with schizophrenia. *Journal of Neurology, Neurosurgery and Psychiatry*, 53, 150–160.

Berman, K.S., Zec, R.F. and Weinberger, D. (1986) Physiological dysfunction of dorsolateral prefrontal cortex in schizophrenia: II. Role of neuroleptic treatments, attention and mental effort. *Archives of General Psychiatry*, 45, 814–821.

Berry, D.T.R., Webb, W.B., Block, A.J., Bauer, R.M. and Switzer, D.A. (1986) Nocturnal hypoxia and neuropsychological variables. *Journal of Clinical and Experimental Neuropsychology*, 8, 229–238.

Blanchard, J.J. and Neale, J.M. (1994) The neuropsychological signature of schizophrenia: Generalised or specific deficit? *American Journal of Psychiatry*, 151, 40–48.

Bliwise, D.L. (1989) Neuropsychological functioning and sleep. *Clinics in Geriatric Medicine*, 5, 381–394.

Boffeli, T.J. and Guze, S.B. (1992) The simulation of neurological disease. *Psychiatric Clinics of North America*, 15, 301–310.

Boone, K.B., Ananth, J., Philpott, I., Kaur, A. and Djenderedjian, A. (1991) Neuropsychological characteristics of non-depressed adults with Obsessive-Compulsive Disorder. *Neuropsychiatry, Neuropsychology and Behavioral Neurology*, 4, 96–109.

Botez, M.I., Botez, T. and Maag, V. (1984) The Wechsler subtests in mild organic brain damage associated with folate deficiency. *Psychological Medicine*, 14, 431–437.

Bowden, C.L. (1993) The clinical approach to the differential diagnosis of bipolar disorder. *Annals of Psychiatry*, 2, 57–63.

Bowden, C.L., Brugger, A.M., Swann, A.C. et al (1994) Efficacy of divalproex versus lithium and placebo in the treatment of mania: The Depakote mania study group. *Journal of the American Medical Association*, 271, 918–924.

Bowers, W.A. (1994) Neuropsychological impairment among anorexia nervosa and bulimia patients. *Eating Disorders: The Journal of Treatment and Prevention*, 2, 42–46.

Braestrup, C. and Nielsen, M. (1980) Benzodiazepine receptors. *Arzneimittel-Forschung/Drug Research*, 30, 852–857.

Braff, D.L. (1993) Information processing and attention dysfunctions in schizophrenia. *Schizophrenia Bulletin*, 19, 233–259.

Braun, C.M. and Chouinard, M.J. (1992) Is anorexia nervosa a neuropsychological disease? *Neuropsychology Review*, 3, 171–212.

Bremner, J.D., Innis, R.B., Staib, L.H., Salomom, R.M., Bronen R.A., Duncan, J., Southwick, S.M., Krystal, J.H., Rich, D., Zubal, G., Dey, H., Soufer, R. and Charney, D.S. (1997) Positron emission tomography measurement of cerebral metabolic correlates of yohimbine administered to combat-related posttraumatic stress disorder. *Archives of General Psychiatry*, 54, 246–254.

Bremner, J.D., Randall, P., Scott, T.M., Bronen, R.A., Seibyl, J.P., Southwick, S.M., Delaney, R.C., McCarthy, G., Charney, D.S. and Innis, R.B. (1995) MRI-based measurement of hippocampal volume in patients with combat-related posttraumatic stress disorder. *American Journal of Psychiatry*, 152, 973–981.

Bremner, J.D., Scott, T.M., Delaney, R.C., Southwick, S.M., Mason, J.W., Johnson, D.R., Innis, R.B., McCarthy, G. and Charney, D.S. (1993) Deficits in short–term memory in Post Traumatic Stress Disorder. *American Journal of Psychiatry*, 150, 1015–1019.

Broadbent, D.E. (1958) *Perception and Communication*. London: Pergamon.

Broadbent, D.E. (1971) *Decision and Stress*. New York: Academic Press.

Brown, R.G. (1989) Models of cognitive function in Parkinson's disease. In *Disorders of Movement*, edited by N.P. Quinn and P.G. Jenner. London: Academic Press.

Brown, R., Colter, N., Corsellis, J.A.N., Crow, T.J., Frith, C.D., Jagoe, R., Johnstone, E.C. and Marsh, L. (1986) Postmortem evidence of structural brain changes in schizophrenia. *Archives of General Psychiatry*, 43, 36–42.

Buchanan, R.W. and Carpenter, W.T. (1994) Domains of psychopathology: An approach to the reduction of heterogeneity in schizophrenia. *Journal of Nervous and Mental Diseases*, 182, 193–204.

Buchanan, R.W., Holstein, C. and Breier, A. (1994) The comparative efficacy and long term effect of clozapine treatment on neuropsychological test performance. *Biological Psychiatry*, 36, 717–725.

Buchsbaum, M.S. (1986) Brain imaging in the search for biological markers in affective disorder. *Journal of Clinical Psychiatry*, 47, 7–10.

Buchsbaum, M.S., Wu, J., DeLisi, L.E., Holcomb, H.H., Kessler, R., Johnson, J., King, A.C., Hazlett, E., Langston, K. and Post, R.M. (1986) Frontal cortex and basal ganglia metabolic rates assessed by positron emission tomography with (-sup-1- sup8F) 2 deoxyglucose in affective illness. *Journal of Affective Disorders*, 10, 137– 152.

Burns, A., Jacoby, R. and Levy, R. (1990) Psychiatric phenomena in Alzheimer's disease. III: Disorders of mood. *British Journal of Psychiatry*, **157**, 81–86.

Butcher, P. (1995) Psychological processes in psychogenic voice disorder. *European Journal of Disorders of Communication*, **30**, 467–474.

Buysse, D.J., Reynolds, C.F., Kupfer, D.J., Houck, P.R., Hoch, C.C., Stack, J.A. and Berman, S.R. (1988) Electroencephalographic sleep in depressive pseudodementia. *Archives of General Psychiatry*, **45**, 568–575.

Cade, J.F. (1949) Lithium salts in the treatment of psychotic excitement. *Medical Journal of Australia*, **36**, 349–352.

Caine, E.D. (1981) Pseudodementia. *Archives of General Psychiatry*, **38**, 1359–1364.

Caine, E.D. (1986) The neuropsychology of depression: The pseudodementia syndrome. In *Neuropsychological Assessment of Neuropsychiatric Disorders*, edited by I. Grant and K. Adams. New York: Oxford University Press.

Calev, A., Edelist, S., Kugelmass, S. and Lerer, B. (1991) Performance of long-stay schizophrenics on matched verbal and visuospatial tasks. *Psychological Medicine*, **21**, 655–660.

Calev, A., Guadino, E.A., Squires, N.K., Zervas, I.M., et al (1995) ECT and memory cognition: A review. *British Journal of Clinical Psychology*, **34**, 505–515.

Calev, A., Nigal, D., Shapira, B., Tubi, N., et al (1991) Early and long-term effects of electroconvulsive therapy and depression on memory and other cognitive functions. *Journal of Nervous and Mental Disease*, **179**, 526–533.

Capel, T.R., Hegley, D.C., Chapman, L.J. and Chapman, J.P. (1990) Facilitation of word recognition by semantic priming in schizophrenia. *Journal of Abnormal Psychology*, **99**, 215–221.

Carlin, A.S. (1991) Consequences of prescription and non-prescription drug use. In *Forensic Neuropsychology: Legal and Scientific Bases*, edited by H.O. Doerr and A.S. Carlin, pp. 99–122. New York: Guilford Press.

Carney, M. (1983) Pseudodementia. *British Journal of Hospital Medicine*, April, 312–318.

Carroll, B.J., Fineberg, M., Greden, J.F., Tarika, J., Albala, A.A., Haskett, R.F., James, N.M., Kronfol, Z., Lohr, N., Steiner, M., deVigne, J.P. and Young, E. (1981) A specific laboratory test for the diagnosis of melancholia: Standardisation, validation and clinical utility. *Archives of General Psychiatry*, **38**, 15–22.

Casper, R.C. and Heller, W. (1991) "La douce indifference" and mood in anorexia nervosa: Neuropsychological correlates. *Progress in Neuropsychopharmacology and Biological Psychiatry*, **15**, 15–23.

Cassens, G., Inglis, A.K., Appelbaum, P.S. and Gutheil, T.G. (1990) Neuroleptics: Effects on neuropsychological function in chronic schizophrenic patients. *Schizophrenia Bulletin,* 16, 477–499.

Cavenar, J.O., Maltbie, A.A. and Austin, L. (1979) Depression simulating organic brain disease. *American Journal of Psychiatry,* 136, 521–523.

Cerletti, U. and Bini, L. (1938) Un neuvo metodo di shockterapie "L'elettro-shock". *Bolletino Academia Medica Roma,* 64, 136–138.

Chavez, E.L., Trautt, G.M., Brandon, A. and Steyaert, J. (1983) Effects of test anxiety and sex of subject on neuropsychological test performance: Finger tapping, trail making, digit span and digit symbol tests. *Perceptual and Motor Skills,* 56, 923–929.

Christensen, A.L. (1979) *Luria's Neuropsychological Investigation* (2nd edn). Copenhagen: Munksgaard.

Chua, S.E. and McKenna, P.J. (1995) Schizophrenia—a brain disease? A critical review of structural and functional cerebral abnormality in the disorder. *British Journal of Psychiatry,* 166, 563–582.

Clyma, E.A. (1975) Unilateral electroconvulsive therapy: How to determine which hemisphere is dominant. *British Journal of Psychiatry,* 126, 372–379.

Coffey, C.E. (1994) The role of structural brain imaging in ECT. *Psychopharmacology Bulletin,* 30, 477–484.

Coffman, J.A., Bornstein, R.A., Olson, S.C., Schwarzkopf, S.B. and Nasrallah, H.A. (1990) Cognitive impairment and cerebral structure by MRI in bipolar disorder. *Biological Psychiatry,* 27, 1188–1196.

Cohen, R.A., Kaplan, R.F., Meadows, M.E. and Wilkinson, H. (1994) Habituation and sensitization of the orienting response following bilateral anterior cingulotomy. *Neuropsychologia,* 32, 609–617.

Cooper, M.J. and Fairburn, C.G. (1992) Selective processing of eating, weight and shape related words in patients with eating disorders and dieters. *British Journal of Clinical Psychology,* 31, 363–365.

Copolov, D. (1995) The dividends of psychiatric research. In *The Decade of the Brain: Australian Brain Research and Theory: Current Understanding,* edited by D. Graham and G.Singer, pp. 1–15. Bundoora, La Trobe University Press.

Corcoran, R. and Frith, C.D. (1993) Neuropsychology and neurophysiology in schizophrenia. *Current Opinion in Psychiatry,* 7, 47–50.

Creasey, H. and Rappoport, S.I. (1985) The aging human brain. *Annals of Neurology,* 17, 2–10.

Crow, T.J. (1980) Molecular pathology of schizophrenia: more than one disease process. *British Medical Journal,* 280, 66–68.

Crowe, S.F. (1992) Dissociation of two frontal lobe syndromes by a test of verbal fluency. *Journal of Clinical and Experimental Neuropsychology*, 14, 327–339.

Crowe, S.F. (1996a) The performance of schizophrenic and depressed subjects on tests of fluency: Support for a compromise in dorso-lateral pre-frontal functioning. *Australian Psychologist*, 31, 204–209.

Crowe, S.F. (1996b) Traumatic anosmia coincides with an organic disinhibition syndrome as assessed by performance on a test of verbal fluency. *Psychiatry, Psychology and Law*, 3, 39–45.

Crowe, S.F. and Hoogenraad, K. (in press) The differentiation of dementia of the Alzheimer's type from depression with cognitive impairment on the basis of a cortical versus subcortical pattern of deficit. *Archives of Clinical Neuropsychology*.

Culebras, A. (1992) Update on disorders of sleep and the sleep-wake cycle. *Psychiatric Clinics of North America*, 15, 467–489.

Cullum, C.M., Heaton, R.K. and Grant, I. (1991) Psychogenic factors influencing neuropsychological performance: Somatoform disorders, factitious disorders and malingering. In *Forensic Neuropsychology: Legal and Scientific Basis*, edited by H.O. Doerr and A.S. Carlin. New York: Guilford Press.

Cumming, S., Hay, P., Lee, T. and Sachdev, P. (1995) Neuropsychological outcome from psychosurgery for obsessive–compulsive disorder. *Australian and New Zealand Journal of Psychiatry*, 29, 293–298.

Cummings, J.L. (1986) Subcortical dementia. *British Journal of Psychiatry*, 149, 682–697.

Cummings, J.L. and Benson, F. (1983) Subcortical dementia. *Archives of Neurology*, 41, 874–881.

Cutting, R.P.J. (1991) Lateralised anomalous perceptual experiences in schizophrenia. *Psychopathology*, 24, 365–368.

Cytowic, R.E. (1996) *The Neurological Side of Neuropsychology*. Cambridge, Massachusetts: MIT Press.

Dalgleish, T. and Watts, F.N. (1990) Biases of attention and memory in disorders of anxiety and depression. *Clinical Psychology Review*, 10, 589–604.

Dalton, J.E., Pederson, S.L. and Ryan, J.J. (1989) Effects of post-traumatic stress disorder on neuropsychological test performance. *International Journal of Clinical Neuropsychology*, 11, 121–124.

Daston, P.G. (1959) Effects of two phenothiazine drugs on concentrative attention span of chronic schizophrenics. *Journal of Clinical Psychology*, 15, 106–109.

David, A.S. (1992) Frontal lobology: Psychiatry's new pseudoscience. *British Journal of Psychiatry*, 161, 244–248.

David, A.S. (1993) Cognitive Neuropsychiatry? *Psychological Medicine*, 23, 1–5.

David, A.S. and Cutting, J.C. (1994) *The Neuropsychology of Schizophrenia*. Hove, East Sussex: Lawrence Erlbaum Associates.

Davison, G.C. and Neale, J.M. (1996) *Abnormal Psychology* (6th edn). New York: John Wiley and Sons.

Delay, J. and Deniker, P. (1956) Chlorpromazine and neuroleptic treatments in psychiatry. *Journal of Clinical and Experimental Psychopathology*, 17, 19–24.

Delvenne, V., Delecluse, F., Hubain, P., Schoutens, A., DeMaertelaer, V. and Mendlewicz, J. (1990) Regional cerebral blood flow in patients with affective disorder. *British Journal of Psychiatry*, 157, 359–365.

desRosiers, G. (1992) Primary or depressive dementia: clinical features. *International Journal of Geriatric Psychiatry*, 7, 629–638.

Devanand, D.P., Dwork, A.J., Hutchinson, E.R., Bolwig, T.G. and Sackheim, H.A. (1994) Does ECT alter brain structure? *American Journal of Psychiatry*, 151, 957–970.

Devanand, D.P., Verma, A.K., Tirumalasetti, F. and Sackeim, H.A. (1991) Absence of cognitive impairment after more than 100 lifetime ECT treatments. *American Journal of Psychiatry*, 148, 929–932.

Diehl, D.J., Keshavan, M.S., Kanal, E., Nebes, R.D., Nichols, T.E. and Gillen, J.S. (1994) Post-ECT increases in MRI regional T-sub-2 relaxation times and their relationship to cognitive side effects: A pilot study. *Psychiatry Research*, 54, 177–184.

DiMascio, A., Havens, L.L. and Klerman, G.L. (1963) The psychopharmacology of phenothiazine compounds: a comparative study of chlorpromazine, promethazine, trifluoperazine and perphenazine in normal males. *Journal of Nervous and Mental Diseases*, 136, 1–28.

Dolan, R.J., Calloway, S.P. and Mann, A.H. (1985) Cerebral ventricular size in depressed subjects. *Psychological Medicine*, 15, 873–878.

Drewe, E.A. (1974) The effect of type and area of brain lesion on Wisconsin Card Sorting Test performance. *Cortex*, 10, 159–170.

Dupont, R.M., Jernigan, T.L., Butters, N., Delis, D., Hesselink, J.R., Heindel, W. and Gillin, J.C. (1990) Subcortical abnormalities detected in bipolar affective disorder using magnetic resonance imaging. *Archives of General Psychiatry*, 47, 55–59.

Emery, O.B and Breslau, L.D. (1989) Language deficits in depression: Comparisons with SDAT and normal aging. *Journal of Gerontology: Medical Sciences*, 44, 85–92.

Falkai, P. and Bogerts, B. (1986) Cell loss in the hippocampus of schizophrenics. *European Archives of Psychiatry and Neurological Science*, 236, 154–161.

Ferber, C., Taillard, J. and Dealberto, M.J. (1992) Sleep apnea syndrome: Psychiatric aspects. *Encephale*, **18**, 361–367.

Figiel, G.S., Krishnan, K.R., Rao, V.P., Doraiswamy, P.M., Ellinwood, E.H., Nemeroff, C.B., Evans, D. and Boyko, O.B. (1991) Subcortical hyperintensities on brain magnetic resonance imaging: A comparison of normal and bipolar patients. *Journal of Neuropsychiatry and Clinical Neuroscience*, **3**, 18–22.

Findley, L.J., Barth, J.T., Powers, D.C., Wilhoit, S.C., Boyd, D.G. and Suratt, P.M. (1986) Cognitive impairment in patients with obstructive sleep apnea and associated hypoxemia. *Chest*, **90**, 686–690.

Flor-Henry, P. (1974) Psychosis, neurosis and epilepsy. *British Journal of Psychiatry*, **124**, 144–150.

Flor-Henry, P. (1976) Lateralised temporal-limbic dysfunction and psychopathology. *Annals of the New York Academy of Sciences*, **280**, 777–795.

Flor-Henry, P. (1986) Electroconvulsive therapy and lateralized affective systems. *Annals of the New York Academy of Sciences*, **462**, 389–397.

Flor-Henry, P., Fromm-Auch, D., Tapper, M. and Schopflocher, D. (1981) A neuropsychological study of the stable syndrome of hysteria. *Biological Psychiatry*, **16**, 601–626.

Flor-Henry, P. and Yuedall, L.T. (1979) Neuropsychological investigation of schizophrenia and manic-depressive psychosis. In *Hemisphere Asymmetries of Function in Psychopathology*, edited by J. Gruzelier and P. Flor-Henry. Amsterdam: Elsevier.

Flor-Henry, P., Yeudall, L.T., Koles, Z.J. and Howarth, B.G. (1979) Neuropsychological and power spectral EEG investigations of the Obsessive-Compulsive Syndrome. *Biological Psychiatry*, **14**, 119–130.

Fodor, J.A. (1983) *The Modularity of Mind*. Cambridge, Mass.: MIT Press.

Fodor, J.A. (1985) Multiple book review of *The Modularity of Mind*. *Behavioral and Brain Sciences*, **8**, 1–42.

Freeman, W. and Watts, J.W. (1947) Psychosurgery during 1936–1946. *Archives of Neurology and Psychiatry*, **58**, 417–425.

Frith, C.D. (1992) *The Cognitive Neuropsychology of Schizophrenia*. Hove, East Sussex: Lawrence Erlbaum and Associates.

Fulton, J.F. and Jacobsen, C.G. (1935) The functions of the frontal lobes, a comparative study in monkeys, chimpanzees and men. *Advances in Modern Biology*, **4**, 113–123.

Garfinkel, P.E. and Garner, D.M. (1982) *Anorexia Nervosa: A Multidimensional Perspective*. New York: Brunner-Mazel.

Gass, C.S. and Daniel, S.K. (1990) Emotional impact on trail making test performance. *Psychological Reports*, **67**, 435–438.

Gerner, R.H. (1993) Treatment of acute mania. *Psychiatric Clinics of North America*, **16**, 443–460.

Gershon, E.S., Hamovit, J. and Guroff, J.J. (1982) A family study of schizoaffective, bipolar I, bipolar II, unipolar and normal control probands. *Archives of General Psychiatry*, **39**, 1157–1167.

Goddard, G.V. (1967) Development of epileptic seizures through stimulation at low intensity. *Nature*, **214**, 1020–1021.

Gold, P.W., Goodwin, F.K. and Chrousos, G.P. (1988) Clinical and biochemical manifestations of depression; Relation to the neurobiology of stress. *New England Journal of Medicine*, **319**, 413–420.

Gold, J.M. and Harvey, P. (1993) Cognitive deficits in schizophrenia. *Psychiatric Clinics of North America*, **16**, 295–312.

Gold, J.M., Randolph, C., Carpenter, C.J., Goldbert, T.E. and Weinberger, D.R. (1992) Forms of memory failure in schizophrenia. *Journal of Abnormal Psychiatry*, **101**, 487–494.

Goldberg, E. (1995) Rise and fall of the modular orthodoxy. *Journal of Clinical and Experimental Neuropsychology*, **17**, 193–208.

Goldstein, S.G., Filskov, S.B., Weaver, L.A. and Ives, J.O.(1977) Neuropsychological effects of electroconvulsive therapy. *Journal of Clinical Psychology*, **33**, 798– 806.

Good, M.I. (1981) Pseudodementia and physical findings masking significant psychopathology. *American Journal of Psychiatry*, **138**, 811–814.

Goodwin, J.S., Goodwin, J.M. and Gary, P.J. (1983) Association between nutritional status and cognitive functioning in a healthy elderly population. *Journal of the American Medical Association*, **249**, 2917–2921.

Gottschalk, L.A., Buchsbaum, M.S., Gillin, J.C. and Wu. J. (1992) The effect of anxiety and hostility in silent mentation on localised cerebral glucose metabolism. *Comprehensive Psychiatry*, **33**, 52–59.

Grafman, J., Jonas, B.S. and Salazar, A. (1990) Wisconsin Card Sorting Test performance based on location and size of neuroanatomical lesion in Vietnam veterans with penetrating head injury. *Perceptual and Motor Skills*, **71**, 1120–1122.

Granick, S. (1971) Psychological test functioning. In *Human Aging II: An Eleven Year Follow-up Bio-medical and Behavioral Study*, edited by S. Granick and R.D. Patterson. Washington, DC: US Government Printing Office.

Grant, I., Adams, K.M., Carlin, A.S., Rennick, P.M., Judd, L.L. and Schoof, K. (1978) The collaborative neuropsychological study of polydrug abusers. *Archives of General Psychiatry,* **35**, 1063–1073.

Grant, D.A. and Berg, E.A. (1948) A behavioral analysis of the degree of reinforcement and ease of shifting to new responses in a Weigl-type card sorting problem. *Journal of Experimental Psychology,* **38**, 404–411.

Gregory, I. and Smeltzer, D.J. (1977) *Psychiatry: Essentials of Clinical Practice.* Boston: Little Brown and Co.

Greenberg, G.D., Watson, R.K. and Deptula, D. (1987) Neuropsychological dysfunction in sleep apnea. *Sleep,* **10**, 254–262.

Gruzelier, J., Seymour, K., Wilson, L., Jolley, A. and Hirsch, S. (1988) Impairments on neuropsychologic tests of temporohippocampal and frontohippocampal functions and word fluency in remitting schizophrenia and affective disorders. *Archives of General Psychiatry,* **45**, 623–629.

Guilmette, T.J. and Guiliano, A.J. (1991) Taking the stand: Issues and strategies in Forensic Neuropsychology. *The Clinical Neuropsychologist,* **5**, 197–219.

Gureje, O., Olley, O., Acha, R.A. and Osuntokun, B.O. (1994) Do young schizophrenics with recent onset of illness show evidence of hypofrontality? *Behavioral Neurology,* 7, 59–66.

Hamsher, K.S., Halmi, K.A. and Benton, A.L. (1981) Prediction of outcome in anorexia nervosa from neuropsychological status. *Psychiatry Research,* **4**, 79–81.

Hart, R.P. and Kwentus, J.A. (1987) Psychomotor slowing and subcortical-type dysfunction in depression. *Journal of Neurology, Neurosurgery and Psychiatry,* **50**, 1263–1266.

Hart, R.P., Kwentus, J.A., Taylor, J.R. and Harkins, S.W. (1987) Rate of forgetting in dementia and depression. *Journal of Consulting and Clinical Psychology,* **55**, 101–105.

Heaton, R.K. and Crowley, T.J. (1981) Effects of psychiatric disorders and their somatic treatments on neuropsychological test results. In *Handbook of Clinical Neuropsychology,* edited by S.B. Filskov and T.J. Boll, pp. 481–525. New York: John Wiley and Sons.

Heimann, H., Reed, C.F. and Witt, P.N. (1968) Some observations suggesting preservation of skilled motor acts despite drug induced stress. *Psychopharmacologia,* **13**, 287–298.

Heller, W., Etienne, M.A. and Miller, G.A. (1995) Patterns of perceptual asymmetry in depression and anxiety: implications for neuropsychological models of emotion and psychopathology. *Journal of Abnormal Psychology,* **104**, 327–333.

Heron, E.A., Kritchevsky, M. and Delis, D.C. (1991) Neuropsychological presentation of Ganser symptoms. *Journal of Clinical and Experimental Neuropsychology*, **13**, 652–666.

Hill, R.D. and Vandervoort, D. (1992) The effects of state anxiety on recall performance in older learners. *Educational Gerontology*, **18**, 597–605.

Hodges, W.F. and Spielberger, C.D., (1969) Digit span: An indicant of trait or state anxiety? *Journal of Consulting and Clinical Psychology*, **33**, 430–434.

Hoff, A.L., Riordan, H., O'Donnell, D.W., Moris, L. and Delisi, L.E. (1992) Neuropsychological functioning of first-episode schizophreniform patients. *American Journal of Psychiatry*, **149**, 898–903.

Hoffman, R.E., Stopek, S. and Andreasen, N.C. (1986) A comparative study of manic versus schizophrenia speech disorganisation. *Archives of General Psychiatry*, **43**, 831–838.

Huron, G.F. and Brown, L.B. (1986) Body images in anorexia nervosa and bulimia nervosa. *International Journal of Eating Disorders*, **5**, 421–439.

Ishimaru, M., Kurumaji, A. and Toru, M. (1994) Increases in strychnine-insensitive glycine binding sites in cerebral cortex of chronic schizophrenics: Evidence for the glutamate hypothesis. *Biological Psychiatry*, **35**, 84–89.

Janer, K.W. and Pardo, J.V. (1991) Deficits in selective attention following bilateral anterior cingulotomy. *Journal of Cognitive Neuroscience*, **3**, 231–241.

Janowsky, D.S. (1982) Pseudodementia in the elderly: differential diagnosis and treatment. *Journal of Clinical Psychiatry*, **43**, 19–25.

Jenike, M.A., Baer, L., Ballantine, T. and Martuza, R.L. (1991) Cingulotomy for refractory obsessive–compulsive disorder: A long-term follow-up of 33 patients. *Archives of General Psychiatry*, **48**, 548–555.

Johanson, A.M., Risberg, J., Silfverskiöld, P. and Smith, G. (1986) Regional changes in cerebral blood flow during increased anxiety in patients with anxiety neurosis. In *The Roots of Perception*, edited by U. Hentscshel, G. Smith and J.G. Draguns, pp. 353–360. Amsterdam: Elsevier.

Jones, B.P., Duncan, C.C., Brouwers, P. and Mirsky, A.F. (1991) Cognition in eating disorders. *Journal of Clinical and Experimental Neuropsychology*, **13**, 711–728.

Jones, M.M. (1980) Conversion reaction: anachronism or evolutionary form? A review of the neurological, behavioral and psychoanalytic literature. *Psychological Bulletin*, **87**, 427–441.

Jones, R.D., Tranel, D., Benton, A. and Paulsen, J. (1992) Differentiating dementia from "pseudodementia" early in the clinical course: Utility of neuropsychological tests. *Neuropsychology*, **6**, 13–21.

Jorm, A.F. (1986) Cognitive deficits in the depressed elderly: A review of some basic unresolved issues. *Australian and New Zealand Journal of Psychiatry*, 20, 11–22.

Judd, L.L., Hubbard, B., Janowsky, D.S., Huey, L.Y. and Takahashi, K.I. (1977) The effect of lithium carbonate on cognitive functions in normal adults. *Archives of General Psychiatry*, 34, 355–357.

Kajaste, S. and Partinen, M. (1985) Neuropsychological findings in obstructive sleep apnoea syndrome as compared with findings in narcolepsy. World Psychiatric Association Symposium: Psychopathology of dream and sleeping (1983, Helsinki, Finland) *Psychiatria-Fennica*, Suppl 41–49.

Kalat, J.W. (1998) *Biological Psychology* (6th edn). Pacific Grove, CA: Brooks/ Cole Publishing.

Katzman, R. (1986) Differential diagnosis of dementing illnesses. *Neurologic Clinics*, 4, 329–340.

Kiloh, L.G. (1961) Pseudo-dementia. *Acta Psychiatrica Scandinavica*, 37, 335–351.

Kim, J.S., Kornhuber, H.H., Schmid-Burgk, W. and Holzmuller, B. (1980) Low cerebro- spinal fluid glutamate in schizophrenic patients and a new hypothesis in schizophrenia. *Neuroscience Letters*, 20, 379–382.

Kimberg, D.Y. and Farah, M. (1993) A unified account of cognitive impairments following frontal lobe damage: The role of working memory in complex, organised behavior. *Journal of Experimental Psychology: General*, 122, 411–428.

King, G.D., Hannay, J., Masek, B.J. and Burns, J.W., (1978) Effects of anxiety and sex on neuropsychological tests. *Journal of Consulting and Clinical Psychology*, 46, 375–376.

Klein, E., Lavie, P., Meiraz, R., Sadeh, A. and Lennox, P. (1992) Increased motor activity and recurrent manic episodes: Predictors of rapid relapse in remitted bipolar disorder patients after lithium discontinuation. *Biological Psychiatry*, 31, 279–284.

Klonoff, H., Fibiger, C.H. and Hutton, G.H. (1970) Neuropsychological patterns in schizophrenia. *Journal of Nervous and Mental Disease*, 150, 291–300.

Kocsis, J.H., Croughan, J.L., Katz, M.M., Butler, T.P., Secunda, R., Bowden, C.L. and Davis, H. (1990) Response to treatment with antidepressants of patients with severe or moderate nonpsychotic depression and of patients with psychotic depression. *American Journal of Psychiatry*, 147, 621–624.

Kolb, B. and Whishaw, I.Q. (1983) Performance of schizophrenic patients on tests sensitive to left or right frontal, temporal or parietal function in neurological patients. *Journal of Nervous and Mental Diseases*, 171, 435–443.

Kovelman, J.A. and Scheibel, A.B. (1984) A neurohistologic correlate of schizophrenia. *Biological Psychiatry*, **19**, 1601–1621.

Kriss, A., Blumhardt, L.D., Halliday, A.M. and Pratt, R.T.C. (1978) Neurological aymmetries immediately after ECT. *Journal of Neurology, Neurosurgery and Psychiatry*, **41**, 1135–1144.

Kronfol, Z., Hamsher, K.D., Digre, K. and Waziri,R. (1978) Depression and hemispheric functions: Changes associated with unilateral ECT. *British Journal of Psychiatry*, **132**, 560–567.

Kuiper, N.A., Derry, P.A. and MacDonald, M.R. (1981) Self-reference and person perception in depression: A social cognition approach. In *Integrations of Clinical and Social Psychology*, edited by G. Weary and H. Mirels. New York: Oxford University Press.

Kuiper, N.A., Olinger, J. and MacDonald, M.R. (1984) Depressive schemata and the processing of personal and social information. In *Cognitive Processes in Depression*, edited by L.B. Alloy. New York: Guilford Press.

Lader, M. (1982) Biological differentiation of anxiety, arousal and stress. In *The Biology of Anxiety*, edited by R.J. Mathew, pp. 11–22. New York: Brunner-Mazel.

Laessle, R.G., Krieg, J.C., Fichter, M.M. and Pirke, K.M. (1989) Cerebral atrophy and vigilance performance in patients with anorexia nervosa and bulimia nervosa. *Neuropsychobiology*, **21**, 187–191.

Lahti, A.C., Holcomb, H.H., Medoff, D.R. and Tamminga, CA. (1995) Ketamine activates psychosis and alters limbic blood flow in schizophrenia. *NeuroReport*, **6**, 869–872.

Lamberty, G.J. and Bieliauskas, L.A. (1993) Distinguishing between depression and dementia in the elderly: A review of neuropsychological findings. *Archives of Clinical Neuropsychology*, **8**, 149–170.

Landro, N.I., Orbeck, A.L. and Rund, B.R. (1993) Memory functioning in chronic and non- chronic schizophrenics, affectively disturbed patients and normal controls. *Schizophrenia Research*, **10**, 85–92.

LaRue, A. (1989) Patterns of performance on the Fuld Object Memory Evaluation in elderly inpatients with depression and dementia. *Journal of Clinical and Experimental Neuropsychology*, **11**, 409–422.

Lee, M.A., Thompson, P.A. and Metzer, H.Y. (1994) Effects of clozapine on cognitive functioning in schizophrenia. *Journal of Clinical Psychiatry*, **55** (Suppl B), 82–87.

Leff, J. (1988) *Psychiatry Around the Globe*. London: Gaskell.

Leibenluft, E. and Wehr, T.A. (1992) Is sleep deprivation useful in the treatment of depression? *American Journal of Psychiatry*, **149**, 159–168.

Legg, J.F. and Stiff, M.P. (1976) Drug related patterns of depressed patients. *Psychopharmacology*, 50, 205–210.

Lester, D. (1993) Suicidal behaviour in bipolar and unipolar affective disorders: A meta- analysis. *Journal of Affective Disorders*, 27, 117–121.

Levin, S., Yurgelun-Todd, D. and Craft, S. (1989) Contributions of clinical psychology to the study of schizophrenia. *Journal of Abnormal Psychology*, 98, 341–356.

LeVine, W.R. and Conrad, R.L. (1979) The classification of schizophrenic neologisms. *Psychiatry*, 42, 177–181.

Levy, R.S. and Jankovic, J. (1983) Placebo-induced conversion reaction: A neurobehavioural and EEG study of hysterical aphasia, seizure and coma. *Journal of Abnormal Psychology*, 92, 243–249.

Levy, R.S. and Mushin, S. (1973) The somatosensory-evoked response in patients with hysterical anaesthesia. *Journal of Psychosomatic Research*, 17, 81–84.

Lewinsohn, P.M. (1973) *Psychological assessment of patients with brain injury.* Unpublished manuscript, University of Oregon.

Lewinsohn, P.M. (1974) A behavioural approach to depression. In *The Psychology of Depression: Contemporary Theory and Research*, edited by R.M. Freidman and M.M. Katz. New York: Wiley.

Lewinsohn, P.M., Youngren, M.A. and Grosscup, S.J. (1979) Reinforcement and depression. In *The Psychobiology of the Depressive Disorders: Implications for the Effects of Stress*, edited by R.A. Depue. New York: Academic Press.

Lezak, M.D. (1995) *Neuropsychological Assessment* (3rd edn). New York: Oxford University Press.

Liddle, P.F. (1987) The symptoms of chronic schizophrenia: A re-examination of the positive-negative dichotomy. *British Journal of Psychiatry*, 151, 145–151.

Liddle, P.F. and Morris, D. (1991) Schizophrenic syndromes and frontal lobe performance. *British Journal of Psychiatry*, 158, 340–345.

Liebson, E., White, R.F. and Albert, M.L. (1996) Cognitive inconsistencies in abnormal illness behaviour and neurological disease. *Journal of Nervous and Mental Disease*, 184, 122–125.

Lingenfelser, T., Kaschel, R., Weber, A. and Zaiser-Kaschel, H (1994) Young hospital doctors after night duty: Their task-specific cognitive status and emotional condition. *Medical Education*, 28, 566–572.

Lishman, W.A. (1987) *Organic Psychiatry* (2nd edn). Oxford: Blackwell.

Liston, E.H. (1977) Occult presenile dementia. *Journal of Nervous and Mental Disease*, 164, 263–267.

Logie, S.A., Murphy, J.B., Brooks, D.N., Wylie, S., Barron, E.T. and McCulloch, J. (1992) The diagnosis of depression in patients with dementia: Use of the Cambridge mental disorders of the elderly examination (CAMDEX) *International Journal of Geriatric Psychiatry*, 7, 363–368.

Loomis, T.A. and West, T.C. (1958) Comparative sedative effects of a barbiturate and some tranquilliser drugs on normal subjects. *Journal of Pharmacology and Experimental therapeutics*, 122, 525–531.

Luchins, D.J., Lewine, R.R. and Meltzer, H.Y. (1984) Lateral ventricular size, psychopathology and medication response in psychosis. *Biological Psychiatry*, 19, 29–44.

Ludwig, A.M. (1972) Hysteria: A neurobiological theory. *Archives of General Psychiatry*, 27, 771–777.

Luria, A. (1973) *The Working Brain: An Introduction to Neuropsychology* (trans. B. Haigh). New York: Basic Books.

Machlin, S.R., Harris, G.J., Pearlson, G.D., Hoehn-Saric, R., Jeffery, P. and Carmargo, E.E. (1991) Elevated medial-frontal cerebral blood flow in obsessive-compulsive patients: A SPECT study. *American Journal of Psychiatry*, 148, 1240–1242.

MacKenzie, T.B., Robiner, W.N. and Knopman, D.S. (1989) Differences between patient and family assessments of depression in Alzheimer's disease. *American Journal of Psychiatry*, 146, 1174–1178.

MacLeod, C. and Donnellan, A.M. (1993) Individual differences in anxiety and the restriction of working memory capacity. *Personality and Individual Differences*, 15, 163–173.

Maletsky, B.M. (1978) Seizure duration and clinical effect in ECT. *Comprehensive Psychiatry*, 19, 541–550.

Malloy, F.W. (1982) Changes in neuropsychological test performance after electroconvulsive therapy. *Biological Psychiatry*, 17, 61–67.

Marinkovic, S.V., Milislavjevic, M.M., Lolic-Draganic, V. and Kovacevic, M.S. (1987) Distribution of the occipital branches of the posterior cerebral artery: Correlation with occipital lobe infarcts. *Stroke*, 18, 728–732.

Markham, R. and Darke, S. (1991) The effects of anxiety on verbal and spatial task performance. *Australian Journal of Psychology*, 43, 107–111.

Marsden, C.D. and Harrison, M. (1972) Outcome of investigation of patients with presenile dementia. *British Medical Journal*, 2, 249–252.

Marshall, G. and Zimbardo, P. (1979) Affective consequences of inadequately explained physiological arousal. *Journal of Personality and Social Psychology*, 37, 970–988.

Martin, A, Brouwers, P., Lalonde, F., Cox, C., Teleska, P., Fedio, P., Foster, N. and Chase, T. (1986) Towards a behavioural typology of Alzheimer's patients. *Journal of Clinical and Experimental Neuropsychology*, **8**, 594–610.

Martin, N.J. and Franzen, M.D. (1989) The effect of anxiety in neuropsychological function. *International Journal of Clinical Neuropsychology*, **11**, 1–8.

Massman, P.J., Delis, D.C., Butters, N., Dupont, R.M. and Gillin, C. (1992) The subcortical dysfunction hypothesis of memory deficits in depression: Neuropsychological validation in a subgroup of patients. *Journal of Clinical and Experimental Neuropsychology*, **14**, 687–706.

Matthews, C.G., Shaw, D.J. and Klove, H. (1966) Psychological test performance in neurologic and 'pseudo-neurologic' subjects. *Cortex*, **2**, 244–253.

McAllister, T.W. (1983) Overview: Pseudodementia. *American Journal of Psychiatry*, **140**, 528–533.

McAllister, T.W., Ferrell, R.B., Price, T.R. and Neville, M. (1982) The Dexamethasone Suppression Test in two patients with severe depressive pseudodementia. *American Journal of Psychiatry*, **139**, 479–481.

McAllister, T.W. and Price, T.R. (1982) Severe depressive pseudodementia with and without dementia. *American Journal of Psychiatry*, **139**, 626–629.

McGuffin, P. and Katz, R. (1989) The genetics of depression: Current approaches. *British Journal of Psychiatry*, **155**, 18–26.

McLean, S. (1987) Assessing dementia. Part i: Difficulties, definitions and differential diagnosis. *Australian and New Zealand Journal of Psychiatry*, **21**, 142–174.

Meehl, P. (1986) Causes and effects of my disturbing little book. *Journal of Personality Assessment*, **50**, 370–375.

Mesulam, M.M. (1985) *Principles of Behavioral Neurology*. Philadelphia: F.A. Davis.

Miceli, G., Caltagirone, C., Gainotti, G., Masullo, C. and Silveri, M.C. (1981) Neuropsychological correlates of localized cerebral lesions in nonaphasic brain damaged patients. *Journal of Clinical Neuropsychology*, **3**, 53–63.

Miller, E. (1983) A note on the interpretation of data derived from neuropsychological tests. *Cortex*, **19**, 131–132.

Miller, E. and Lewis, P. (1977) Recognition memory in elderly patients with depression and dementia: A signal detection analysis. *Journal of Abnormal Psychology*, **86**, 84–86.

Miller, L. (1984) Neuropsychological concepts of somatoform disorders. *International Journal of Psychiatry in Medicine*, **14**, 31–46.

Miller, W.R. (1975) Psychological deficit in depression. *Psychological Bulletin*, **82**, 238–260.

Milner, B. (1963) Effects of different brain lesions on card sorting. *Archives of Neurology*, 9, 90–100.

Milner, B. (1964) Some effects of frontal lobectomy in man. In *The Frontal Granular Cortex and Behavior*, edited by J.M. Warren and K. Akert. New York: McGraw Hill.

Mineka, S. and Sutton, S.K. (1992) Cognitive biases and the emotional disorders. *Psychological Science*, 3, 65–69.

Mitchell, P., Parker, G., Jamieson, K., Wilhelm, K., Hickie, I., Brodaty, H., Boyce, P., Hadzi-Pavlovic, D. and Roy, K. (1992) Are there any differences between bipolar and unipolar melancholia? *Journal of Affective Disorders*, 25, 97–106.

Mogg, K., Mathews, A., Bird, C. and MacGregor-Morris, R. (1990) Effects of stress and anxiety on the processing of threat stimuli. *Journal of Personality and Social Psychology*, 59, 1230–1237.

Moniz, E. (1936, 1994) Prefrontal leucotomy in the treatment of mental disorders. *American Journal of Psychiatry*, 151(6, Suppl), 237–239.

Morice, R. (1990) Cognitive inflexibility and pre-frontal dysfunction in schizophrenia and mania. *British Journal of Psychiatry*, 157, 50–54.

Mortimer, A.M., Smith, A.,, Lock, M. and Lekh, S. (1995) Clozapine and neuropsychological function: Preliminary report of a controlled study. *Human Psychopharmacology, Clinical and Experimental*, 10, 157–158.

Mountain, M.A. and Snow, W.G. (1993) Wisconsin card sorting test as a measure of frontal pathology: A review. *The Clinical Neuropsychologist*, 7, 108–118.

Mowrer, O.H. (1960) *Learning Theory and Behavior*. New York: Academic Press.

Nasrallah, H.A., McCalley-Withers, M. and Pfohl, B. (1984) Clinical significance of large cerebral ventricles in manic males. *Psychiatry Research*, 13, 151–156.

Ndetei, D.M. and Vadher, A. (1984) A cross-cultural study of the frequencies of Schneider's first rank symptoms of schizophrenia. *Acta Psychiatrica Scandinavica*, 70, 540–544.

Nolte, J. (1993) *The Human Brain: An Introduction to its Functional Anatomy* (3rd edn). Mosby: St Louis.

O'Carroll, R. (1992) Neuropsychology of psychosis. *Current Opinion in Psychiatry*, 5, 38–44.

O'Dea, J.A. (1995) Body image and nutritional status among adolescents and adults: A review of the literature. *Australian Journal of Nutrition and Dietetics*, 52, 56–67.

Otto, M.W. (1992) Normal and abnormal information processing. A neuropsychological perspective on Obsessive–Compulsive Disorder. *Psychiatric Clinics of North America*, 15, 825–848.

Otto, M.W., McNally, R.J., Pollack, M.H. and Chen, E. (1994) Hemispheric laterality and memory bias for threat in anxiety disorder. *Journal of Abnormal Psychology*, 103, 28–831.

Palazidou, E., Robinson, P. and Lishman, W.A. (1990) Neuroradiological and neuropsychological assessment in anorexia nervosa. *Psychological Medicine*, 20, 21–527.

Pande, A.C. and Gruhaus, L.J. (1990) ECT for depression in the presence of myasthenia gravis. *Convulsive Therapy*, 6, 176–180.

Pantellis, C. and Nelson, H.E. (1994) Cognitive functioning and symptomatology in schizophrenia: The role of frontal-subcortical systems. In *The Neuropsychology of Schizophrenia*, edited by A.S. David and J.C. Cutting. Hove, East Sussex: Lawrence Erlbaum Associates.

Park, S and Holzman, P.S. (1992) Schizophrenics show spatial working memory deficits. *Archives of General Psychiatry*, 49, 975–982.

Paykel, E. (1974) Recent life events and clinical depression. In *Life Stress and Illness*, edited by E.K. Gunderson and R.H. Rahe. Springfield, Illinios: Thomas.

Paykel, E., Myers, J., Dienelt, M., Klerman, G., Lindenthal, J. and Pepper, M. (1969) Life events and depression. *Archives of General Psychiatry*, 21, 753–760.

Pearlson, G.D., Garbacz, D.J, Breakey, W.R., Ahn, H.S. and DePaulo, J.R. (1984) Lateral ventricular enlargement associated with persistent unemployment and negative symptoms in both schizophrenia and bipolar disorder. *Psychiatry Research*, 12, 1–9.

Pearlson, G.D., Garbacz, D.J, Moberg, P.J., Ahn, H.S. and DePaulo, J.R. (1985) Symptomatic, familial, perinatal and social correlates of computerised axial tomography changes in schizophrenics and bipolars. *Journal of Nervous and Mental Diseases*, 173, 42–50.

Pearlson, G.D., Garbacz, D.J, Tompkins, R.T., Ahn, H.S., Gutterman, D.F., Veroff, A.E. and DePaulo, J.R. (1984) Clinical correlates of lateral ventricular enlargement in bipolar affective disorder. *American Journal of Psychiatry*, 141, 253–256.

Pearlson, G.D., Rabins, P.V., Kim, W.S., Speedie, L.J., Moberg, P.J., Burns, A. and Bascom, M.J. (1989) Structural brain CT changes and cognitive deficits in elderly depressives with and without reversible dementia ('pseudodementia'). *Psychological Medicine*, 19, 573–584.

Pearlson, G.D., Ross, C.A., Lohr, W.D., Rovner, B.W., Chase, G.A. and Folstein, M.F. (1990) Association between family history of affective disorder and the depressive syndrome of Alzheimer's disease. *American Journal of Psychiatry*, 147, 452–456.

Perret, E. (1974) The left frontal lobe of man and the suppression of habitual responses in verbal categorical behavior. *Neuropsychologia*, 12, 323–330.

Pinel, J.P.J. (1997) *Biopsychology* (3rd edn). Needham Heights, MA: Allyn and Bacon.

Posner, M.I., Early, T.S., Reiman, E., Pardo, P.J. and Dhawan, M. (1988) Asymmetries in hemispheric control of attention in schizophrenia. *Archives of General Psychiatry*, 45, 814–821.

Posner, M.I. and Raichle, M.E. (1994) *Images of Mind*. New York: Scientific American Library.

Post, F. (1975) Dementia, depression, and pseudodementia. In *Psychiatric Aspects of Neurologic Disease*, edited by D.F. Benson and D. Blumer. New York: Grune and Stratton.

Pratt, R.T.C. and Warrington, E.K. (1972) The assessment of cerebral dominance with unilateral ECT. *British Journal of Psychiatry*, 121, 327–328.

Prudic, J. and Sackheim, H.A. (1996) Electroconvulsive therapy. *Current Opinion in Psychiatry*, 9, 35–39.

Rabins, P., Merchant, A. and Nestadt, G. (1984) Criteria for diagnosing reversible dementia caused by depression: Validation by 2-year follow-up. *British Journal of Psychiatry*, 144, 488–492.

Rapee, R. (1993) The utilisation of working memory by worry. *Behaviour Research and Therapy*, 31, 617–620.

Reed, G. (1977) Obsessional personality disorder and remembering. *British Journal of Psychiatry*, 130, 177–183.

Reilly, J.J., Crowe, S.F. and Lloyd, J.H. (1991) Neuroleptic toxicity syndromes: A clinical spectrum. *Australian and New Zealand Journal of Psychiatry*, 25, 499–505.

Reitan, R.M. (1986) Theoretical and methodological bases of the Halstead-Reitan neuropsychological test battery. In *Neuropsychological Assessment of Neuropsychiatric Disorders*, edited by I. Grant and K. M. Adams. New York: Oxford University Press.

Reynolds, C.F., Hoch, C., Kupfer, D.J., Buysse, D.J., Houck, P.R., Stack, J.A. and Campbell, D.W. (1988) Bedside differentiation of depressive pseudodementia from dementia. *American Journal of Psychiatry*, 145, 1099–1103.

Richelson, E. (1993) Treatment of acute depression. *Psychiatric Clinics of North America*, 16, 461–478.

Robinson, A.L., Heaton, R.K., Lehman, R.A.W. and Stilson, D.W. (1980) The utility of the Wisconsin Card Sorting Test in detecting and localising frontal lobe lesions. *Journal of Consulting and Clinical Psychology*, 48, 605–614.

Roehrs, T., Merrion, M., Pedrosi, B. and Stepanski, E. (1995) Neuropsychological function in obstructive sleep apnea (OSAS) compared to chronic obstructive pulmonary disease. *Sleep*, 18, 382–388.

Roth, M. (1955) The natural history of mental; disorders in old age. *Journal of Mental Science*, 101, 281–301.

Rovner, B.W., Broadhead, J., Spencer, B.A., Carson, K. and Folstein, M.F. (1989) Depression and Alzheimer's disease. *American Journal of Psychiatry*, 146, 350–353.

Sackheim, H.A., Decina, P., Portnoy, S., Neeley, P. and Malitz, S. (1987) Studies of dosage, seizure threshold, and seizure duration in ECT. *Biological Psychiatry*, 22, 249–268.

Sackheim, H.A., Freeman, J., McElhiney, M., Coleman, E., Prudic, J. and Devanand, D.P. (1992) Effects of major depression on estimates of intelligence. *Journal of Clinical and Experimental Neuropsychology*, 14, 66–80.

Sackheim, H.A., Prohovnik, I., Moeller, J.R., Brown, R.P., Apter, S., Prudic, J., Devanand, D.P. and Mukherjee, S. (1990) Regional cerebral blood flow in mood disorders: I. Comparison of major depressives and normal controls at rest. *Archives of General Psychiatry*, 47, 60–70.

Sagawa, K., Kawakaisu, S. and Shiboya, I. (1990) Correlation of cerebral blood flow with performance on neuropsychological tests in schizophrenic patients. *Schizophrenia Research*, 3, 241–246.

Savard, R.J., Rey, A.C. and Post, R.M. (1980) Halstead-Reitan Category Test in bipolar and unipolar affective disorders: Relationship to age and phase of illness. *Journal of Nervous and Mental Diseases*, 168, 297–304.

Saykin, A.J., Gur, R.C., Gur, R.E., Mosley, P.D., Mosley, L.H., Resinch, S.M., Ketser, B. and Stafiniak, P. (1991) Neuropsychological function in schizophrenia: Selective impairment in memory and learning. *Archives of General Psychiatry*, 48, 618–624.

Schachter, S. and Singer, J.E. (1962) Cognitive, social and physiological determinants of emotional state. *Psychological Review*, 69, 379–399.

Schlegal, S. and Kretzschmar, K. (1987) Computed tomography in affective disorder, I. *Biological Psychiatry*, 22, 4–14.

Schneider, K. (1959) *Clinical Psychopathology*. New York: Grune and Stratton.

Scott, A.I.F., Dougall, N., Ross, M. and O'Carroll, R.E. (1994) Short-term effects of electroconvulsive treatment on the uptake of -super(99 m)Tc-exametazime into brain in major depression shown with single photon emission tomography. *Journal of Affective Disorders*, 30, 27–34.

Scott, M.L., Golden, C.J., Ruedrich, S.L. and Bishop, R.J. (1983) Ventricular enlargements in major depression. *Psychiatry Research*, 8, 91–93.

Seal, M., Crowe, S.F. and Cheung, P. (1997) Deficits in source monitoring in subjects with auditory hallucinations may be due to differences in verbal intelligence and verbal memory. *Cognitive Neuropsychiatry*, 2, 273–290.

Seligman, M.E. (1974) Depression and learned helplessness. In *The Psychology of Depression: Contemporary Theory and Research*, edited by R.M. Freidman and M.M. Katz. New York: Wiley.

Selye, H. (1936) A syndrome produced by diverse nocuous agents. *Nature*, 138, 32–38.

Selye, H. (1976) *Stress in Health and Disease*. Boston: Butterworths.

Shagass, C. (1965) The EEG in affective psychosis. In *Applications of Electroencephalography in Psychiatry*, edited by W.P. Wilson. Durham, North Carolina: Duke University Press.

Shallice, T. (1988) *From Neuropsychology to Mental Structure*. Cambridge: Cambridge University Press.

Sher, K.J., Frost, R.O., Kushner, M., Crews, T.M. and Alexander, J.E. (1989) Memory deficits in compulsive checkers: replication and extension in a clinical sample. *Behavior Research and Therapy*, 27, 65–69.

Shulman, R. (1967) A survey of vitamin B_{12} deficiency and psychiatric illness in an elderly psychiatric population. *British Journal of Psychiatry*, 113, 241–251.

Shutts, D. (1982) *Lobotomy: Resort to the Knife*. New York: Van Nostrand Reinhold.

Small, I.F., Small, J.G. and Milstein, V. (1986) A critical review of ECT: Past, present and future. In *The American Handbook of Psychiatry*, edited by P.A. Berger and H.K.H. Brodie, pp. 999–1028. New York: Basic Books.

Small, J.G., Milstein, V., Miller, M.J., Sharpley, P.H., Small, I.F., Malloy, F.W. and Klapper, M.K. (1988) Clinical, neuropsychological, and EEG evidence for mechanisms of action of ECT. *Convulsive Therapy*, 4, 280–291.

Smeets, M.A.M., Panhuysen, G.E. (1995) What can be learned from body size estimation? It all depends on your theory. Special Issue: Body experience. *Eating Disorders: The Journal of Treatment and Prevention*, 3, 101–114.

Smith, P.F. and Darlington, C.L. (1996) *Clinical Psychopharmacology: A Primer*. New Jersey: Lawrence Earlbaum Associates.

Sorg, B.A. and Whitney, P. (1992) The effect of trait-anxiety and situational stress on working memory capacity. *Journal of Research in Personality*, 26, 235–241.

Southmayd, S.E. (1989) Diagnosing pseudodementia. *Hospital and Community Psychiatry*, 40, 753–754.

Spar, J.E. and Gerner, R. (1982) Does the Dexamethasone Suppression Test distinguish dementia from depression? *American Journal of Psychiatry*, **139**, 238–241.

Speed, M., Toner, B.B., Shugar, G. and Gasbarro, I.D. (1991) Though disorder and verbal recall in acutely psychotic patients. *Journal of Clinical Psychology*, **47**, 735–744.

Spielberger, C.D., Lushene, R.E. and McAdoo, W.G., (1977) Theory and measurement of anxiety states. In *Handbook of Modern Personality Theory*, edited by R.B. Cattell and R.M. Dreger, pp. 239–253. Washington: Hemisphere.

Spohn, H.E., Lacoursiere, R.B., Thompson, K. and Coyne, L. (1977) Phenothiazine effects on psychological and physiological dysfunction in chronic schizophrenics. *Archives of General Psychiatry*, **34**, 633–644.

Spreen, O. and Benton, A. (1965) Comparative studies of some psychological tests for cerebral damage. *Journal of Nervous and Mental Disease*, **140**, 323–333.

Spreen, O. and Strauss, E. (1998) *A Compendium of Neuropsychological Tests* (2nd edn). New York: Oxford University Press.

Squire, L.R. (1977) ECT and memory loss. *American Journal of Psychiatry*, **134**, 997–1001.

Squire, L.R., Chance, P.M. and Slater, P.C. (1976) Retrograde amnesia following electroconvulsive therapy. *Nature*, **260**, 775–777.

Steffens, D.C., Tupler, L.A. and Krishnan, K.R.R. (1993) The neurostructural/neurofunctional basis of depression/mania. *Current Opinion in Psychiatry*, **6**, 22–26.

Stephens, D.N., Duka, T. and Andrews, J.S. (1991) Benzodiazepines, betacarbolines and memory. In *Memory: Neurochemical and Abnormal Perspectives*, edited by J. Weinman and J. Hunter, pp. 11–42. London: Harwood Academic Publishers.

Sternberg, D.E. and Jarvik, M.E. (1976) Memory functions in depression: Improvement with antidepressant medications. *Archives of General Psychiatry*, **33**, 219–224.

Stuss, D.T. and Benson, D.F. (1984) Neuropsychological studies of the frontal lobes. *Psychological Bulletin*, **95**, 3–28.

Stuss, D.T., Benson, D.F., Kaplan, E.F., Della Malva, C.L. and Weir, W.S. (1983) The effect of prefrontal leucotomy on visuoperceptive and visuoconstructive tests. *Bulletin of Clinical Neuroscience*, **49**, 43–51.

Stuss, D.T., Benson, D.F., Kaplan, E.F., Weir, W.S. and Della Malva, C. (1981) Leucotomized and nonleucotomized schizophrenics: Comparison on tests of attention. *Biological Psychiatry*, **16**, 1085–1100.

Stuss, D.T., Kaplan, E.F., Benson, D.F., Weir, W.S., Naeser, M.A. and Levine, H.L. (1981) Long-term effects of prefrontal leucotomy: An overview of neuropsychologic residuals. *Journal of Clinical Neuropsychology*, **3**, 13–32.

Stuss, D.T., Kaplan, E.F., Benson, D.F., Weir, W.S., Chiuli, S. and Sarazin, F.F. (1982) Evidence for the involvement of orbitofrontal cortex in memory functions: An interference effect. *Journal of Comparative and Physiological Psychology*, **6**, 913–925.

Stuss, D.T., Kaplan, E.F., Benson, D.F., Weir, W.S., Naeser, M.A., Lieberman, I. and Ferrill, D. (1983) The involvement of orbitofrontal cerebrum in cognitive tasks. *Neuropsychologia*, **21**, 235–248.

Stuss, D.T., Kaplan, E.F., Benson, D.F. et al. (1986) Language functioning after bilateral prefrontal leukotomy. *Brain and Language*, **28**, 66–70.

Suhara, T., Nakayama, K., Inoue, O., Fukuda, H., Shimizu, M., Mori, A. and Tateno, Y. (1992) D_1 dopamine receptor binding in mood disorders measured by positron emission tomography. *Psychopharmacology*, **106**, 14–18.

Summefeldt, A.T., Alphs, L.D., Wagman, A.M.I., Funderburk, F.R., Hierholzer, R.M. and Strauss, M.E. (1991) Reduction of perseverative errors in patients with schizophrenia using monetary feedback. *Journal of Abnormal Psychology*, **100**, 613–616.

Sutker, P.B., Allain, A.N. and Johnson, J.L. (1993) Clinical assessment of long-term cognitive and emotional sequelae to WWII POW confinement: Comparison of twin pilots. *Psychological Assessment*, **5**, 3–10.

Sutker, P.B., Allain, A.N., Johnson, J.L. and Butters, N.M. (1992) Memory and learning performances in POW survivors with a history of malnutrition and combat veteran controls. *Archives of Clinical Neuropsychology*, **7**, 431–444.

Sutker, P.B., Vasterling, J.J., Brailey, K. and Allain, A.N. (1995) Memory, attention and executive function in POW survivors: Contributing biological and psychological factors. *Neuropsychology*, **9**, 118–125.

Sweeney, J.A., Keilp, J.G., Haas, G.L., Hill, J. and Weiden, P.J. (1990) Relationships between medication treatments and neuropsychological test performance in schizophrenia. *Psychiatry Research*, **37**, 297–308.

Szmukler, G.I., Andrewes, D., Kingston, K., Chen, L., Stargatt, R. and Stanley, R. (1992) Neuropsychological impairment in anorexia nervosa: Before and after refeeding. *Journal of Clinical and Experimental Neuropsychology*, **14**, 347–352.

Taylor, M.A. and Abrams, R. (1984) Cognitive impairments in schizophrenia. *American Journal of Psychiatry*, **141**, 196–201.

Taylor, M.A. and Abrams, R. (1985) Short-term cognitive effects of unilateral and bilateral ECT. *British Journal of Psychiatry*, 146, 308–311.

Tomer, R. (1989) Asymmetrical effects of neuroleptics on psychotic patients' performance on a tactile discrimination task. *Journal of Nervous and Mental Disease*, 177, 699–700.

Torrey, E.F. (1980) Neurological abnormalities in schizophrenic patients. *Biological Psychiatry*, 15, 381–388.

Touyz, S.W., Beumont, P.J. and Johnstone, L.C. (1986) Neuropsychological correlates of dieting disorders. *International Journal of Eating Disorders*, 5, 1025–1034.

Tucker, D.M., Roth, R.S., Arneson, B.A. and Buckingham, V. (1977) Right hemisphere activation during stress. *Neuropsychologia*, 15, 697–700.

Tucker, D.M., Antes, J.R., Stenslie, C.E. and Barnhardt, T.M. (1978) Anxiety and lateral cerebral function. *Journal of Abnormal Psychology*, 87, 380–383.

Tucker, D.M. and Williamson, P.A. (1984) Asymmetric neural control systems in human self–regulation. *Psychological Review*, 91, 185–215.

Tucker, D.M. and Derryberry, D. (1992) Motivated attention: anxiety and frontal executive functions. *Neuropsychiatry, Neuropsychology and Behavioral Neurology*, 5, 233– 252.

Tyler, S.K. and Tucker, D.M. (1982) Anxiety and perceptual structure: Individual differences in neuropsychological function. *Journal of Abnormal Psychology*, 91, 210–220.

Uddo, M., Vasterling, J.J., Brailey, K. and Sutker, P.B. (1993) Memory and attention in combat-related post-traumatic stress disorder (PTSD) *Journal of Psychopathology and Behavioural Assessment*, 15, 43–52.

Valencia-Flores, M., Bliwise, D.L., Guilleminault, C., Cilveti, R. and Clerk, A. (1996) Cognitive function in patients with sleep apnea after acute nocturnal nasal continuous positive airway pressure (CPAP) treatment: Sleepiness and hypoxemia effects. *Journal of Clinical and Experimental Neuropsychology*, 18, 197–210.

Valenstein, E.S. (1986) *Great and Desperate Cures: The Rise and Decline of Psychosurgery and other Radical Treatments for Mental Illness.* New York: Basic Books.

van Zomeren, A.H. and Brouwer, W.H. (1994) *Clinical Neuropsychology of Attention.* New York: Oxford University Press.

Victor, M., Adams, R.D. and Collins, G.H. (1989) *The Wernicke-Korsakoff Syndrome and Related Neurological Disorders due to Alcoholism and Malnutrition* (2nd edn). Philadelphia: F.A. Davis Company.

Waller, G. and Hodgson, S. (1996) Body image distortion in anorexia and bulimia nervosa: The role of perceived and actual control. *Journal of Nervous and Mental Disease*, 184, 213–219

Walsh, K.W. (1994) *Neuropsychology: A Clinical Approach* (3rd edn). Melbourne: Churchill Livingstone.

Weinberger, D.R., Berman, K.S. and Zec, R.F. (1986) Physiological dysfunction of dorsolateral prefrontal cortex in schizophrenia: 1. Regional cerebral blood flow evidence. *Archives of General Psychiatry*, 43, 1114–1124.

Weinberger, D., Berman, K.S. and Illowsky, B.P. (1988) Physiologic dysfunction of dorsolateral prefrontal cortex in schizophrenia III: a new cohort of evidence for monoaminergic *Archives of General Psychiatry*, 45, 609–615.

Weiner, R.D., Fink, M., Hammersley, D., Moench, L., Sackheim, H.A. and Small, I. (1990) *American Psychiatric Association: The Practice of ECT: Recommendations for Treatment, Training and Privileging*. Washington DC: American Psychiatric Press.

Weingartner, H. (1986) Automatic and effort-demanding cognitive processes in depression. In *Handbook for Clinical Memory Assessment of Older Adults*, edited by L. Poon. Washington, DC: American Psychological Association.

Weingartner, H., Cohen, R.M., Murphy, D.L., Martello, J. and Gerdt, C. (1981) Cognitive processes in depression. *Archives of General Psychiatry*, 38, 42–47.

Wells, C.E. (1979) Pseudodementia. *American Journal of Psychiatry*, 136, 895–900.

Whitehead, A. (1973) Verbal learning and memory in elderly depressives. *British Journal of Psychiatry*, 123, 203–208.

Williams, K.M., Iacono, W.G., Remick, R.A. and Greenwood, P. (1990) Dichotic perception and memory following electroconvulsive treatment for depression. *British Journal of Psychiatry*, 157, 366–372.

Wirz-Justice, A. and Wehr, T.A. (1983) Neuropsychopharmacology and biological rhythms. *Advances in Biological Psychiatry*, 11, 20–34.

Witt, E.D., Ryan, C. and Hsu, L.K.G. (1985) Learning deficits in adolescents with anorexia nervosa. *Journal of Nervous and Mental Disease*, 173, 182–184.

Wood, F.B. and Flowers, D.L. (1990) Hypofrontal versus hypo-sylvian blood flow in schizophrenia. *Schizophrenia Bulletin*, 16, 413–424.

Wu, J.C. and Bunney, W.E. (1990) The biological basis of an antidepressant response to sleep deprivation and relapse: Review and hypothesis. *American Journal of Psychiatry*, 147, 14–21.

Yergelun-Todd, D., Craft, S., Levin, S., Kaplan, E. and Aizley, H. (1987) Process analysis of the Rey Osterreith Complex Figure in patients with schizophrenia and manic depressive illness (Abst). *Journal of Clinical and Experimental Neuropsychology*, 9, 61.

Yergelun-Todd, D., Craft, S., O'Brien, C., Kaplan, E. and Levin, S. (1988) Wisconsin Card Sort in schizophrenia and manic depressive illness (Abstract). *Journal of Clinical and Experimental Neuropsychology*, **10**, 71.

Yerkes, R.M and Dodson, J.D. (1908) The relation of strength of stimulus to rapidity of habit formation. *Journal of Comparative Neurology and Psychology*, **18**, 459–482.

Yesavage, J.A., Brink, T.L., Rose, T.L., Lum, O., Huang, V., Adey, M.B. and Leirer, V.O. (1983) Development and validation of a geriatric depression screening scale: A preliminary report. *Journal of Psychiatric Research*, **22**, 165–170.

Young, L.T., Warsh, J.J., Kish, S.J., Shannak, K. and Hornykeiwicz, O. (1994) Reduced brain 5-HT and elevated NE turnover and metabolites in bipolar affective disorder. *Biological Psychiatry*, **35**, 121–127.

Young, R.C., Manley, M.W. and Alexopoulos, G.S. (1985) 'I don't know' responses in elderly depressives and in dementia. *Journal of American Geriatrics Society*, **33**, 253–257.

Young, M.A., Schefter, W.A., Fawcett, J. and Klerman, G.L. (1990) Gender differences in the clinical features of unipolar major depressive disorder. *Journal of Nervous and Mental Disease*, **178**, 200–203.

Zajecka, J.M. and Fawcett, J. (1991) Innovative somatic treatments for depression. *Psychiatric Medicine*, **9**, 77–103.

Zervas, I.M. and Fink, M. (1991) Electroconvulsive therapy. *Current Opinion in Psychiatry*, **4**, 73–77.

Zervas, I.M. and Jandorf, L. (1993) The Randt Memory Test in electroconvulsive therapy: Relation to illness and treatment parameters. *Convulsive Therapy*, **9**, 28–38.

Zielinski, C.M., Taylor, M.A. and Juzwin, K.R. (1991) Neuropsychological deficits in Obsessive–Compulsive Disorder. *Neuropsychiatry, Neuropsychology, and Behavioral Neurology*, **4**, 110–126.

Zornberg, G.L. and Pope, H.G. (1993) Treatment of depression in bipolar disorder: new directions for research. *Journal of Clinical Pharmacology*, **13**, 397–408.

Zucker, D.K., Livingston, R.L., Nakra, R. and Clayton, P.J. (1981) B_{12} deficiency and psychiatric disorders: case report and literature review. *Biological Psychiatry*, **16**, 197–205.

INDEX

Abnormal illness behaviour 86
Activation 49
Acute stress response 63, 66–7
Adrenocorticotrophic hormone
   (ACTH) 66, 114
Adynamia 109
Affective disorders 39–62
   biological origins 42–44
   hemispheric contribution to 50–1
   neuropathological investigations 44
   neuropathology 44–5
   neuropsychological features 47–50
   pseudomentia 51–2
   psychological origins 44
   structural and functional imaging
      data 45–7
   treatment of 125-7
Aggression 57
Agoraphobia 65
Akithisia 125
Alcoholism 98
Alogia 22
Alzheimer's disease 1, 15, 48, 52, 88
Anorexia nervosa 93, 96–105
Anterior cingulate 26
Anterograde amnesia 116
Antidepressant drugs 130
Antidepressant drug therapy 41

Anti-manic drugs 130
Antipsychotics 124
Anxiety 63
   free-floating 65
   state 65
   trait 65
Anxiety disorders 65–80
   due to a general medical condition
      65
   generalised 65–6
   substance-induced 65
Anxiolytic drugs 127, 131
Anxiolytics 130
Aplasia 26
Approximate answers 83
Apraxia 6
Arithmetic 12 see also Wechsler Adult
      Intelligence Scale-Revised
Arithmetic and Digit Symbol Substi-
      tution tasks 59
Arousal 13, 49, 57, 64
Association areas
   heteromodal (higher order) 9
   unimodal (modality specific) 9
Atrophy 54
Attention 57
Atypical antipsychotic agents 25, 124
Austin Maze Test (AMT) 11, 13, 59

Automatic tasks 30
Autopsychagnosia 33
Avolition 22

Barbiturates 130
Basal ganglia 47
Benton Visual Retention Test 49
Benzodiazepines 67, 127, 131
Binge eating 96 *see also* bulimia nervosa
Bipolar affective disorders 39–62
Bipolar disorders 41
    treatment of 126
Bizarre behaviour 22
Black swan approach 3
Block design 12 *see also* Wechsler
    Adult Intelligence Scale-Revised
Body dysmorphic disorder 82
Boston Diagnositic Aphasia
    Examination 14
Bottom-up modules 139
Brain stem 7, 14
Breathing-related sleep disorder 93
Bucco-lingual masticatory 125
Bulimia nervosa 93, 96–97
Burton 40
Butyrophenones 124

Capsulotomy 109
Carbamazepine 126
Catatonia 19
Catechol O Methyl Transferase
    (COMT) 15
Catecholamines 16
    levels 42
Caudate 47
    nucleus 68
Cell doctrine of brain function 5
Central sulcus 7
Checking behaviour 73 *see also*
    obsessive–compulsive disorder
Chimeric faces test 75
Chlorpromazine (CPZ) 20, 124, 128

Chronic sleep deprivation 94
Chronic stress 67
    condition 67
Cingulotomy 109
Circadian rhythms 55
Classical conditioning 67
Clinical decision making 2
Clozapine 25, 35, 129
Cognition
    drug effects on 127–131
Cognitive behaviour therapy for
    depression 44
Comprehension 12 *see also* Wechsler
    Adult Intelligence Scale-Revised
Computed tomography (CT) 26
Confabulation 98
Confrontational naming 14
Consciousness 93
Continuous positive air pressure
    (CPAP) treatment 94–6
Controlled Oral Word Association Test
    (COWAT) 11, 13
Conversion disorder 82
Cortical 56
Cortical tone 13
    and arousal 6
Corticotrophin releasing factor (CRF)
    66
Cortisol 114

Delirium 99
Delusion 22, 42
Delusions 1, 19
Dèmence prècoce 19
Dementia
    in depression 51
Dementia of the Alzheimer type
    (DAT) 10
    differential diagnosis of 52
Dementia paranoides 19
Dementia praecox simplex 20
Dementia syndrome of depression 51

Depression 39
  cognitive behaviour therapy of 44
  dementia in 51
  dementia syndrome of 51
  endogenous form of 40
  monoamine hypothesis of 42
  neurotic form of 40
  psychotic form of 40
  reactive 40
Depression-induced organic mental
  disorder 51
Depressive disorders 41
Depressive pseudodementia 51
Derailment 29
Dexamethasone 43
Diazepam 127
Digit span 12
Digit span and similarities 50
Digit span task 69
Digit Symbol 12 *see also* Wechsler
  Adult Intelligence Scale-Revised
Digit Symbol Substitution Task 48
Disordering of thought 1
Disorders of sleeping and eating 93–105
Disorders of neurovegetative
  functioning 93
Disorganisation syndrome 23
Dissociative disorders 81, 83
Dissociative fugue 83
Distinctiveness 30
Distractability 42
Dopamine 14–5
  hypothesis 25
Dorso-Lateral Pre Frontal Cortex
  (DLPFC) 26, 32
Double dissociation 140
*Diagnostic and Statistical Manual of
  Mental Disorders* (DSM)
  criteria (DSM-III) for the diagnosis
    of dementia of the Alzheimer
    type 52

  criteria (DSM-IV)
    for the diagnosis of eating
     disorders 96–7
    for the diagnosis of mood
     disorders 41–2
    for the diagnosis of schizophrenia
     23–4
    for the diagnosis of somatoform
     disorders 82
Dysplasia 26

Eating disorders 9, 96–102
  biological origins 97
  hemispheric contribution to the
    affective disorders 101
  neuropsychological features 98–100
  nosology 96
  psychological origins 97
  structural and functional imaging
    data 98
Effortful tasks 30
Electoconvulsive therapy (ECT) 41,
  107, 111–18
  bilateral 111
  biological basis 113–14
  neuropsychological and structural and
    functional image data 114–15
  unilateral 111
Encoding of material 30
Endogenous depression 40
Epilepsy 111
Equipotential 6
Execution 14
Extrapyramidal side effects 125

Factitious disorders 81, 82, 84
Fear 63
Fight/flight response 16, 57, 63, 67
Figural Memory 12
Finger gnosis 14
First rank symptoms 21
Flattening of affect 22

Flight of ideas 42
Fluency
    depression of 13
Fluoxetine 125
Folate deficiency 99
Free-floating anxiety 65
Freedom from distractability 12
Frontal cortex 47
Frontal lobes 3, 7
Frontal lobology 138
Fuld Object Memory Evaluation 49
Functional 4

Gain 84
Gall 5, 6
gamma-aminobutyric acid (GABA)
    67, 114, 127
Ganser response 83
Ganser syndrome 83
General adaptation response (GAR)
    67
Generalised anxiety disorder 65–6
Glove and stocking anaesthesias 86
Glucocorticoids 66
Gnosis 48
    and praxis 13
Goal orientation
    loss of 29
Grandiosity 42

Hallucination 1, 22, 42
Halstead Reitan Battery (HRB) 115,
    129
Hebephrenia 19
Hierarchical structure 7
Hippocampus 26
Hippocrates 40
HM 3
Hydrocortisone 43
Hyothalamic pituitary adrenal axis 43
Hypochondriasis 82
Hypofrontal blood flow 31

Hypokalaemia 99
Hyponatraemia 99
Hypothalamus 9, 66
Hypothesis testing 2
Hypoxemia 95
Hysteria 85

Idiotypic 9
Illogical 29
Imipramine 126, 130
Impairment
    frontal/executive 11
Impulsivity 42
Incoherent 29
Information 12 see also Wechsler
    Adult Intelligence Scale-Revised
Information and orientation 12
Information processing modules 3
Iproniazid 126
Irritability 42

Judgement of Line Orientation and
    Facial Recognition 116

Kindling 113
Kraepelin 40

L-dopa 15
La belle indifference 82
Language functions 13, 48
Lashley, Karl 6
Late Onset Depression (LOD) 47
Lateralisation 74
Law of hierarchical structure of the
    cortical zones 7
Law of diminishing specificity of the
    hierarchically arranged cortical
    zones 7
Law of the progressive lateralisation of
    functions 7
Leucotomy 108
Limbic areas 8–9, 68
Limbic leucotomy 109

Limbic system 15, 47
Lithium 43, 130
Lithium carbonate 126
Locus coeruleus 16, 42
Logical Memory 1, 12
Luria 6
Luria Nebraska Battery 115

Magnetic resonance imaging (MRI) 26
Malingering 82, 83, 85
Mania 40
Manic episode 42
Meclobemide 126
Medial frontal areas 32
Memory encoding 49
Mental Control 12
Mesocortical pathway 15, 125
Mesolimbic pathway 15, 125
Mesulam, Marcel 8
Meta-memory 49
Minnesota Multi-phasic Personality
    Inventory (MMPI) 59
Modularity 139
Monoamine oxidase inhibitor (MAOI)
    15, 125–6
Monoamine hypothesis of depression 42
Monoamine oxidases (MAO) 15
Mood disorders 39–62
Motor planning and output 6
Munchausen's syndrome 83

Narrow localisation 6
Negative symptoms 22
Neocortex 15
Neologism 29
Neuroanatomical 6
Neurobehavioural battery 14
Neuroleptics 124, 127–130
Neuromodulators 14
Neuropsychological disorders
    and psychiatric illness 1-18
Neurotransmitters 14

Neurovegetative 93
Nigrostriatal pathway 15, 125
Nonspecific central systems 140
Noradrenaline 14, 16, 66, 67
Norepinephrine 42

Object assembly 12 see also Wechsler
    Adult Intelligence Scale-Revised
Object Assembly and Picture
    Completion 50
Obsessive–compulsive disorder 65–6
Obstructive Sleep Apnoea Syndrome
    (OSAS) 94–6
Oestrogen 66
Orbital gyri 68
Orbital PreFrontal Cortex (OPFC) 32
Organic 4

Pain disorder 82
Panic attacks 65
Panic disorder
    with and without agoraphobia 65
Paralimbic areas 9
Parallel distributed processing
    networks 140
Paranoia 19, 42
Parkinsonian 25
Parkinson's disease 15
Paroxetine 125
Perceptual organisation 12
Performance scale 12
Pernicious anaemia see vitamin B_{12}
    deficiency
Perseveration 29, 50
Pharmacotherapy 107
Phenothiazenes 124
Phenothiazine 124
Phineas Gage 3
Phobias 66
Phrenology 5

Picture arrangement 12 *see also* Wechsler Adult Intelligence Scale-Revised
Picture completion 12 *see also* Wechsler Adult Intelligence Scale-Revised
Poppelreuter figures 14
Positive symptoms 21–2
Positron emission tomography (PET) 25
Post-mortem 53
Post-traumatic stress disorder 65–6, 70
Praxis 48
Prefrontal cortices 26
Prefrontal lobotomy 107
Pressor amines 126
Pressure of speech 42
Primary insomnia 93
Process approach 2
Progressive lateralisation 7
Projection 7
Projection-association 7
Prolactin 66, 114
Pseudodementia 51–2
Psyche 20
Psychiatric disorders
pharmacological treatment of 123–136
physical treatments of 107–122
Psychiatric Illness
neuropsychological disorder 1
Psychomotor agitation 42
Psychomotor poverty syndrome 23
Psychosurgery 107–10
Putamen 47
Pyramidal cells 26

Rapid cycling bipolar 46
Reactive depression 40
Reality distortion syndrome 23
Reductionism 17
REM 55
Renaissance, the 5

Repetition 14
Reserpine 20
Reticular activating system (RAS) 93
Retrograde amnesia 116
Retrograde memory impairment 116
Rey Complex Figure Test 49
Right/left orientation 14
Roth, Sir Martin 40

Schizophrenia 19–38
biological origins 24–5
catatonic type 24
disorganised type 24
hemispheric contributions 33
neuropathology 26
neuropsychological features 27
paranoid type 24
structural and functional imaging data 26–7
treatment for 124–5
undifferentiated 24
Sedative hypnotics 127
Selegiline 126
Self-esteem 42
Self-reference
heightened 29
Self-schemata 44
Self-talk 44
Semantic priming 30
Sensitisation 113
Serotonergic tracts 16
Serotonin 14, 16, 67
Serotonin-selective re-uptake inhibitors (SSRIs) 125
Sertraline 125
Serum cortisol 43
Similarities 12 *see also* Wechsler Adult Intelligence Scale-Revised
Single-case methodology 3
Sleep apnoea 94–5
Sleep deprivation 54–5
chronic 94

Sleep disorder, breathing-related *see* breathing-related sleep disorder
Sleeping disorders 93–6
Social phobia 65
Somatization disorder 82
Somatoform disorders 81, 82, 84
SPECT 68
Spurzheim 6
State anxiety 65, 69
Statistical clinical decision making 2
Stress response, acute 63
Stressor 63
Striatal areas 68
Stroop Test 32, 70, 94
Subcaudate tractotomy 109
Subcortical 45, 56
Substance-induced anxiety disorder 65
Symptoms
　first rank 21
　negative 22
　positive 21
Syndrome analysis 6

Tangentiality 29
Temporal lobe epilepsy 50
Temporal lobes 47
Temporal-hippocampal system 31
Testosterone 66
Thioridazine 128
Thioxanthenes 124
Thought disorder 22
Threshold seizure 113
Thyroid axis 43
Thyroid-stimulating hormone (TSH) 43
　levels 114
Trail Making Test (TMT) 11–13
Trait anxiety 65, 69
Tri-cyclic antidepressants (TCAs) 16, 125
Trifluoperazine (TFP) 128
Tryptophan 16
Tubero-infundibular pathway 15

Tyrosine 15
Unipolar affective disorders 39
Uric acid 123–4

Valium 130
Valproate 126
Vasopressin 66
Vegetative 39
Ventral tegmental area 15
Ventricular dilatation 98
Ventricular enlargement 45
Ventricular to brain ratios (VBR) 45
Ventriculomegaly 47
Verbal, recall deficits 29
Verbal comprehension 12
Verbal paired sssociates 1, 12
Verbal scale 12
Visual, recall deficits 29
Visual paired asssociates 1, 12
Visual reproduction 1, 12
Vital spirit 5
Vitamin B_{12} 99
　deficiency 99
Vocabulary 12 *see also* Wechsler Adult Intelligence Scale-Revised

Waking 7
Wechsler Adult Intelligence Scale (WAIS) 50, 115
Wechsler Adult Intelligence Scale-Revised (WAIS-R) 11–12, 59
Wechsler Memory Scale-Revised (WMS-R) 11–12, 59
Wernicke Korsakoff Syndrome 98
Wisconsin Card Sorting Test (WCST) 10, 26, 50
Working brain 3
Working memory 73

Yerkes Dodson Law 66, 73

Zones of overlapping 7